Vedic View of the
EARTH

Reconstructing Indian History & Culture
(ISSN 0971-3824)

1. Society in Ancient India; by Sures Chandra Banerji.
2. Political Thought in Ancient India; by G.P. Singh.
3. Early Indian Historical Tradition and Archaeology; by G.P. Singh.
4. Vasantotsava: The Spring Festivals of India; by Leona M. Anderson.
5. Ecological Readings in the Veda; by M. Vannucci.
6. Vṛndāvana in Vaiṣṇava Literature; by Maura Corcoran.
7. Social History of the Tamils (1707-1947); by P. Subramanian.
8. Ancient Indian Coinage; by Rekha Jain.
9. Buddhism and Socio-Economic Life of Eastern India; by Bimal Chandra Mohapatra.
10. Chandragupta Maurya; by P.L. Bhargava.
11. Mṛtyu: Concept of Death in Indian Traditions; by Gian Giuseppe Filippi.
12. Yama: The Glorious Lord of the Other World; by Kusum P. Merh.
13. Sacred Complex of Ujjain; by D.K. Samanta.
15. Society in the Atharvaveda; by B.S. Kharade.
16. Orissan History, Culture and Archaeology; by S. Pradhan.
17. Education in Ancient India; by Mitali Chatterjee.
18. Surā: The Liquor and the Vedic Sacrifice; by M.B. Kolhatkar.
19. Human Ecology in the Vedas; by Marta Vannucci.
20. Governance in Ancient India; by Anupa Chandra Pandey.
21. The Cultural Glory of Ancient India: A Literary Overview; by Sures Chandra Banerji.
22. Kauṭilya's Arthaśāstra in the light of Modern Science & Technology; by Sunil Sen Sarma.
23. History of Jainism — With Special Reference to Mathurā; by V.K. Sharma.
24. Cultural Tourism in India: Museums, Monuments & Arts — Theory and Practice; by S.P. Gupta; Krishna Lal; Mahua Bhattacharya.
25. Ancient Indian Historiography — Sources and Interpretations; by G.P. Singh.
26. Republics, Kingdoms, Towns and Cities in Ancient India; by G.P. Singh.
27. Facets of Ancient Indian History and Culture — New Perception; by G.P. Singh.
28. Kamakhya — A Socio-cultural Study; by Nihar Ranjan Mishra.
29. History and Culture of Tamil Nadu as Gleaned from the Sanskrit Inscriptions Vol. 1 (up to c. AD 1310); by Chithra Madhavan.
30. Life Style of the Vedic People; by Pranati Ghosal.
31. History and Culture of Tamil Nadu as Gleaned from the Sanskrit Inscriptions Vol. 2 (up to c. AD 1310 - *c.* 1885 AD); by Chithra Madhavan.
32. Matrimonial Alliances and Ancient Indian Polity (*c.* 600 BCE to *c.* 650); by Preeti Prabhat.
33. Artisans and Craftsmen of Northern India; by Kuldeep Singh Thind.
34. The Evolution of Historiographical Tradition in Ancient and Medieval India by G.P. Singh.

Reconstructing Indian History & Culture, no. 14

Vedic View of the EARTH

— A Geological Insight into the Vedas —

S.R.N. Murthy

DK PRINTWORLD

Publishers of Indian Traditions

Cataloging in Publication Data — DK
[Courtesy: D.K. Agencies (P) Ltd. <docinfo@dkagencies.com>]

Murthy, S. R. N. (Sindhughatta Ramasastry
Narasimha), 1936-

Vedic view of the earth.
(Reconstructing Indian history and culture, no. 14).
Includes bibliographical references (p.).
Includes index.
ISBN 9788124600917

1. Geology in the Vedas. 2. Geology in
Vedic literature. 3. Geology in Sanskrit literature.
4. Earth in the Veḍas. I. Title. II. Series:
Reconstructing Indian history and culture, no. 14.

ISBN 13: 978-81-246-0091-7
First published in India in 1997
Second impression in India in 2013

Published and printed by:
D.K. Printworld (P) Ltd.
Regd. Office: 'Vedaśrī', F-395, Sudarshan Park
Ramesh Nagar Metro Station
New Delhi-110 015-11
Phones: (011) 2545 3975; 2546 6019; *Fax*: (011) 2546 5926
e-mail: indology@dkprintworld.com
Website: www.dkprintworld.com

ॐ धनुर्धरायै च विद्महे
सर्वसिद्धयै च धीमहि
तन्नो धरा प्रचोदयात् ॥

Oṁ dhanurdharāyai ca vidmahe
sarvasiddhayai ca dhīmahi
tanno dharā pracodayāt ॥

[May we know the Goddess Earth
On whom we meditate to bestow on us
The fruits of my accomplishments
May the Earth impel us towards it]

to my revered teachers
in
Sanskrit and Earth Science

Preface

After going through the book *The Earth* by H. Jeffrys (Cambridge, 1924) I was, as a student of earth science, interested in bringing out a book on the same subject incorporating thoughts from the Vedic heritage of India. But the work was postponed for many reasons. During the period of my service as a scientist of the federal Geological Survey, the Survey, appreciating my efforts, sponsored me for the Third International Sanskrit Conference held at Paris in 1977 for presenting the following papers — (i) The Vedic Theory of the Earth, (ii) Varāhamihira's Contribution to the Vedic Theory of the Earth, and (iii) An Integrated Theory of the Earth. The proceedings of the Conference, however, published only one paper, i.e., "Varāhamihira's Contribution to the Vedic Theory of the Earth". Later, the Bangalore-based Kalpataru Research Academy published all the three papers in the form of a book titled *An Integrated Theory of the Earth* (Murthy, 1987) which contains the rudiments of a Vedic theory of the earth.

In the year 1992, Professor V.N. Jha, Director, Centre of Advanced Study in Sanskrit, University of Poona, invited me to give a series of ten lectures on "Ancient Indian Theories of the Earth", which were later published (Murthy, 1992). These books, however, could not bring out the essentials of earth sciences in detail as culled from Sanskrit literature.

My endeavour here has been to present all data relating to earth sciences in the *Vedas* for determining the veracity of a Vedic theory of the Earth. The material had been with me for a long time but I was waiting for a suitable opportunity. It finally came when Shri Kireet Joshi, the then Member-Secretary, Rashtriya Veda Vidya Pratishthan, New Delhi evinced great interest in the subject. The present endeavour is a consequence of that. The material presented in this book has been culled by me over a period of three-to-four decades. Here, I present my researches to the modern students of the earth science as well as students of Sanskrit specialised in the *Bhūśāstras* (for *śāstra* means science in Sanskrit).

Since the appearance of the book *The Principles of Geology* by Lyell in 1830, when the modern discipline of geology took shape as a science, much geological information has been accumulated. The latter half of the present century, in particular, has seen an unprecedented collection of geologic information. Similarly, mining activity and other aspects of geology have also developed manifold. When examining such a vast literature pertaining to geology, one wonders whether such information might have existed in the Orient, since almost all the information that can be called modern are occidental. Actually, the way the oriental people, especially the Indians, treated the earth and exploited earth material for advancement of human civilisation, geo-philosophy, etc. has not been dealt with by any book in a comprehensive manner. In this context, though this book alone may not fill the gap of information, it is an effort to help modern students appreciate the eastern views as compared to the Western views.

It is well-known that the Middle East, the Indus and the Chinese people developed the most ancient civilisations (Lockyer, N.J., 1964, *The Dawn of Astronomy*, Massachusetts Institute of Technology, p. 432). Lockyer states, "I have already remarked that the ideas of the early Indian Civilisation, crystallised in their sacred book called *Vedas*, were known to us long before either the Egyptian or Babylonian and Assyrian records had been deciphered. Enough, however, is now known to show that we may take the *Vedas* to bring before us the remnants of the first ideas which dawned upon the minds of the earliest dwellers in Western Asia—that is, the territory comprised between the Mediterranean, the Black Sea, the Caucasus, the Caspian Sea, the Indus, and the waters which bound the southern coasts — say, as far as Cape Comorin." Further, he observes, "But the *Vedas* speak fully, while as yet information on this special point is relatively sparse from the other regions. It is wise, therefore, to begin with India, whence the first complete revelations of this kind came. Max-Müller and others during recent years have brought before us an immense amount of most interesting information, of the highest importance for our present subject". He continues, "They tell us that in 1,500 BC there was a ritual, a set of hymns called *Veda* (*Veda* meaning 'knowledge'). These hymns were written in Sanskrit, which few years ago was almost an unknown language; we know now that it turns out to be the nearest relation to our English tongue. The thoughts and feelings expressed in these early hymns contain the first roots and germs of that intellectual growth which connects our own generation with the ancestors of the Āryan race. Those very people who, as we now learn from the *Vedas*, at the rising and the setting of the Sun, listened with trembling hearts to the sacred songs chanted by their priests. The *Veda*, in fact, is the oldest book in which we can study the first beginnings of our language and of everything which is embodied in all the languages under the Sun. The oldest, most primitive, most simple form of Āryan Nature-worship finds expression in this wonderful hymnal, which doubtless brings before us rituals of the ancient Āryan populations represented also by the Medes and Persians." This royal astronomer of England should have lived to see the later developments in Indology when it was recognised that the *Vedas* are first texts in the library of mankind. Lockyer is believed to be the founder of the *Nature* magazine.

While there is the absence of any solid monument that may prove that the *Vedas* or the Vedic Civilisation is **the oldest**, one may also note the absence of such a text as the *Vedas* in the other most ancient civilisations on the earth. The antiquity of the Vedic Civilisation has been debated to a great extent. There is the vague possibility of the Āryan people belonging to the Europoidal race originating in the lap of the Western Himālayas in the foothills of the Śiwālik Ranges, and possibly accounting for the earliest of human beings originating from the highly advanced primates of this region. Some clues to the highly-advanced primates of this region from Hari-Talyangar, Ramnagar and other places are described by Pascoe (1973), who says, "There is no other part of the world in which the anthropoid apes are represented in such numbers and variety as in India and the inference follows that the original centre of distribution of the group could not have been far from northern India". This, according to me, is enough to lay to rest the immigration theory of Āryans (that Āryans came to India from outside) and to reduce the theory of the Āryan immigration into a myth. The so-called Āryans would have originated in the Brahmāvartta, that is, the area of present Ambālā district which was drained in the north by the river Sarasvatī and in the south by the river Draṣadvatī by about the beginning of the present (fifth) ice age — taking the Āryan Civilisation some 10 millennia backwards from the present date, if not more. There is no civilisation known to humanity with such antiquity as Vedic Āryan Civilisation. In *The Geological Foundations of Indology*, (1994, p. 91) I have dispelled all doubts about the theory of Āryan immigration into India and clearly established the origin of the Āryans in the western sector of the Śiwālik range in the foothills of the Himālayas.

When we talk of the Vedic Āryans, especially in terms of their contribution, it is the name of Max-Müller that stands out boldly amongst the Sanskrit scholars of Europe. He has given his observations on India in glowing terms. In *India, What can it Teach us*? (Nilakantha Shastry, 1961, p. 230), comprising his Cambridge lectures delivered in 1882 and published in 1883, he says, "If I were to look over the whole world to find out the country most richly endowed with all the wealth, power and beauty that nature can bestow — in some parts, a very paradise on earth — I should point to India. If I were asked under what sky the human mind has most fully developed some of its choicest gifts, has most deeply pondered on the greatest problems of life, and has found solutions to some of them which well deserve the attention even of those who have studied Plato and Kant — I should point to India. And, if I were to ask myself from what literature we, here in Europe, we who have been nurtured almost exclusively on the thoughts of Greeks and Romans, and of one Semitic race, the Jewish, may draw that corrective which is most wanted in order to make our inner life more perfect, more comprehensive, more universal, in fact more truly human, a life, not for this life only, but a transfigured and eternal life — again I should point to India."

According to Nilakantha Shastry (*ibid.*), in 1846, the Board of Directors of the East India Company commissioned Max-Müller to bring out at their expense — of the order of some £10,000, a huge sum of money then — a complete edition of the *Ṛgveda* with Sāyaṇa's commentary. This was the first time that the complete *Ṛgveda*, which had never been committed to writing since thousands of years, was put in black and white. The intention of such a stupendous job was not without any strings. According to S. Navaratna Rajaram (*Aryan Invasion of India : The Myth and the Truth*, *Voice of India*, 1993, New Delhi, p. 63), "There can be no question, however, that he (Max-Müller) saw his scholarly work as a mission to convert India to Christianity. Writing about his translation of the *Ṛgveda* to his wife in 1866, he was to observe — "This edition of mine and the translation of the *Veda* will hereafter tell to a great extent on the fate of India and on the growth of millions of souls in that country. It is the root of their religion and to show them what the root is, I feel sure, is the only way of uprooting all that has sprung from it during the last three thousand years."

Speaking about the *Upaniṣads*, it was Dara Shikoh, the eldest son of Emperor Shahjahan, who took interest in the

Upaniṣads when he visited Kashmir in AD 1640 and got them translated into Persian in AD 1657. This Persian version of the *Upaniṣads* was translated into Latin in 1775 by Anquetil Duperron under the title 'Oupnekhat'. Schopenhauer was greatly influenced by this translation, and he observed that, "In the whole world there is no study, except that of the originals, so beneficial and so elevating as that of the Oupnekhat. It has been the solace of my life, it will be solace of my death." (Max-Müller, 1988, p. 324).

However, much of the study in comparative religion and philosophy has been carried out to the conspicuous exclusion of any scientific discussion related to the *Vedas* and the *Upaniṣads*. Modern students of the earth sciences have hardly been exposed to the information related to the earth contained in these works. Even the scientific commentary on them in Sanskrit is wanting. It is stated that the *Vedas* were commented by as many as some 16 commentators prior to Yāska (Anantarangachar, 1956, p. 72) and later by Sāyana (Swamy Satyaprakash Saraswati, 1990, p. 60). The pre-Yāskan commentaries are not available to us today. But most, if not all, of the commentaries have tried to give the *Vedas* a colour of religion and sacrifice. Vālmikī, the author of *Rāmāyana*, observed that without the application of the *Vedas*, scientific disciplines get degenerated; however, not many others have tried to study scientific aspects in the *Vedas* let alone bring them to light.

Writing about the age of the earth, Arthur Holmes (Murthy, 1982, pp. 441-43) observed that "Hutton's genius received scant recognition in his lifetime, mainly because of the prevalent belief that the world had been created in the year 4004 BC. Far from being welcomed, Hutton's discoveries were generally regarded with righteous horror. Had he lived in India, however, Hutton would have found a readymade system of world chronology fully adequate for the needs of geology at that time. According to the Hindu Calendar, as recorded in the ancient books of Vedic philosophy, the year AD 1960 corresponds to 1,972,949,061 years since the present world came into existence. This astonishing concept of the Earth's duration has at least the merit of being of the right order." Professor Arthur Holmes, who had examined all the calendars that were available from the very ancient countries of the world, highly praised the Hindu Calendar. This alone suffices to substantiate the view that the geological information that is available in the Vedic and later literature in Sanskrit is most scientific and not primitive. The religion that is spoken of by the Vedic and the later periods is simply scientific and that was the type recommended by Professor Einstein when he said that "Science without religion is blind and religion without science is lame". In this sense, the Hindu or the Vedic religion is neither blind nor lame; hence it is one of the most dynamic religions of the world. It must be emphasised here that the Vedic religion is not fundamentalistic and it cautioned the support of some of its followers to that effect. It is most secular and universal in all its appeal, since it is essentially scientific and rational.

It is necessary to note here that the Vedic literature is a theistic school investing divinity in all its geological and universal agents. Whether such an approach is necessary may be debated; but its absence in the modern Western science developed on the dicta of the Royal Society of London has left it at the end of the space-time continuum while the former has ended with the concept of *Brahman*. According to Ronan (1964, p. 232), "The Royal Society, or more precisely The Royal Society of London for Improving Natural Knowledge, had been formed in 1660 by a number of men whose main interests were in the new scientific movement or new philosophy, as they called it. Granted a royal charter of rights and privileges in 1662 by Charles II, it is still one of the foremost scientific societies in the world . . . . Its fellows were for the most part men who were forging ahead with the new experimental approach to knowledge of the natural world. They all insisted on the importance of verifying theories of every kind by experimental evidence, and had broken away completely from the older view of turning to ancient authority as the test of any new idea. Their motto, *nullius in verba*, which has been freely translated most aptly by Professor E.N. da C. Andrade, himself a Fellow, as 'We don't take anybody's word for it', succinctly expresses their approach to natural knowledge." There was no such Royal Society in India in the ancient times and the responsibility of such a society was taken by the school of the *Upaniṣads*. While the school of the *Upaniṣads* did not invalidate the school of scriptures but built their foundation on its premise, the Western school of science completely ignored their scriptures in understanding nature. Thus, the motto of the Upaniṣadic school was the same as that of the Royal Society of London but with the difference that it did not derecognise the Vedic authority. The Ṛgvedic compositions were simply geo-poetry to a major extent with very less human code of conduct or corrective spirits, like the Gambler's *Sūkta*. The Upaniṣadic school did not require a Royal Charter for its inception or for its scientific analyses of nature. There are many anecdotes to prove this from the Upaniṣadic literature. Drawing upon the Vedic authority, the Upaniṣadic school which may be seen as the rationalistic dimension of nature — the geo-philosophy, as it may be called — was developed.

Without investing divinity into the natural geological agencies, the Western school, as already stated, finally arrived at a point of no return in the space-time continuum, which lacked a life spirit or living substratum. This is the grave error in Western philosophy. The point, however, was taken into consideration by the Indian sages in their deliberations as a result of which they devised the school of the *Brahman*. The data taken by the Indian seers was complete in all respects right from the definition of the 'Universe' — the term meaning everything living and non-living in the words of Fred Hoyle (*Frontiers of Astronomy*, London, 1957). The Western school has taken only the infrastructure without the spirit of life, as it is partial in its outlook of the 'universe'. Hence the Western philosophy cannot be considered wholesome.

In this monograph information available in the *Veda*s on the earth and geoelectrical/magnetic, hydro-spherical, geothermal and atmospheric shields, the luminaries and planets of the solar system, and the starry zodiac of the celestial sphere has been presented. The realisation that the earth represents the universe as emphasized by the great sages is brought out. The earth's relationship with the various universal bodies is established to some extent. Information about the earth in the *Veda*s has been theorised. In addition, information culled from one of the most important *Upanisad*s, i.e., the *Taittirīya Upanisad,* has been discussed to trace the evolution of the earth from space which is confirmed by modern views. This theory, however, may read incoherently at places. This is due to the lack of a clear objective in the *Veda*s.

The application of such a theory has been given in Part II of this book. Data about the origin of the earth and the planets, age of the earth, shape of the earth, dimensions of the earth and movements of the earth are presented as also a special chapter on the earthquakes, with a proposed method for predictive seismology based on a Vedic theory of the earth. It is hoped that the material thus presented will help modern students in the field appreciate the views of ancient Indian seers and their development in later ages.

This monograph claims to have brought out the geological aspects of the *Veda*s to a good extent though it cannot be considered as exhaustive. The task of presenting each and every detail has been left to more diligent students. My aim in this monograph is to bring out the salient features of the geological aspects of the *Veda*s, the *Vedānta* and the *Upaniṣad*s. And I believe that this aim has been fulfilled substantially. It is now left to the scientific and religious communities to examine my claim and introduce the matter in the college curriculum for the study of natural philosophy from the Vedic angle. In this context, it may be remarked that scientific discussions based on the *Veda*s and related to other disciplines both within and outside the scope of earth sciences may be taken up by others. The results would certainly be interesting. Before the compartmentalisation of scientific disciplines in the Western universities a few centuries ago, these disciplines were treated under Natural Philosophy. So, for instance, Physics, Chemistry, Botany and Zoology were studied under the unified discipline of Natural Science. This approach is very apt for the study of Vedic literature. Where a student of natural philosophy is concerned, unless such a division is discarded and a total picture is given, he will be in a great fix and unable to comprehend the truth of the universe. If this point is realised and the purport of the material studied here is noted, the author would feel amply rewarded for all the studies/researches that he has done in the past decades and presented in this monograph.

The thoroughness and details of the modern disciplines of science may not be found in the *Vedas* which are rather instructive and suggestive. But, at the same time, the grandeur and brevity of the *Vedas* are not found in the disciplines of modern science. The *Vedas* and the disciplines of modern science are rather complementary and not contradictory. If modern science is seen or read through Vedic eyes, the students will be much benefited. Keeping this in mind, modern students of earth science may attempt to search for the earliest of the ideas about the earth in Vedic literature. This book is intended to help all such students. It is the first of its kind as well, for it can be safely said that there exists no book such as this which gives a modern student in this field the ideas of oriental sages.

As a student of the earth and the *Vedas* myself, I have endeavoured to bring to light the various aspects of the *Vedas* which could be interpreted from the modern angle of earth science notwithstanding their religious significance. I believe that if the Vedic students can have the kind of background provided in this work, they would be able to perform their religious activities with added vigour and friendly nature. The advantage in this would be two-fold; for science with religion is knowledge and religion with science is power.

1-1-1997 **S. R. N. Murthy**

Contents

Part II
APPLICATION

Acknowledgements

I AM most grateful to the Maharshi Sandipani Rashtriya Vedavidya Pratishthanam, Ujjain for sponsoring the research *A Vedic Theory of the Earth*. I am thankful to all its members and, in particular, Mr. Sarvasri T.N. Dhar, Mr. K.C. Dube, and Mr. M.C. Jain (consultants) for the help rendered to me during my work on this project. I am overwhelmingly indebted to Shri Kireet Joshi, the then Member-Secretary of the Rashtriya Veda Vidya Pratishthan, Delhi, for arranging a Senior Fellowship for me to carry out this project. But for their fullest cooperation, it would not have been possible for me to complete this project.

Sarvasri C. Karunakaran and V.K.S. Varadan, former Directors General, Geological Survey of India who helped me present my earlier works to the Third International Sanskrit Conference held in Paris in 1977 deserve special mention for evincing interest in this project.

I acknowledge the kind help extended by Dr. B.P. Radhakrishna, President, Geological Society of India, Bangalore and Professor K.T. Pandurangi, Retired Professor and Head of the Department of Sanskrit, and formerly President, Mythic Society, Bangalore who reviewed the work of the project (Part I) and gave directions for further research. Here, I would also mention the 'anonymous referee' who made constructive criticisms and helped me revise and improve the Manuscript.

I am grateful to D.K. Printworld, Delhi who were keen to publish this work under their imprint.

S.R.N. Murthy

Abbreviations

AIOC	:	All India Oriental Conference.
CASS	:	Centre of Advanced Study in Sanskrit.
ELBS	:	English Language Book Society.
INSA	:	Indian National Science Academy.
KSRI	:	Kuppuswamy Sastry Research Institute.
MIT	:	Massachusetts Institute of Technology.

Plate 1

Stellar Arcs of the Formation of Luminaries, Planets and Nodes

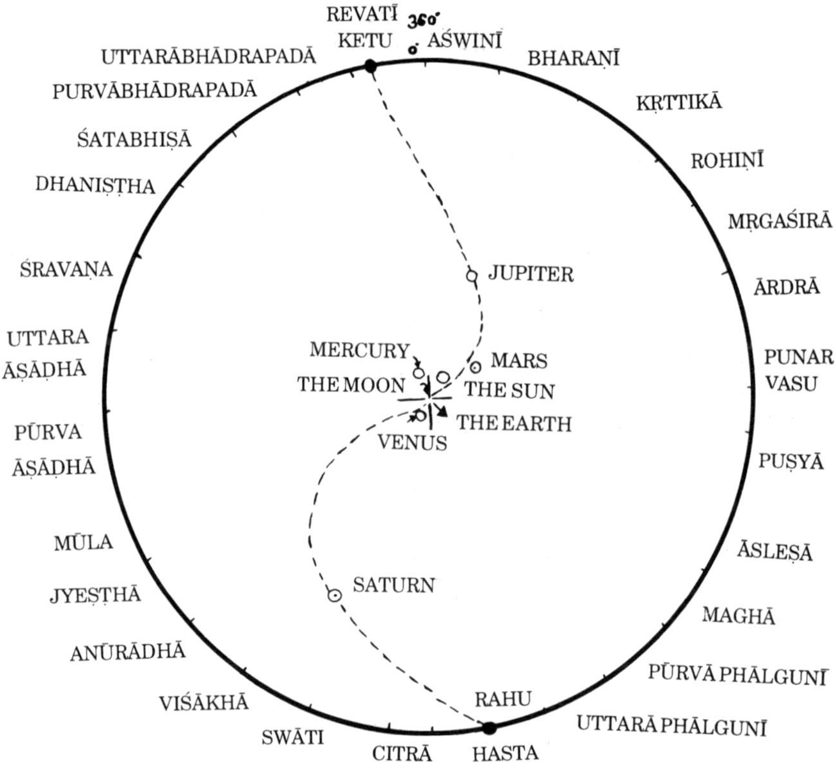

The Geocentric Concept with the possible reversed 'S' type of solar nebula.

The earth could be considered to be formed in the arc of anūrādhā star.

Introduction

THE Vedic foundations of the 'cultural heritage' of India have received tremendous appreciation through the ages. But the Vedic foundations of the 'scientific heritage' of India are hardly known. All the post-Vedic literature including the *Brāhmaṇas*, *Āraṇyakas*, *Upaniṣads*, *Darśanas*, *Purāṇas*, *Smṛtis* and even *Kāvyas* emphasise man's spiritual development alone. Even the commentaries that are available on the *Vedas* focus on the spiritual aspect of the *Vedas* only. It appears that there were as many as sixteen commentaries on the *Vedas* by the time of Yāskācārya, none of which are available to us today apart from the commentary of Yāska and later that of Madhva-Sāyaṇācārya in the thirteenth century AD. Madhva-Sāyaṇācārya's commentary is the standard one and referred to by one and all. Even this focuses on the spiritual aspects of the *Vedas*. It is understood, perhaps rightly to a large extent, that the *Vedas* form the foundations of spiritual thought in India. Though the recent commentaries on the *Vedas* by Aurobindo and Maharṣi Dayānanda Sarasvatī give an impression of a scientific temper in the *Vedas*, these mostly emphasise their spiritual and symbolic views and not their scientific value. As a result, the world knows the *Vedas* to be a compendium of religious and spiritual spells only. What emerges is a most disturbing situation arising, one may say, out of a kind of bias on the development of post-Vedic literature of India. But getting down to the problem itself, what Physics, Chemistry or Biology can be deciphered in the *Vedas*? Can there be anything of modern science in the *Vedas*? What kind of literature is contained in the *Vedas* which would help in propounding of scientific thoughts? Why is the scientific value of these texts not brought out for the appreciation of modern scientists?

The Sanskrit term *śāstras* mean 'sciences'. Almost all of the *śāstras* known in Sanskrit literature owe their origin to the *Vedas*, like *jyotiṣa, sāṁkhya, rasa, dharma* or religion, etc. The term, *dharma* or religion has been suffixed to *śāstra* to give the former a scientific outlook. Vālmīki in his *Rāmāyaṇa* mentions that *āmnāyānām ayogena śāstram praśithilām iva* — meaning, without the application of the *Vedas*, the scientific disciplines become degenerated and obsolete. Hence, any *śāstra* had to have the foundation of the *Veda* especially for its sustenance and development. This being the case, why is it that the *Vedas* are clearly partial towards religion and spiritualism? Millions of people over thousands of years have been made to believe in the religious and spiritual aspects of the *Vedas* with the result that inquiry into the Vedic sciences has taken a back seat, even totally forgotten.

The *Vedas* were plenty during the pre-Vyāsa period as per the dictum *anantā vai vedāḥ*, meaning that the *Vedas* are endless. Whether, at this time, the Vedic statements were employed only for performing sacrifices is uncertain. But during the post-Vyāsa time, it is certain that the Vedic literature, having been edited by him, was employed essentially for performance of sacrifices. Vyāsa is credited with having edited the then available *Vedas* into *Ṛg*, *Yajur* and *Sāma* sections so as to help the *hotṛ*, *adhvaryu* and *udgātṛ* priests in sacrifices. Later restriction was laid down on growth of the *Vedas* and the *Vedas* edited by Vyāsa, which is what is available to us today, gained currency.

In the pre-Vyāsa period, the Vedic compositions were made by the *ṛṣi-kulas* after considerable observation and they were codified in the form of hymns. On discovering changes or shortcomings, they composed new hymns and called the old ones perhaps *khila* or invalid. The observations made by them were put in the kula *maṇḍalas* of the *Ṛgveda*. The books of the *Ṛgveda* along with the names of sages they are attributed to are given below:

Kula-Maṇḍalas	Ṛṣi-kulas
Second *Maṇḍala*	Ghṛtsamada
Third *Maṇḍala*	Viśvāmitra
Fourth *Maṇḍala*	Vāmadeva
Fifth *Maṇḍala*	Atri
Sixth *Maṇḍala*	Bharadvāja
Seventh *Maṇḍala*	Vasiṣṭha

These books of the *Ṛgveda* were a result of continuous and unstinted efforts of dynasties of sages over several centuries especially with regard to various observations of nature around them. The hymns of the eighth *maṇḍala* are mostly attributed to the dynasty of Kaṇva and the hymns of the ninth *maṇḍala* to Somapavamāna. The first and the tenth *maṇḍalas* are known to be of later origin.

The original extent of the *Vedas* is not available to us today. That which is available to us now, it appears, is a small fraction of the extensive Vedic literature that was available in the pre-Vyāsa period.

THE VEDIC LITERATURE

The *Vedas* as codified by Vyāsa appears to have consisted of only the *Ṛg*, *Yajur* and *Sāma Vedas*. Hence, they were called *Trayī*. Amarasiṁha observed this when he said "*. . . ṛksāma yajuṣī iti vedāstrayastrayī*" in his *Amarakośa*, the well-known Sanskrit lexicon. That the *Vedas* then consisted of only the *Ṛg*, *Sāma* and *Yajur Vedas* is supported by the *mantra* called *Gāyatrī* attributed to Viśvāmitra in the third *maṇḍala* of the *Ṛgveda*. *Gāyati anena trayena iti gāyatri* — it is observed. Hence, the original classification of the Vedic literature into three is justified.

By and large, the *Ṛgveda* is the oldest and the largest of all the three *Vedas*. The *Ṛgveda* is divided into 10 *maṇḍalas*, 1028 *sūktas* (hymns) and 10552 *ṛks* (verses). Another system of classification of the *Ṛgveda* divides it into eight *aṣṭakas* or *khaṇḍas* (sections), each *aṣṭaka* with eight *adhyāyas* (chapters). Similarly, the *Yajurveda* is divided into *Kṛṣṇa* and *Śukla* parts: the *Kṛṣṇa Yajurveda* consisting of seven *khaṇḍas* (books), 44 *adhyāyas* (chapters) and 651 *anuvākas* (sections), and the *Śukla Yajurveda* comprising 40 *adhyāyas* and 1975 *mantras*. With regard to *Sāmaveda*, out of its 1549 *ṛks*, only 75 are original to this *Veda* and the remaining are drawn from the *Ṛgveda*.

The *Atharvaveda* emerged later than the other three *Vedas*. It did not enjoy the sanctity of the other *Vedas* even though the Brahmā of the sacrifices was considered to be conversant with this *Veda*. This could have been due to its contents not being in harmony with the aims of the other *Vedas*. The *Atharvaveda* is noted to contain 20 *khaṇḍas* with some 731 *sūktas*. There is some confusion regarding the number of the *sūktas*, as some state it to be 730, 759 or even 798. This itself is an indication that many additions were made to the original in course of time. This is also reflected in the number of its *mantras* which is stated to be 5028, 5849, 5987 or 6000. One can find some 1200 *mantras* of *Ṛgveda* included in the 20th *khaṇḍa* of this *Veda*.

The Vedic Śākhās

According to *Maukitkopaniṣad*, there are a total of 1180 *śākhās* in the four *Vedas*. *Ṛgveda* has 21 *śākhās*, the *Yajurveda* has 109, the *Sāmaveda* has 1000 and the *Atharvaveda* has 50. According to *Kūrma Purāṇa*, the total *śākhās* of the four *Vedas* are 1130 with 21 in *Ṛgveda*, 100 in *Yajurveda*, 1000 in *Sāmaveda* and nine in *Atharvaveda*. However, many of these *śākhās* were lost a long time back. These *śākhās* were established for specialisation in certain sections of the *Vedas* by some schools of teachers and their students especially for purposes of rendering and practice. Only two *śākhās* of the *Ṛgveda*, viz., *Āśvalāyana* and *Sāṁkhyāyana* are to be found. Of the many *śākhās* in *Yajurveda*, it is observed that those belonging to *Taittirīya* are found in South India, those of *Maitrāyāṇī* in Gujarat, and to *Kaṭha* in Kashmir. Out of the 1000 *śākhās* of *Sāmaveda*, only thirteen have been provided with names. They are *Rāṇāyaṇa*, *Satyamugra*, *Vyāsa*, *Bhāguri*, *Oulunḍi*, *Gaulmulāvi*, *Bhānumanupamanyava*, *Karata*, *Maśaka*, *Gārgyā*, *Varṣājña*, *Kauthumi* and *Jaimini*. Only *Rāṇāyaṇīya*, *Kauthumīya* and *Jaiminīya śākhās* are available, with not much difference between the first two.

We would like to restrict the literary survey of the *Vedas* to this *śākhā* classification to the exclusion of the *Brāhmaṇas*, *Āraṇyakas*, *Upaniṣads* and other literature which are considered post-Vedic. They are of a contemplative nature and involve an in-depth study of the Vedic literature and explain the significance of the *mantras* in the sacrifices in elaborate forms, especially with a view to emphasise religious aspects of human conduct. The literature dealing with the six adjuncts of the *Vedas* referred to as *Śikṣā*, *Vyākarana*, *Chandas*, *Nirukta*, *Jyotiṣa* and *Kalpa* is considerable and it has not been taken up for study in this monograph. However, wherever necessary, it will be drawn upon for scientific interpretations.

Origin and Development of the Vedic Literature

The problem of origin and development of the Vedic literature is directly connected with the origin and evolution of Indo-Āryans. The origin and evolution of the Indo-Āryans is a fascinating problem where research related to the geological foundations of

Indological studies is concerned (Murthy, 1994, p. 91). Many theories have been put forward to the effect that the Āryans immigrated into India from parts of Central Asia where the temples of Varuṇa and other deities were discovered at a place called Bogos Koi. This idea, probably attributed to William Jones, gained currency early and helped Indologists to trace the connection between the mother language of Vedic Sanskrit and other European languages, including Zend, Avesta, Latin, Greek, Babylonian, Assyrian, Phoenician, etc. It was believed that the Āryans originated in Central Asia and migrated towards south and south-east in branches and the south-eastern branch immigrated into India and established themselves in the region of the present-day Jammu and Kashmir, Punjab and Himachal Pradesh. This idea got strengthened by the publication of the book *Arctic Home in the Vedas* by Bāl Gaṅgādhar Tilak in 1936. The theory put forward by B.G. Tilak contended that the home of the Vedic Āryans was the Arctic region based on certain geological data, especially on the 'Theory of Ice Ages' in the Quaternary period. However, many students of the *Veda*s argued on the basis of the description of the geographical environment in the region of Jammu and Kashmir, Punjab and Himachal Pradesh, drained by the Sapta-Sindhus and the rivers Sarasvatī and Dṛśadvatī, that the Āryans emigrated from the north-western parts of India rather than immigrated into India. Though the book on Vedic geography brought out by Bhargava (1964, p. 157) suggests that the north-western parts of India were the original home of the Āryans, the problem is to be studied in the field of anthropology to focus on the question of origin of man in that region. Where the origin of the early man is concerned, the first skull fossil was collected in Heidelberg in Germany. Then scholars announced that traces of the earliest men could be identified and grouped into the Jāvā Man, Sumātrā Man, Cromagnan Man, China Man, Neanderthal Man and Africa Man. The problem has since become more and more complex.

The appearance of man on the surface of the earth is very recent and the period of his presence on earth is only a fraction of the long history of the earth extending over 4.5 billion years. Life originated on the earth about 3.6 billion years ago or earlier in the form of microcellular organisms and slowly evolved into multicellular organisms such as algae, ferns, flowering plants, fishes, reptiles and mammals.

There is difference of opinion among scientists as to the true ancestors of man. The gorilla, the chimpanzee and the orangutan, at one time, were considered as man's ancestors respecting 'The Theory of Evolution' by Darwin that propounded the concept of the survival of the fittest. Yet others were of the view that man originated out of Tarsius of Borneo. It was also suggested that the Neanderthal Man developed in Central and Eastern Asia while *Sapiens* evolved in Europe, Africa, Asia Minor and India. The Neanderthal Man disappeared during the fourth ice age and *Homo Sapiens* evolved and began to live in caves, hunted big games, used fire, buried their dead, made special tools, clothed themselves and produced religious arts.

In this connection it is relevant to consider the palaeontological records of the Śiwālik hills of the Himālayas. According to Pascoe (1973, p. 2130),

> At Haritalyangar, which is near the Ḳangra boundary, remains of vertebrates have been found by Pilgrim and Vinayak Rao throughout a vertical section of some 600 feet of strata in the Siwalik Himalayas. In the Nagri stage of Haritalyangar, fossils are plenty in the upper 2000 feet of the total 3500 feet thick sediments. Primates, as many as ten species, have been listed to occur in this stage. Further Pascoe observed that, "There is no other part of the world in which the anthropoid apes are represented in such numbers and variety as in India, and the inference follows that the original centre of distribution

of the group could not have been far from northern India.

The Śiwālik hills which are about 20 million years old contain well-preserved mammalian remains of prehistoric animals including man-like apes and hominids like *Ramapithecus*. The Miocene formations in Himachal Pradesh near Haritalyangar and Rāmnagar in Udhampur, Jammu have yielded hominid remains in association with artefacts of the early period. Prasad (1975, pp. 382-90 and 1989, pp. 93-110) made a valuable collection of hominid remains from Himachal Pradesh and suggested the possibility of radiation of higher apes including hominids in the Śiwālik region. These data have suggested that the origin of man-like apes and hominids like *Ramapithecus* took place in the Śiwālik region of the Himālayas.

All these palaeontological evidence may go to show that man originated in the western section of the Śiwālik Himālayas, perhaps giving rise to the Europoidal race of human beings to which the Indo-Āryans belong (Murthy, 1993, p. 17). This proposition does not exclude the origin of man in other parts of the world. The China Man, Jāvā Man, Sumātrā Man, etc. might have given rise to the Mongoloid race while the Africa Man might have evolved into the Negroid and Australoid races. While all these races are represented in India, that of the Indo-Āryans appears to have been much advanced in the faculty of speech and entrepreneurship. It is to be observed that where race is concerned, the area where the greatest mixing has occurred and which is hardest to classify should be the most central one, that is, India.

Based on the above-mentioned observations, Āryan immigration into India from outside can be ruled out and their origin in the Śiwālik Himālayas of Himachal Pradesh, Punjab and Jammu and Kashmir established. Instead of immigration they emigrated from that original place to various places within India, and mid-Europe and western Europe in the distant past, and have peopled the world. These facts have been brought out in various

Purāṇas and recently by Josyer (1966, p. 265) and Sārada (1975, p. 383). The Āryanisation of south India has been discussed by Nilakantha Sastry (1958).

Being indigenous to the Śiwālik hills of the western Himālayas, the Āryans were the children of nature. From their speliological background they developed a riparian culture on the banks of the now-dried-up river Sarasvatī and the Sapta-Sindhus. There are a number of references to the river Sarasvatī in the *Ṛgveda* (Murthy, 1978, pp. 193-218). The river Sarasvatī was praised by the Āryan sages in superlative terms who elevated her to the status of motherhood and godhood. The river was much responsible for the sustenance and prosperity of the Vedic civilisation; and it was, hence, befittingly praised. According to Krishnan (1956, p. 555),

> When the Saraswati was a live river, it must have irrigated an area of perhaps 7000 sq miles of what is now practically a desert . . . . The Saraswati has been described in the Vedic literature (probably 5000 BC or earlier) as a great river — greater than even the Indus and the Ganges. Between the time of Manu and the *Mahābhārata* its upper course had dried up, probably because of the easterly diversion of the waters of the Yamuna. The lower course in Bikaner, Bahawalpur and Sind continued to be well watered, for during the invasion of Alexander of Macedonia in the fourth century BC and of the Arabs in the 9th century AD the Rann of Kutch was a fairly deep gulf and ships moved up the river into Sind. In Todd's Annals of Rajasthan it is stated that the Hakra (identified with the extinct Saraswati) in Bikaner became dry for the first time about the year 1044 AD.

Krishnan also notes,

> The river Saraswati appears to have been originated in

> the Siwalik hills of Sirmur on the borders of the Ambala district between the telus fans of the rivers of Yamuna in the east and of Sutlej in the west and was flowing in a general south-westerly direction, finally debouching into the Rann of Kutch. The dry bed of Hakra, which is as wide as 3 to 5 miles in the territory of Bikaner, has been recognised as the course of the now-extinct river Saraswati. On the banks of Hakra it is stated that several mounds containing remnants of prehistoric and historic settlements have been identified which revealed the ruins of temples, dwellings, pot shreds, etc. of the Mohanjo-Daro type. The withdrawal of the waters from the Sutlej and possibly from the Jamuna, dried up Saraswati.

This is a geological truth and archaeologists and Indologists have plenty of scope for establishing the existence of river Sarasvatī and Vedic civilisation.

It is well-known that the northern part of the present Ambālā district was drained by rever Sarasvatī and the river southern part by river Dr̥śadvatī. The region between the two rivers was known as Brahmāvartta while the region south of the river Dr̥śadvatī was called Brahmarṣideśa. This region is the actual place of the seven *brahmarṣis*, namely, Kaśyapa, Atri, Bharadvāja, Viśvāmitra, Gautama, Jamadagni and Vasiṣṭha. All of them are *mantradr̥ṣṭāras* and leaders of the *kula-maṇḍalas* of the *Ṛgveda.*

These *r̥ṣis* who were inhabitants of the banks of the Sarasvatī and Dr̥śadvatī were astonishing observers of nature. They studied the nature surrounding them and came up with uncanny details. They measured time and had their own calendar. They were, in all cases, attuned to simple living and high thinking. They were extraordinary poets. They developed and practised the Vedic Sanskrit and composed hymns pregnant with meaning. Their observations were spread over several generations and they codified their observations in the form of hymns.

Age of the Ṛgveda

There is considerable controversy about the age of the *Ṛgveda* and the other *Vedas*. *Ṛgveda* being the oldest amongst the *Vedas*, its age has been under debate for a very long time. According to Macdonell (1976),

> The *Ṛigveda* is undoubtedly the oldest literary monument of the Indo-European languages. But the exact period when the hymns were composed is a matter of conjecture. All that we can say with any approach to certainty is that the oldest of them cannot date from later than the thirteenth century BC. . . . On astronomical grounds, one Sanskrit scholar has concluded that the oldest Vedic hymns date from 3000 BC while another puts them as far back as 6000 BC.

In *The Orion* B.G. Tilak (1972, p. 243) observed that "the oldest period in the Aryan Civilisation may therefore be called Aditi or the pre-Orion and we may roughly assign 6000-4000 BC as its limit."

The fixing of the age of the *Vedas*, *Brāhmaṇas*, *Āraṇyakas* and the *Upaniṣads* at intervals of 200 years from 1200 BC was due to Max-Müller. The reason for such identification is not known. But it is difficult to say why Max-Müller who observed, "I doubt whether any real book can rival it (the *Vedas*) in antiquity' (*My Autobiography*, 1976, p. 176) fixed these ages for the *Ṛgveda* and other related Sanskrit literature. Probably being nurtured in the Biblical school, he did not venture to take the *Vedas* out of the ambit of 4004 BC — the date of creation claimed in the *Bible*. Is it not commonsense to look at this problem from a different angle and observe that the present *kaliyuga* commenced from17th/18th February, 3102 BC, the chronology being maintained by all the Indian almanacs, when the great *Mahābhārata* war ended? And were the *Vedas* not there at the time of the *Mahābhārata* war? Were the *Vedas* not existing at the time of the *Rāmāyaṇa* which is much earlier than the *Mahābhārata* period? There is no mention of any of these epic stories in the *Vedas*. That itself indicates that the *Vedas* must be older to these events. Also considering the occurrence of equinoxes in the arc of Aditi (Punarvasu star), it is possible to consider the Ṛgvedic compositions earlier than the oldest date available to us today by another two to three thousand years. In the absence of the first or the oldest hymns in the Ṛgvedic compositions, it is futile to declare when the exact age of the *Rgveda* commenced.

Many archaeologists are happy fixing the age of the *Ṛgveda* at about 1200 BC and have gone to the extent of saying that the Vedic civilisation followed that of the Harappa and Mohenjo-Daro i.e., the Indus Valley civilisation. According to Srikantha Sastry (1962, pp. 9-18), the Harappan culture is a development over the Vedic culture, and this does not substantiate the view that the Āryans immigrated into India and destroyed the Harappan and related cultures. The Harappan culture is noted to be of the age of some 2500 BC. Yet the bottom layers of the cultural terrain have not been exposed and studied which may take its age back by some additional centuries. And for the development of such a culture, it is broadly estimated that it would take another two to three thousand years. If the Indus Valley civilisation owes its origin to the Vedic civilisation, it is justifiable to believe that the age of the *Vedas* is something of the order of seven or eight thousand BC.

From the geological point of view, the present world exists between the fourth and the fifth glacial ages with the fourth inter-glacial period commencing from about 10 000 years ago. In the context of the above, the origin and evolution of man in the

Himālayan lap agrees with this age and its evolution, and it can be well related to the period of early Vedic era.

Authors of the Vedas

The traditional school of the *Vedas* claims that the *Vedas* are not man-made, i.e., *apauruṣeya*, and they has come directly from the mouth of the *Brahman* at the beginning of creation. It is rather difficult to substantiate the traditional view from a scientific and pragmatic point of view. The truth is that the Āryan *ṛṣis*, the previously mentioned *brahmarṣis* and others have been the authors of the *Vedas*. The *ṛṣis* were great poets who composed the Vedic hymns to well-recognised metres, the major ones being *gāyatrī, uṣṇik, anuṣṭubh, bṛhatī, paṅkti, triṣṭubh, jagatī, virāṭ, kakup, dvipadī*, etc. Each *mantra* is known by the deity, metre and the sage who 'saw' the *mantra*. In this sense, a *ṛṣi* perceived the *mantra* with respect to a deity and composed the *mantra* to some definite metre. It is possible to understand that the significance of the *mantra* existed before the *ṛṣi* perceived it, when he perceived it and after he had perceived it—thus, the significance being eternal and impersonal. But it will be inviting a debate if it is claimed that the *Vedas* appeared overnight at the hour of universal creation from the mouth of Brahmā. It is wisdom to state that the *ṛṣis* were *mantra-dṛṣṭaras*, i.e., who had 'seen' the *mantras* and hence could compose them. They were rather superior souls or keen observers of nature and were able to perceive the truths of nature. The eternal value of such perceptions has stood the test of time.

Commentaries on the Vedas

The *Brāhmaṇas* came into existence in order to convey the true meaning of the Vedic *mantras*. Later, to understand the exact meaning of the *Vedas*, the texts of *Nirukta* became useful. *Niś kṛṣṭā uktā idam ittham* (for "this is its meaning") was the way these texts explained the Vedic *mantras*. Of the many texts of *Nirukta*, that of Yāskācārya is well-known and the earlier ones are not available to us now. Yāskācārya is also the author of *Nighaṇṭu* which lists the synonymous words in the *Vedas*. *Sarvānukramaṇī* of Kātyāyana and *Bṛhaddevatā* texts have also been of help in interpreting the Vedic *mantras*. Also, many texts in *Pūrva Mīmāṁsā* of Jaimini, *Advaita Vedānta* of Śaṅkara, *Dvaita Vedānta* of Madhva and *Viśiṣṭādvaita Vedānta* of Rāmānuja have helped understand the Vedic *mantras*.

The most important one of such Vedic commentaries is by Madhva-Sāyaṇācārya in the fourteenth century AD and it is titled *Vedārtha Prakāśa* (Sontakke. N.S., *et al.*, 1951-92). There are also commentaries by Skandasvāmī, Mādhavabhaṭṭa and others on the *Vedas*. As already mentioned, all these commentaries tried to emphasise a religious and spiritual aspect of the *Vedas*, that is characteristic of the Vedic traditional school.

During the nineteenth century AD Western contributions on the *Vedas* began pouring in. Initiated in AD 1805 by Colebrook through his article "About the *Vedas* — the Sacred Books of the Hindus", the West came to know about the existence of the *Vedas*. After two decades, Frederich Rosen began to edit and print the *Ṛgveda* in Germany but died even before the first *aṣṭaka* was completed. In 1846, Rudolf Roth wrote on the poetry and history in the *Vedas*. This created an interest in the West to study the *Vedas*. Later the contributions of Muir, Haug, Bühler, Grossman, Jacobi, Benfey, Schelling, Böhtling and others like Wilson, Goldstucker, Weber, Ludwig, Monier-Williams, Oldenberg, Geldner, Peterson, Griffiths started flowing from the West. Most of these also to the line of traditional views.

The commentary, though partial, by Maharṣi Dayānanda Sarasvatī in his *Ṛgvedādibhāṣyabhūmikā* (1976, p. 361) is of a mixed kind with a scientific temper. Aurobindo's commentary (1993, p. 581) attributed to the *Vedas* is of pure symbolic nature.

The one and only commentary or rather explanation of some *mantras* in terms of their importance to eclipses is *Drapsa — The Vedic Cycle of Eclipses* by Shamasastry which was published in 1938. Shamasastry (p. 227) opens up a grand new chapter for evaluating the Vedic hymns in terms of what they observe regarding eclipses. He has given detailed explanations of many of the Vedic hymns in which it is evident that the Vedic poets resorted to religious practices with an intention to prevent eclipsing of the Sun and the Moon, especially to save them from the clutches of Svarbhānu and Ketu. Though it was unscientific to think that the Sun and the Moon were being devoured during the eclipses, which opinion continued to persist till very late in the cultural heritage of India, yet such an interpretation of sheer grandeur merits our attention as it may be a possible true explanation of many of the Vedic hymns — especially in the absence of any other kind of explanation than the traditional kind which expounds spiritual and religious feelings.

Max-Müller did the singular service of editing and publishing the *Ṛgveda* with Sāyaṇa's commentary in Sanskrit from AD 1849 to 1885, and also translated portions of the *Ṛgveda* and published them in his *Sacred Books of the East* series. This was the first time that the *Ṛgveda* had been completely edited and printed. According to Max-Müller (1961, p. 229),

> Let it not be supposed that because there are several translations of the Ṛgveda in English, French and German, therefore all that the Veda can teach us has been learned. Far from it. Every one of these translations has been put forward as tentative only. I myself, though during the last thirty years I have given translations of a number of the more important hymns, have only ventured to publish a specimen of what I think a translation of the Veda ought to be; and that translation, that *traduction raisonee*, as I ventured to call it, of twelve hymns only, fills a whole volume. We are still on the mere surface of the Vedic

literature.

From all these considerations it becomes evident that there is great scope for examining the Vedic literature for their scientific content, if any. It is all the more important to think that the *Vedas* contain scientific truths since they have been the eternal springs from where the various *śāstras* (sciences) have originated in Sanskrit.

Ambiguity of Vedic Definitions

Sāyaṇa observed, *pratyakṣeṇānumityā vā yastūpāyo na budhyate. énam vidanti védéna tasmād védasya védatā*, meaning that one finds in the *Vedas* such means (to attain things) which are not possible to obtain by means of direct or inferred observations. This definition of the *Vedas* perhaps restricts the vast scope that the *Vedas* possess. Perhaps Sāyaṇa saw the Vedic deities employed in various kinds of sacrifices as important only for attainment of material prosperity. If such material prosperity is difficult to gain by means of direct and inferred observations, by hard work and labour, it could be obtained by resorting to Vedic injunctions like *svarga kāmo yajéta* — meaning, one desirous of attaining *svarga* should perform a sacrifice. In the performance of a sacrifice the deities are invited by chanting Vedic hymns and presenting the *havis* to them in *agni*; thus, they are pleased and they fulfil the desire of the performer. This kind of interpretation was very much welcomed by one and all for it appealed to all persons. This view perhaps did not change in spite of the later Upaniṣadic dicta, *kurvannévéha karmāṇi jijīviśét śatam samāḥ* — meaning, one should live for hundred years performing his duties. But what kind of duties? Again it was interpreted as those duties which have been prescribed to various *varṇas* by the *smṛtis*, since the human code of conduct had already been instituted. All these made the person embrace or succumb to the religious way of life with the utmost desire to get liberated from the cycle of birth and death. Liberation or *mokṣa,* as it has come to be understood, was the only best aim of life. Towards this end most, if not the entire, literature of Vedic and post-Vedic schools and all sorts of interpretations were directed.

If a methodology (to attain something) does not have a direct or inferred evidence, how can it come within the ambit of modern science? Hence, Sāyaṇa's definition of the *Vedas* excludes them from being capable of generating a method which can be verified by direct or indirect observation, for as such the *Vedas* do not contain any science. This idea was perhaps dominant about the fourteenth century AD though it had been nourished in India for a very long time.

There were not a few *arthavādins* of the *Vedas*, and Śabara Svāmī was one of them. His arguments (Ganguli, 1989, pp. 139-52) are more pragmatic. He does not talk of a god or deity for a natural process of human importance. According to Ganguli,

> Shabara has shown how Prajāpati's sacrifice mentioned in Taittirīya Samhita (2/1/1) is a symbolic representation of the process of rain produced by co-operation of natural elements, ensuring on the earth an abundant wealth of children, cattle and crops. Prajāpati is a synthesis of pronounced material elements responsible for rain and sustenance of living beings.

Further, Ganguli (1989) observes,

> We have reason to be proud that even as early as the seventh century BC, India had produced thinkers whose well-reasoned atheism and materialism, evident in their interpretation of the Vedas, sounded a note of modernity which is an object of surprise and admiration to a modern mind. It is no mean achievement that the first and the most authoritative interpreters of the Vedas in ancient

> India enunciated the theory of personification and primitive metaphor along with the comprehensive doctrine of *Arthavāda* relegating gods and heaven to the domain of fictive imagination, useful but unreal. Yet it is true, nevertheless, that in the final count, class and caste, intercastes prevailed over the rational approach in deference to the social reality of those days. Many instances may be shown to illustrate the unholy marriage of rationalism and obscurantism. Thus the theory of *Apūrva*, basically a scientific concept has been to serve the obscurantist faith in the power of rituals to produce the desired results. Yet, quite undeniably, a correct scientific and historical outlook is evident in the assertion that the original significance of the Vedas lies in the emphasis on action relating to man's survival and not in the spiritual profoundity of absolute monism. It is not for nothing that in his commentary on the very first sutra of the Brahmasūtras, Shankara has to reckon with the *Mīmāmsa* position that the Vedas are *Sadhyapara* not *Siddhapara*. This is a field of elaborate research encompassing the history of man and society.

In the context of the above, it becomes clear that despite a pragmatic approach to the *Vedas* of many an inquirer from very early times, it is only the orthodox traditional spiritual school that has survived to the detriment of any scientific appraisal of the *Vedas*. The *Vedas* have lost significance as the source of all *śāstras* or sciences. While plenty of logic (*tarka*) was applied to the so-called *mahāvākyas* in the *Veda* for proving the faith to accept the existence of some supernatural force or field as *Brahman* — on which plenty of literature exists, no such study of this kind appears to have taken place regarding the positive natural agencies described in the *Vedas*. It is my earnest belief that had it been possible to apply logic for an analysis of the natural agencies described in the *Vedas*, it would have been a great thing, for the ancient Indian scientists could then have discovered many a new natural phenomena.

In the absence of any such scientific interpretations of the natural agencies described in the *Vedas*, I make an attempt in the following pages to bring out the essence of the early human-nature interaction presented in the Vedic literature as a full-fledged data collection programme of the early Āryans in the development of a 'Theory of the Earth' in the post-Vedic period.

SCOPE OF THE WORK

The scope of this work is to examine the Vedic literature with an express view to studying their geoscientific descriptions and evaluating the data for the development of a theory of the earth which prevails in Sanskrit literature of the later period as presented by the author of the *Bṛhatsaṁhitā*, Varāhamihira in the fifth century AD.

What is a 'Theory of the Earth'? For that matter, any theory is a supposition explaining something based on principles independent of the phenomenon, according to the *Oxford Dictionary*, as in the case of gravitation, atomic, light, heat, magnetism, etc. It involves collection of data, experimental observation and processing of the data, and formulation of general principles. A theory may work when put into practice and it may yield results — when it will be called a working theory. A theory may not work, yet may be retained in a theoretical form needing further improvement. Such are many theories in scientific literature, earth science being no exception. There are theories of the origin of the earth, plate tectonics, continental drift, origin of mountains and oceans, origin of ores and rocks, prediction of earthquakes and volcanoes, etc. in earth sciences. Geological mapping of the earth, petro-mineralogical studies of the rocks of the earth's crust, especially to ascertain their physico-chemical conditions of formation, etc. are going on since geology became a recognised science in the early part of the nineteenth century when the famous book *Principles of Geology* was published by Charles Lyell (in AD 1833). All these data being collected worldover are part and parcel of a bigger project of formulating principles of a 'Theory of the Earth' by which we can predict the future of the earth, as per Scheidegger (1963). Till now modern science has not a theory of the earth worth its name for predicting the future course of the earth despite its spectacular development over two centuries. By collecting vast data, it, however, has a modern 'Theory of Plate Tectonics' which tries to explain the drifting of continents and origin of mountains and oceans. It has not been possible by such a theory to predict day-to-day and annual features of movement of wind, occurrence of rainfall, crop pattern, public health, political changes, etc. which are directly connected with the motion of the earth for want of data. Of course there are computerised meteorological data and satellite data for predicting rain, etc. but assessment of crop pattern, political and other changes cannot be done from the data that are available to us now. But this type of assessment is being made in India at least from the time of the fifth century AD, i.e., from the time of the *Bṛhatsaṁhitā* which is very well-known. It is the earnest duty of the earth scientists to formulate such a theory and give guidance to the people on the climate, rainfall and the types of crop that can be grown and geological and ecological changes that may take place based on a sound 'Theory of the Earth'. Data is being collected for the world at large but it has been difficult to process the vast amount of data to formulate principles though the world has shrunk due to the revolution in communication. Anyhow, such a theory may not be expected in modern science in the near future.

While scientific developments are taking place rapidly in the West, we in the Orient should make an attempt to at least consolidate the information that is available in the Eastern literature. Sanskrit is unrivalled in its antiquity and scope, and India has been fortunate to possess such a grand treasure.

It has been mentioned that the Vedic Āryans were childern of nature. They saw and attributed divinity to whatever aspect of nature they encountered in the place of their origin. Their interaction with nature resulted in their appreciation of each aspect of nature after a good deal of observation. These appreciations have formed the basis of the Vedic hymns. They have found divinity in the rains, forests, air, fire, thunderstorms, morning, the sun, moon, planets, night, oceans, etc. There is no fear in their description of these aspects of nature. Their appreciation is very bold and they pray to these aspects for bestowing plenty and prosperity on them. One can view the personification of these aspect in the Vedic hymns as a reflection of the people themselves. According to Ganguli (1989),

> In his commentary on Jaimini Sūtras 1/2 and 9/1 Shabara has elaborately shown how the mantras apparently describing the limbs and deeds of gods, are really arthvādas, the significance of which ends in inducement to perform the appropriate sacrifice. They do not assert the factual existence of embodied gods who eat the havis and favour the sacrificers with the benefits asked for. The theory of arthvāda is ultimately related to the theory of personification of nature through primitive metaphorical construction. The theory of personification and primitive metaphor had developed long before 650-500 BC the assumed approximate period of Yāska who refers to the Yāgnika tradition of Vedic interpretation and faithfully records in view that gods are inanimate objects of nature personified in metaphorical construction. According to the school of Nirukta, of which Yāska is the only known representative whose work has come down to us, all gods are derived from their original god, fire, the

> terrestrial god; air (or Indra) the atmospheric god and the Sun, the god of outer space. Durgācārya comments that there is no question of these gods being animate personal beings (Purushavidha), for they are perceptibly inanimate objects of nature. Similar is the case with all other gods, who are metaphorically personified. It is well known that Yāska interprets the myth of Indra's slaying of Vrtra as the metaphorical expression of thunderclouds charged with lightning bursting into rain. Sometimes Vrtra is conceived as a huge black serpent which is a metaphor for the dark rainy clouds covering the sky.

A good deal of discussion had ensured in the post-Vedic period amongst the *darśanakāras* as to the divine attributes of the natural agencies. I shall not go into all such details here. However, it is relevant to quote some of the observations which support the present endeavour. Ganguli (1989) notes,

> A section of ritualists hold the view that Vedic mantras are relevant to rituals only as incantations, but not as meaningful expressions. Some mantras have no comprehensible meaning at all, some have meanings which are patently self contradictory. Again there are some whose meanings, though befitting relation to conscious persons, have been absurdly bound up with inanimate objects. For example, in a certain mantra even stones are supposed to hear an address. This is absurd. So recitation of mantras in a ritual does not involve any understanding of their meaning.

Ganguli (1989) observes

> the Sāmkhya contention that the Brahman as the absolute consciousness cannot be the material cause of the unconscious material world. The material cause of the material world can only be the primordial matter which

> is called prakrti or pradhāna by the Sānkhya. To this the Vedantin may reply that the so called material objects are only seemingly material. They are really conscious elements. Otherwise how can we explain Sruti texts such as 'Thus spake the earth', 'Thus spake water?' So these are conscious objects; inert unconscious matter cannot speak.

Further Ganguli (1989) says,

> Jaimini declares that all gods are basically material objects which are defied through personification involving superimposition of consciousness on the unconscious. In his commentary Sankara asserts that material objects like the Sun, etc. are not unconscious things, but are really conscious deities.

These arguments of the ancient schools of *darśana*s lead us to believe that all objects of nature are personified metaphors in the *Veda*s with the field of consciousness existing within them in a passive way. Perhaps this is the crux of the problem distinguishing the Indian philosophy from Western philosophy, where nature is dealt with as nature only and nothing else.

Take the case of a seed or an egg; the process of sprouting or hatching is merely a process. Life exists in the seed or egg. By the natural process it gets life. According to Caraka (Ray and Gupta, 1965, p. 120),

> The individual is a replica of the universal; both the external world and the individual are the manifestations of one and the same eternal spirit (Brahman). In other words, *spirit and matter are not two separate entities but one integral whole.* Both man and the visible world are composed of six elements. Prithwi (earth), Ap (water or liquid), Tejas (fire), Vāyu (air) and Ākāśa (ether) are

common to both. The sixth element, the spirit or self in the individual, is equivalent to Brahman in the Universe.

Further, it is observed that

> Conception occurs inside the womb by the union of semen, ovum and the spirit. By the physical act of mating, union takes place between the semen (sperm) and the female ovum (germ); then the spirit, associated with the mind, descends and enters into the zygote formed, and a new embryonic life is created. If the spirit does not descend, no life is created and conception fails to occur.

Further,

> It is the mind which yokes the living organism to the spirit and holds the senses together. With the departure of mind, the organism becomes a life-less matter.

The interaction of life with the material earth is 3600 million years old or more from the point of view of the geological records. Unless the subtler spirit of *Brahman* which is omnipresent and omnipotent exists, the grosser spirit of life cannot get manifested. The grosser life spirit is then encased within the grosser matter of the earth for life to manifest itself. This idea makes us think that consciousness is not superimposed over the unconscious matter, but the field of consciousness (*Brahman*) exists everywhere and is within the field of material universe also. Otherwise the omnipresence of *Brahman* cannot be substantiated. By this, all the natural agencies are to be regarded as living in the sense that life exists in the seed or egg. Since modern science does not subscribe to the concept of the *Brahman* as put forward by Indian philosophy and it sees the seed or egg as matter without life, it has remained confined to the threshold of the material world. Such an exposition has been the bane of Western philosophy especially as the one based on modern science.

It is not without reason that the Vedic Āryans instilled a kind of divinity into the natural agencies. They could have sung and praised these natural aspects without personifying them but then they would have had a drab and matter-of-fact existence devoid of life and the ability to influence the environment, especially the human environment. Their philosophy then would have ended with some material end as has been the case in the world of Western science. That would have led man to an agnostic end. This is the kind of argument advanced by the Cārvāka school of Indian philosophy. By instilling divinity into the aspects of nature, the Vedic Āryans at once graduated from the just material world to a spiritual world, the advantage of which was immense. It is rather difficult to assess the potential benefit of the *Vedas* to humanity. The philosophy based on this instilling of divinity in the natural aspects has helped great thinkers from time immemorial to realise the truth of existence.

In the above context, it is the earnest endeavour of the writer to interpret the true nature of the various geological agencies described in the *Vedas* in their proper perspective. Though the subject-matter of the *Vedas* has to do with only data collection — part of a wider 'Theory of the Earth', it will be brought out in its full scope for the researcher. The information from the modern physical geology will rather supplement the Vedic idea which is usually suggestive as well as conceptual. The whole earth and its aspects have been the subject-matter of the *Vedas*. It contains information pertaining to the modern scientific compartments of geomathematics, geoastronomy, geochemistry, geophysics, geobotany and the geological discipline. One may wonder that the first book of nature, the *Vedas* contain all such information not in primitive form but to an advanced extent compared to many civilisations in the contemporaneous world. It may be mentioned that the *Vedas* contain the earliest discourses on the earth and its various aspects.

Not only have the rivers, mountains, plants and even the stones been elevated to godhood, but the sun, the moon, the planets and the stars, the dawn, night, rains, thunderstorm, and other aspects of nature have also been personified as gods. What is then the nature of godhood of the Vedic Āryans? This is a very important question. God or divinity is a word derived from 'divine' or day or *dyu*. All these aspects of nature observed in the day time as full of vigour and force appealed to the Āryan mind. They saw the air, fire, rains, sunlight, moonlight, etc. as superior powers or forces of nature. These happen to be superior for, the work that such natural agencies do cannot be done by any individual, however powerful one may be. The water can be drunk by many simultaneously and it will help all at the same time. However, a man can only attend to one person at a time. A man is elevated to godhood sometimes when he is addressing his students as a teacher, for then he can influence the minds of all his students at a time. That is how '*guru brahma* . . .' is repeated. Thus godhood is a superior power and this was attributed to the natural geological agencies by the Āryans. It is generally expressed in the concept of field in the sense of a magnetic field, an electric field or a geothermal field, atmosphere, hydrosphere, lithosphere, etc. In the two-dimensional approach, the ratio between circumference and the radius of a circle is roughly 10/3 — what is called pie value. This is the actual term *tri-daśāḥ* used to address the gods. The field concept was prevalent amongst the Vedic Āryans when they defined the *kosas* or shells like *annamayakoṣa*, *prāṇamayakosa*, *manomayakoṣa*, *vijñānamayakoṣa* and *ānandamayakosa*. Also. the concept of evolution of *ākāśa*, *vāyu*, *āgni*, *āp* and *pr̥thvī* presumes that those in one field for successive *bhutas* have the qualities of the previous *bhūtas* invested in them. It is similar to the fact of the gravitational, geomagnetic, geoelectric fields simultaneously existing through the earth. Each field is subtler than the previous one, and thus the grossest being is manifested in the form of matter for easy perception.

Superiority and action have been the most fundamental factors attributing divinehood to the various natural geological agencies. Similarly, the light that is shed by the Sun and Moon, the fall of night and the onset of day all around, the fall of rains over large tracts, the flow of rivers with force, the overall growth of forests, the vastness of land and sea, the lofty mountains, etc. had a scintillating effect on the Āryan mind. They simply addressed them as gods. The vastness of the sky, the distant lights from planets and stars, the force of the thunderstorm, the universal effect of fire, etc. also had similar salutary effects. The Āryans faced the nature surrounding them boldly, and interacted with it in a manner of a child with its father. The result was the composition of the Vedic hymns.

Each *r̥ṣi-kula* had its own set of observations which continued for several generations. The *r̥ṣi-kula*s had a common nomenclature for many of the geological agencies and there was a kind of similarity in their praise of these agencies as can be observed in the various *kula-maṇḍala*s of the *Ṛgveda*. Though there are a good number of synonyms for each and every aspect of the natural agency, the Aryan *r̥ṣi*s employing them meant the object for which the synonyms were applied. Though the use of some of them suggests that at times their appreciation disappeared and boredom crept in, it also shows how much the natural agencies meant to them in their day-to-day lives.

In the above context, the Vedic Āryans are the earliest students of the earth; their studies incorporated in the *Veda*s form the foundation of the most elegant natural philosophy which has not been surpassed even to this day. Though the Vedic data cannot be made a substitute for the modern geological data, the latter is supplementary to the Vedic data. An integration of the two, it is felt, would pave the way for formulating the principles of a sound 'Theory of the Earth' based on which the future course of the earth can be predicted satisfactorily.

PART I

THEORETICAL OBSERVATIONS

1

Bhū Maṇḍala

SUBJECT-MATTER OF THE VEDIC LITERATURE

It is a general estimate that there are some 20,000 hymns in all the four *Veda*s. More than half of this make up the *Ṛgveda*. The *Yajurveda* and *Sāmaveda* contain considerable portions of the *Ṛgveda* with some additions. The *Atharvaveda* also owes much of its compositions, more than 1000 *mantras*, to *Ṛgveda*. Broadly, we may say that the *Ṛgveda* is the right representative of all the *Veda*s, being the oldest and the grandest.

It has also been mentioned that the Vedic literature was stupendous in the pre-Vyāsa period and Vyāsa grouped them into the *Ṛg*, *Yajur* and *Sāma* divisions, mostly to help in the performance of the sacrificial ceremonies. This was also to help commit the voluminous literature of the *Veda*s to memory. From then onwards, the singular institution of the *Veda*s has been transmitted by one generation to the next by word of mouth, a system which has no comparison in the whole world. That is how the *Veda*s have come to us down four or five millennia without change of a single spelling or accent. This may be called the eighth wonder of the world. Only in the later part of the nineteenth century was the *Ṛgveda* edited (by Max-Müller), printed (funds provided by the East India Company) and published (in 1885).

Later, Śrīpāda Dāmodara Sātavalekar, with the help of many scholars, edited all the *Vedas* and published them from the Svādhyāya Maṇḍala, Pāradi. Though the commentary on the *Vedas*, i.e., *Vedārtha Prakāśa* was brought out by Madhva-Sāyaṇācārya in the fourteenth century, the original *Vedas* were printed only in the latter part of the nineteenth century and the early part of the twentieth century. Since the entire *Vedas* could not be had at a single source, that too with the commentary, it was not possible for any individual to undertake serious research into the *Vedas* prior to their printing. What they contained was a bugbear for many and even those who could expound them. It was not possible to easily interpret the *Vedas* for the simple reason that they had been learnt by heart just for the sake of preservation.

The Ṛgveda

The Ṛgvedic hymns can be divided into the following five groups: (1) Natural or Geological, (2) Geographical, (3) Historical, (4) Social, and (5) Religious.

Majority of the *sūktas* come under the natural or geological division; some give data on the geographical aspects of the Ṛgvedic period; a few give the dynastic history of the solar and lunar kings to trace the history of the kings of the *Ṛgveda*; many *sūktas* concern themselves with various sociological aspects like the game of dice, the song of the frogs, the marriage-ceremony, conversation between separated lovers, importance of farming and protection of cows, importance of *dāna* and healthy living; and finally, most of these *sūktas* are concerned with religious discourse. Here we are concerned only with the natural or geological aspects of the *Ṛgveda* since they are the most important *sūktas* with the earliest interpretation of the physical-geological aspects.

The *sūktas* which have a description of geological aspects are also those with much religious significance. As mentioned earlier, the natural geological aspects have been described as Indra, Agni, Vāyu, Varuṇa, Uṣas, Sandhyā, etc. Some 33 dieties have been described in all the *Vedas*. They are the 8 Vasus, 11 Rudras, 12 Ādityas, Indra and Prajāpati. The Vasus are Agni, Pṛthvī, Vāyu, Antarikṣa, Āditya, Dyu, Candramā and Nakṣatras; the Rudras are the 10 Prāṇa Vāyus in the human body and Ātmā; and the Ādityas are the names of the 12 zodialc constellations of the Sun.

A distressing factor in the editing of the *Vedas* by Vyāsa is the imbalanced treatment of literature pertaining to the above aspects. Vyāsa thus probably took the entire collection of the *kula-maṇḍalas* and formed them into various books of the *Ṛgveda*. There is no uniform treatment of all deities in them. For example, more than a quarter of the entire Ṛgvedic *sūktas* are devoted to Indra alone; some 200 *sūktas* are attributed to Agni; about 120 *sūktas* praise Soma; Viśvedevas are described by some 40 *sūktas*; about 12 *sūktas* are devoted to Varuna; more than 50 *sūktas* deal with Aśvins; the Sun is described in about 40 *sūktas*; Āpas in about four; Pūṣan in about eight; Parjanya in about three of them; Uṣas in about 20; Bṛhaspati in about 11; Rudra in about three; Viṣṇu in about six; Maruts in about 33; Savitṛ in about 11; Dyāvāpṛthivī in about six and Mitra-Varuṇa in many. There is scope for editing the Ṛgvedic *mantras* dealing with Indra alone, Agni alone, Varuṇa alone, Vāyu alone, and so on. All those *sūktas* pertaining to the Rudras, the Vasus, the Ādityas, etc. can be regrouped and examined to get a complete picture. Even for religious purposes, such a classification of the *Vedas* would be of great help.

The distribution of the *sūktas* may probably indicate the relative importance of these geological agencies. Had the *Vedas* been only religious texts, there would not have been scope for the inclusion of historical, social, geographical and geological *sūktas* in the Vedic literature. Vyāsa, when he edited the *Ṛgveda*, probably wanted to abridge the then existing vast Vedic literature into a few books of standard education so that a person acquainted with the *Vedas* could get a perspective of the world at large to deal with sociological problems, know some useful history and also practise religious injunctions to lead a happy life as a good citizen.

Apart from the above, there are a couple of *sūktas* dealing with the profound aspects of creation of the universe and inquiring into the most fundamental aspects of nature. The concern of the Vedic sages to unravel the very foundation of the universal order is something to be admired. Though there is no clear-cut answer for such deep inquiries in the *Vedas*, the earnest desire of the students to know the first principles of nature is the crowning glory of the Vedic literature.

The Yajurveda

The essential feature of *Yajurveda* is its relevance to the performance of sacrifices. The *mantras* that are to be employed in performing *Rājasūya*, *Aśvamedha*, *Somayāga*, *Agniṣṭoma*, etc. are found in this *Veda*. There are two divisions of this *Veda*, viz., *Kṛṣṇa* and *Śukla*. The *Kṛṣṇa Yajurveda* is noted to have both prose and poetry in its *mantras* while *Śukla Yajurveda* is purely poetry. The available literature of *Yajurveda* consists of 7 *kāṇḍas*, 44 *adhyāyas* and 650 *anuvākas* (some say it is 631). The *Kṛṣṇa Yajurveda* has five *kāṇḍas*, namely *Prājāpatya*, *Saumya*, *Āgneya*, *Viśvedeva* and *Svāyambhuva*. Compared to this, *Śukla Yajurveda* is very limited; it is noted to have 40 *adhyāyas* and 1975 *mantras*. It is also said that this *Veda* was not edited by Vyāsa but edited by Yājñavalkya.

It is believed that there were some 85 *śākhās* in the *Kṛṣṇa Yajurveda* but only four are available now. They are the *Taittirīya*, *Maitrāyaṇī*, *Kaṭha* and *Kapisthala* of which only the *Taittirīya* is most prevalent in south India. Two *śākhās* of the *Śukla Yajurveda* are known, namely, Yājñavalkya and Vājasaneyi. Though there are two traditions in the *Śukla Yajurveda* called

Kāṇva and Mādhyandina, it appears that there is not much difference between them. The Kāṇva tradition is found in the south and the followers of Mādhyandina are more in north India.

Though this *Veda* is not as important as the *Ṛgveda* for students of earth science, yet there are some interesting features in *Iṣṭividhāna* and *Citi nirūpaṇa* for expounding early mathematics and geometry. But the fifth hymn of Vasordhārā which includes *rudra camaka prśna* is interesting from the geological point of view especially for its metallurgical information.

The Sāmaveda

Of the 1549 *ṛk*s constituting this *Veda*, all except 85 are drawn from the *Ṛgveda*. This *Veda* is the foundation for Indian music and there is very little information concerning earth science in it.

The Atharvaveda

As mentioned earlier, this *Veda* was a later addition to the Vedic literature. This *Veda* is also called *Brahmaveda*. Since there was the need for a *ṛtvik* in a *yajna* to look after the successful completion of the *yajña*, a person was nominated as Brahmā with that responsibility. He was supposed to know the means and methods to ward off impediments to the sacrifice and remove *doṣa*s of the *yajña*. Hence, that person acting as Brahmā was to be acquainted with the knowledge of destroying the impediments both outside and inside the family of the *yajña* performer. The methods for these have been enumerated in this *Veda*.

Of the 20 *kāṇḍa*s (with 730 *sūkta*s and 5987 hymns), the first thirteen deal with *abhicāra*; the 14th deals with marriage *mantra*s, the 15th is called *Vrātyakānda* and it deals with *mantra*s of Vrātya goddess; the 16th deals with *mantra*s for destroying bad dreams; the 17th *kānda* deals with *mantra*s for prosperity; the 18th deals with *mantra*s employed in *pitṛyajña*; the 19th deals with medical science; and the 20th with *mantra*s employed in some *yāga*. *Mantras* for growth of kingdoms and some philosophical aspects are also found in the 19th *kāṇḍa*. As already noted, some 1200 *mantras* of the 20th *kāṇḍa* have been drawn directly from the *Ṛgveda*. The *Atharvaveda* is noted to be the foundation of the science of Indian medicine. Many aspects, however, deal with the destruction of adversaries of a king or the family head. It is also observed that this *Veda* is the source of the science of Indian archery (*Dhanurveda*).

In addition to the above, there are *mantras* concerned with agricultural farming, environment, appeasement, use of precious vegetative crystals and organic shells, cleanliness, war, constitution, depoisoning, destruction of harmful insects, sociological and domestic issues etc. The most important from the point of view of earth-science studies is the first hymn entirely devoted to the earth, though the earth is praised in the *Ṛgveda* in combination with *dyāvā*. There are hymns on the aspects of time and on stars — the stars were known by the time of the *Ṛgveda* itself as is clear in the *Vedāṅgajyotiṣa* by Lagadha.

Thus the *Vedas* were texts prescribed for detailed study by heart in Āryan India. It contained geology, geography, history, botany, sociology, polity, agriculture, religion, environment among others, all blended in one. There was no education other than the *Veda* required at that time and the *Vedas* used to be learnt at the feet of a teacher for not less than 12 years, extendable up to 32 years. The earth sciences included the study of physical geology and geo-astronomy, and ore-geological studies. There might have been studies pertaining to gemmology. With the background of the studies concerning the geological agencies, the planets, the Moon and the Sun as well as the starry heaven, the Vedic sages initiated the formulation of the rudiments of a 'Vedic theory of the Earth' that culminated in the Upaniṣadic period which involved deep studies and contemplation. Most of the Ṛgvedic and some of the other Vedic literature were all concerned with the earth. Since there was no compartmentalisation of knowledge into various disciplines as in modern science, all such information remained scattered causing incoherency in the Vedic literature.

Amongst the six *aṅgas* or adjuncts of the *Vedas*, importance was given to mathematics and geo-astronomy in preference to all other disciplines. Grammar, teaching and science of metres, language, etc. were also emphasised. But scientific disciplines such as botany, chemistry, geology etc. did not receive individual attention; all these disciplines found a backseat when logic was applied to the *mahāvākyas* (statements with pregnant meaning to indicate the superior force underlying the visible universal manifestation), and various schools of *darśanas* and systems of Indian philosophy mushroomed. Alas! Not a single instance is available of incisive philosophical discourse involving the natural geological agencies, the luminaries, the planets, the stars and other aspects of nature! There was spectacular advancement in philosophy, astronomy, medicine, metallurgy, musicology, dance, drama, fine arts but hardly any advance appears to have been made in positive sciences including physics, chemistry, biology, geology etc.

The most important factor is the tracing of the origin of the Āryans to the Brahmāvartta and the Brahmarsideśa which are very close to the Spiti valley of the Himālayas. There is a geological section which brings the history of the earth from the Cambrian period to that of the Cretaceous, measuring a time gap of some 500 million years, which is included in the standard book on geology of those periods. There is some difference between the geology of the Spiti valley indicated to us and the standard geological record of the European stratigraphy. It would have been the singular fortune of India if the geology of the Spiti valley had been traced by the Āryan sages who dwelt in that place for millennia. That apart, the Indian philosophical approach for all local problems gave them some fanciful Purāṇic interpretations. For example, ammonite shells were found in the Spiti shales up the river Nārāyaṇī in Nepal which, having drained, supplied those shells to the lower stretches of the river joining the Gaṇḍakī. Instead of their correct identification as fossils, they have been worshipped as *śāligrāms* (Krishnan, 1956, p. 555) since ages. According to Krishnan, they (the Spiti shales) contain numerous fossils, particularly ammonites, which are often found enclosed in nodules. These ammonites called *śāligrāms* are brought down by the Gaṇḍak and other rivers in Nepal and are considered sacred by the Hindus. Some of the fossils have a coating of pyrites which gives them a golden colour. These golden-coloured ammonites have been addressed as *svarṇa śāligrāms*. This confirms that the Hindu thought is essentially spiritual.

GEOLOGICAL ASPECTS OF HINDU RELIGION

The above facts lead us to a few more interesting points. Though fundamentally the Hindu philosophy is most scientific particularly in terms of the Einsteinian observation that "Science without religion is lame and religion without science is blind", yet the later Sanskrit literature especially the *Purāṇas* and *Sthalamāhātmya* shows unscientific attitudes to many geological factors. For instance, on bathing in the various hot and cold water springs, some of which are charged with sulphur and radioactive elements, persons may find relief from some of the skin diseases. Such springs — the Rājgīrkuṇḍa, the Puttur springs, the thermal springs of Phugā valley etc. — are numerous in the subcontinent and they have been declared *tīrtha-kṣetras*. There is considerable Purāṇic literature to back them up with the most unscientific interpretations.

Similarly, the *liṅgas* in certain places of worship which have been designated as *udbhava liṅgas* are nothing but forms that have been a result of prolonged differential weathering of the ground or rocks. They, however, hold the religious spellbound and receive considerable appreciation. There are many such things throughout the country.

Again, there is the filling-up of a spoonful of water in the small hole on the head of the famous Agastyeśvara. The hole is said to fill up as soon as the water is removed from it. It is probably connected to a small spring underneath and so the filling-up is no miracle at all. It is simply a geological truth. Some *Purāṇas* describe the magnesite occurrences of the Chalk hills, Sālem in Tamil Nadu as the severed wings of Jaṭāyu (the eagle) that fought the epic villain Rāvaṇa at the time of Sītā's kidnapping. It is just that the material magnesite with its hacked appearance looks like severed bone structures to a non-geological mind. Innumerable anecdotes of this kind can be listed. Their mention here is only to clarify that such material does not constitute the data for a scientific interpretation of the *Vedas*.

The above observations do not in any way depreciate the acumen of the later architecture of the Hindus, Jains and Buddhists. The famous Jagannātha temple of Orissa is made out of rocks called Khoṇḍalites; the famous Hoysala Temples of Karnataka are carved out of steatite; those of Bādāmī are of sandstone. Many of the South Indian temples are made of granites, charnockites and similar rocks. Those of Maharashtra are made of basalt. The famous Ajantā and Ellorā cave temples — the marvels of carving — are of basalt, rocks which are highly jointed and break into angular pieces when even hammer weight is applied. The carvers deserve our utmost appreciation for their skill in dealing with such tricky rocks. Most of the temples in Gujarat and Rajasthan are of marble. The Sthāpatis or carvers have classified rocks by genders. They used to distinguish rocks into male, female and hermophrodite based on their acoustic property. Those rocks which produced a bronze sound on the application of hammer weight were called male, those producing a brass sound as female, and those distinct from both these as hermophrodite. In *Śilpa-śāstra*, the male rocks should be used for carving male deities, the female rocks for female deities and the hermophrodite rocks for making the base and other parts. But this has been flouted in many cases, as for example, as in the case of the Hoysala temples of Karnataka made of steatite which do not produce either male or female sound, and hence are 'hermophrodite' rocks. The icons made of this rock are simply left out of the discussion in the *Śilpa-śāstra.*

Another geological truth misinterpreted or camouflaged by Purāṇic literature is concerning the Triveṇī Saṅgam at Allahabad. There is only Dviveṇī Saṅgam at present due to the great confluence of the Gaṅgā and the Yamunā rivers. But it is believed that the third river Sarasvatī joins these rivers in sub-surface and hence it is called 'Suptanadī'. The existence of river Sarasvatī during the Vedic times, draining the present-day Ambālā district and flowing south-westwards to join the Arabian Sea (Murthy, 1980, pp. 189-92), has been explained earlier. But how can the river Sarasvatī join the Gaṅgā and Yamunā at Prayāga? The concept of 'Suptanadī' might be due to the fact that the waters of Sarasvatī were diverted to that of the Yamunā before its total extinction. Here, the geological facts have been camouflaged. This is a case of 'river piracy' in geomorphological terminology.

Thus there is the tendency to give religious colour to a geological truth since the Vedic period. This attitude is rooted in the Vedic times. Even the various geological agencies have been personified with metaphorical expressions. Instilling a religious faith into a natural phenomenon is in itself not bad; rather it has paved the way for a grand Indian philosophy. But when it is inculcated to the level of becoming a superstition and to the detriment of scientific truths, it leaves much to be desired in a person following this kind of 'scientific religion'. It is my endeavour here to remove unscientific aspects of the sacred texts and positively propound the science underlying the Vedic compositions. It is not my intention to find loopholes in Hindu religion but to expound scientific aspects in the Vedic texts to support their data from a scientific angle in order to substantiate their claim of a scientific natural philosophy. With this kind of conceptual or suggestive interpretation of the Vedic texts, it is hoped to find out the possibility of advancing modern science on the lines suggested therein for the benefit of science and humanity.

Indra

According to Macdonell (1976, p. 41):

> Indra is invoked alone in about one-fourth of the hymns of the *Ṛgveda*, far more than are addressed to any other deity; for he is the favourite national God of the Vedic people. He is more anthropomorphic on the physical side and more invested with mythological imagery, than any other member of the pantheon. He is primarily a god of the thunderstorm who vanquished the demon drought or darkness, and sets free the waters or wins the light. He is secondarily the god of battle who aids the victorious Āryan in overcoming his aboriginal foes.

Indra is the Lord of eastern directions. He is the chief of gods (Devarāja). According to the text of *Prapañcasārasaṁgraha*, Indra is conceived as seated on the all-white elephant of divine origin, Airāvata in the garden called Nandana containing the divine trees, Mandāra, Pārijāta, Santhāna, Kalpavṛkṣa and Haricandana. Indra is seated on a lotus seat and is four-armed. The right hand is depicted as bestowing a boon and the left hand is in a gesture of giving protection. He is holding a thunderbolt in the third hand and an elephant goad in the fourth. Alternatively, he may also be depicted as holding *śakti-āyudha* and *vajra*. He is given as one wearing red garments and applying fine unguents. He is surrounded by Śaci, his wife, to the right, Mātali, his driver, to the left and by Viśvedevas, Maruts, the eight Vasus, the two Aśvins, the eleven Rudras and Prajāpati. He is also sometimes depicted as holding a golden pot from which jewels stream out.

His weapons are said to be fashioned by Tvaṣṭṛ. His capital is called Amarāvatī. He is regarded as the first son of the twelve sons of Aditi from Kaśyapa, the sage. Thus he came to be regarded as Āditya. As per the Vedic hymns there will be an Indra to preside over the assembly of gods in each of the *Manvantaras* — a *Manvantara* being the duration of a Manu. This is more of an office than a person. His horse is called 'Uccaiśravas'. His assembly is *Sudharma*. He is represented as handsome and bedecked with ornaments including a splendid crown.

His weapon, the thunderbolt, prepared by Tvaṣṭṛ out of iron, is golden, tawny, sharp and many-pointed. Sometimes it is known to be made out of stone or stock. They have made a golden car drawn by two tawny steeds for him which he employs in wars. He sometimes fights with the bow and arrow. He is a great *soma*-drinker and drink will enthuse him to fight with Vṛtra, Śambara, Vala and other demons.

Though Indra has been mentioned as the son of Kaśyapa, he is also mentioned as one born to Dyau. Agni is his brother. Indra is often associated with the Maruts — his allies, Varuṇa, Vāyu and less often with Soma, Bṛhaspati, Pūṣan and Viṣṇu. Indra is mighty and he may be ten times bigger than the earth. Exhilarated by drinking *soma* and escorted by the Maruts, he attacks demon Vṛtra and due to this war, the heaven and earth tremble. He shatters Vṛtra with his bolt; the result is that Indra pierces the clouds and causes heavy rains which were denied by the demon Vṛtra. This is renewed each time. The clouds are compared to the mountains and the held-up water as cows imprisoned. Says Macdonell (1976),

> The physical elements in the conflict are nearly always the bolt, the mountain, waters or rivers, while lightning, thunder, cloud, rain are seldom directly named. The waters are often terrestrial, but also often aerial and celestial. The clouds are the mountains (parvata, giri) on which the demons dwell or from which Indra casts them down or which he cleaves to release waters. Or the cloud is rock (adri) which encompasses the cows (as the waters

> are sometimes called), and from which he releases them. Clouds as containing waters, figure as cows also; they further appear under the names of udder (udher), spring (utsa), cask (kavandha), pail (kohsa). The clouds moreover appear as the fortresses (puras) of the aerial demons, having described as moving, autumnal, made of iron or stone, and as 90, 99 or 200 in number. Indra shatters them and is characteristically called the 'fort destroyer' (purabhid).

The last attribute of Indra is interpreted by the historians as referring to the destruction of cities like Harappā and Mohenjo-Daro by the Āryans coming from outside of India and occupying the present area of Punjab, Jammu and Kashmir and Himachal Pradesh, driving the Draviḍas from there. This is nothing but a historical fallacy.

The destruction of the clouds and causing of rains resulted in sunshine and so Indra is attributed to have won the light, the sun and the dawn. He is supposed to have gained the sun from the darkness of the clouds. He is also said to have won *soma* by driving away the serpentine clouds and he is called 'Somapā'. His name 'Indra' itself is interpreted by Kshiraswamy commenting on the *Amarakośa* (K.G. Oka, 1913) as *indraha paramaiśvarya yogāt iti*, meaning 'since Indra is the lord of prime wealth, he is called so'. Giving synonyms Amarasiṁha mentioned Indra, Marutvān, Maghavān, Bidaujāha, Pākaśāsanaha, Vrddhaśravāḥ, Śunāsīraha, Puruhūtaha, Pūrṇadaraha, Jiṣṇuhu, Lekharśabaha, Śakraha, Śatamanyuhu, Divaspatihi, Sutrāmā, Gotrabhid, Vajrī, Vāsavaha, Vṛtrahā, Vṛṣā, Vāṣtoṣpatihi, Surapatihi, Balārātihi; Śacīpatihi, Jambabhedi, Harihayaha, Svarāṭ, Namucisūdanaha, Sankrandanaha, Duścyavanaha, Turāṣād, Meghavāhanaha, Pracīnabarhi, Ahihā, Pṛtanāśāt, Pulomajit, Ākhaṇḍalaha, Sahasrākṣaha, Ṛbhukṣā, etc.

The most important attribute of Indra is his control over the quaking mountains and plains. This is expressed in more than a single hymn. He is supposed to hold the earth and heaven separately, as two wheels kept apart. He stretches out heaven and earth like a hide, and holds them asunder. He is supposed to have defeated the demon who held the earth and the heaven together. Indra is also said to be the god of tempest. Storm is described as a violent disturbance of atmosphere with thunder or heavy rain, snow or hail, and is equated with tempest. (Griffiths, 1986)

> Thou art the Mighty one; when born, O
> Indra, with power thou terrified earth and heaven;
> When, in their fear of thee, all firm-set mountains and
> monstrous creatures shook like dust before thee.
> (Śatarcinas) (*Ṛ*V, I.63.1)

Perhaps this is the first reference in any literature describing the shaking of the mountains or earthquakes.

> When at thy shout, O Thunder-armed each thing
> both fixed and moving shook, Even Tvastar trembled
> at the wrath and quaked with fear because of thee,
> lauding thine own imperial sway. (Śatarcinas)
> (*Ṛ*V, I.80.14)

Like this, there are many *ṛ*ks describing the quaking of mountains and earth.

This aspect of the god Indra is found in almost all *maṇḍalas* of the *Ṛgveda.*

> By whom this universe was made to tremble
> (*Ṛ*V, II.12.4)
>
> Even the Heaven and Earth bow down before his very
> breath the mountains tremble.
> (*Ṛ*V, II.12.13)
>
> For him who followeth the Law the mountains and

Heaven and Earth stand as if firmly stabilised.
(*ṚV*, III.30.4)

Heaven trembled at the birth of thine effulgence;
Earth trembled at the fear of thy displeasure.
The steadfast mountains shook in agitation;
the waters flowed, and the desert spots were flooded.
(*ṚV*, IV.17.2)

It is observed :

With thou might cleavest even the rock under as :
(*ṚV*, V.30.4)

It is observed by Bharadvāja thus :

Thou, Wonderous, Shaker of things firm,
(*ṚV*, VI.18.5)

And, Mightiest! roaring! boldly rent in pieces things that were firmly fixed and Never shaken .....
(*ṚV*, VI.22.6)

Through fear of thee, O Indra, all the regions of Earth, though naught may move them, shake and tremble. All that is firm is frightened at thy coming —
The earth, the heaven, the mountains and the forests.
(*ṚV*, VI.31.2)

O Indra, thou hast filled mid-air's wide region
and given the gods by battle room and freedom.
(*ṚV*, VII.98.3)

Kaṇvas have observed :

Before thee, Thunder-armed! all beings tremble
the heaven and earth before thee shake with terror.
(*ṚV*, VIII.86.14)

By his truth supported earth's foundation

> The counterpart of heaven and earth is Indra.
>
> (*Ṛ*V, X.111.4-5)

> Thou (Indra) in the heavens hast set the ordering of the Moon.
>
> (*Ṛ*V, X.138.6)

The most important of all these hymns is the one that says :

> He who fixed fast and firm the earth that strengthened and set at rest the agitated Mountains,
> Who measured out the air's wide middle region and gave the heaven support, He man is Indra.
>
> (*Ṛ*V, II.12.2)

In all the above hymns, it is clear that Indra is not a person or God but that force which separates the earth from the sky or space and holds them in order as well as the moon, fixing them in their orbit of rotation to prevent a wobbling condition.

The first attribute of Indra is destroying the clouds and causing rains. The second attribute of Indra is causing the earthquake and fixing the earth firmly on its path of movement.

That these two attributes have been the characteristics of Indra from a scientific point of view is clear from the Ṛgvedic texts. These observations have been made by not one *ṛṣi* but all *kulapatis* in their respective *maṇḍalas*. Hence, they require a detailed prognosis from the more scientific point of view.

As far as the first tribute is concerned, the reference is to the natural principle underlying the formation of clouds from the oceans owing to the sun's heat and causing of rains by dissolving such clouds. Indra endowed with the weapon of *vajrāyudha* or thunderbolt is personification. Thunder is the loud noise following the flash of lightning due to discharge of electricity through the air. It is a geomagnetic/electric phenomenon. Thus, the concept of Indra is the Sanskrit Vedic nomenclature for the usual geophysical phenomena.

This geophysical phenomena has a lot to do with the origin and evolution of the earth. It is now understood that after the earth material was separated and forming into the earth, the earth underwent what is called Primary Geophysical Differentiation. As a result of this process the earth got differentiated into an outer shell, an inner mantle and an interior core. The outer shell is essentially made of silicates of alumina and magnesia and hence called SIAL and SIMA; the core is essentially made of iron and nickel and addressed as NIFE; and the mantle has a composition comparable to that of the chromosphere of the sun. The most interesting feature of this differentiation is the generation of a geomagnetic field due to the earth's core, which generates a shell outside the earth from which all harmful rays of the external world are filtered through paving the way for the origin of the sedimentary cycle and life on earth. It is impossible to fully evaluate the contribution of this process, for its later evolution has been unique in the whole visible universe. The formation of clouds and causing of rains and the cycle of weathering, denudation, transportation of sediments and their deposition in the oceans began in due course (Shankara Narayana, 1989).

The word *vidyut* has been employed at many places in the *Ṛgveda*. Since the interaction between the Vedic sages and the natural phenomena was of first hand, it is rather difficult to expect the early human understanding to go beyond the usual observation made by *ṛṣis*. However, it is very clear that they meant a geophysical phenomenon in their personification called Indra.

Why did the Ṛgvedic sages address a geophysical phenomenon as Indra is rather difficult to answer. Probably they attributed to the rains all kinds of prosperity and believed that prosperity was invested in the phenomenon of release of rains from the clouds.

They were right and even to this day prosperity can be measured as per the amount of rain a land receives. Since all prosperity was to be measured from the amount of rains, the Ṛgvedic sages named this phenomenon as Indra — which has been defined earlier as giver of supreme wealth or *paramaiśvaryatvāt-indraha.*

That Indra has been praised by all the ṛṣis of the *kula-maṇḍalas* shows the kind of appreciation the Vedic sages had for the phenomenon of cloud formation and the rains. Since this is the fundamental measure of national prosperity, the sages have rightly composed so many *sūktas* on it, numbering more than a quarter of the *Ṛgveda.* Even to this day, the prosperity of the subcontinent of India is based on the monsoon rains it receives. Can there be any objection to the fact that the Vedic Āryans praised such a grand phenomenon in many terms as per their own understanding?

It is hard to believe that even though the Vedic ṛṣis praised Indra in many *sūktas*, no temple of Indra was constructed in later ages as per the directives of the *Kalpa* literature. Indra, however, occupies an important seat amongst the *Aṣṭa Dikpālas*, as he is the lord of the eastern directions. This also has scientific significance. The solar flares influencing the geomagnetic field is from the eastern direction. Perhaps this signifies the true direction of Indra.

That Indra causes floods and the Āryans witnessed heavy rains filling the streams and rivers with high current in the region occupied by them in Brahmāvartta and Brahmarṣideśa is evident from many a hymn in the *Ṛgveda.* It has been described to such an extent that one can feel the monotony of repetition. This may be because the Āryans made an emphatic effort realising the fundamental importance of the phenomenon in the generation of wealth and prosperity.

It can be seen that even the iconographic description of Indra fits in most admirably. His vehicle is the elephant which can be compared to the dark clouds; his tawny colour itself is the colour of the rains; his weapon, the thunderbolt is the one causing the rains or generated during the fall of rains; his one hand depicting benediction refers to the all-round prosperity brought about by the rains for humanity.

The second attribute of Indra has to do with firmly fixing the shaking earth and mountains. This is a very important aspect from the geological point of view. According to Bhat (1986, p. 1106),

> In bygone days the Earth, being shaken severely by the winged mountains which flew up and came down heavily, spoke bashfully to the creator (Brahma) in the assembly of Gods — 'My Lord, the name you have given me, namely *Acala* (Immovable), is falsified by the flying mountains, and I am unable to put up with this suffering'. Hearing these words of Mother Earth, who was choked with tears and whose lower lip quivered slightly, and observing her downcast face with tears flowing from eyes, the Creator spoke thus: 'Indra, remove this humiliation of Mother Earth; throw your thunderbolt and chop off the wings of the mountains'. At this, Indra said, 'So be it', and consoled her with the words 'Do not fear'; but Wind, Fire, myself and Varuna will shake you in the four parts of the day and night put together respectively in order to reveal the good and bad effects of actions to the world.

This is a story couched with the geological facts. Soon after the consolidation of the earth from its molten conditions originating out of hot clouds from the sun, micro-continents and micro-oceans appeared on the surface of the earth. Because of the early instability of the crust, probably it raised itself at some points and lowered itself at some other points with frequency. This instability is the fact that made the earth complain to the creator in the story. Though the earth has attained some kind of stability in some of its landmasses of ancient crystalline substance, it is still unstable along the plate margins and numerous earthquakes originate at these points even to this day. This is probably what was told by Indra to the earth when he said that he and others will shake her in certain parts of the day. According to Varāhamihira (Bhat, 1986),

> Some sages hold that an earthquake is brought about by the huge animals living in the waters of the ocean, while others (like Garga) opine that it is the result of the rest that is resorted to by the elephants of the quarters that are tired by the weight of the earth. Yet other sages like Vasishtha declare that it is caused by the atmospheric wind colliding with another and falling to the earth with a booming sound. There are still others like Vriddhagarga who maintain that it is occasioned by some unseen power.

These observations on the causes of earthquakes may make the modern students of seismology consider the Ṛgvedic sages as the earliest students of earthquake studies in the world. A considerable study has been made by the sages on the occurrences and causes of earthquakes. This theory needs deep study and examination by modern scholars for its veracity and for any support it may offer to a theory for prediction of earthquakes, which is still due. Located in the foothills of the Western Himālayan region which is prone to earthquakes, the sages were curious about them in those ages. According to Parāśara,

> The earthquakes are caused by eclipses of luminaries, unnatural phenomena occurring in the planets and special movements of the heavenly bodies.

Adopting the views of sages Garga and Ṛṣiputra which differ from those of Vṛddhagarga, Parāśara and Kaśyapa, Varāhamihira has made the following observations in predictive seismology:

> The stellar circle or group presided over by the Wind God (Vāyu) consists of the seven constellations, viz., Uttarāphālguṇī, Hasta, Chita, Swāti, Punarvasu, Mrigashira and Aświni. The following symptoms of this circle will appear a week in advance: the quarters will be covered with smoke; a strong wind will blow throwing the dust of the earth breaking down trees; and the Sun will not shine brightly. The effects of an earthquake of the Wind Circle (Vāyu Maṇḍala) are the following: Destruction of crops, water, forests and herbs, outbreak of swellings, asthma, lunacy, fever and phlegmatic affections, and trouble to the trading class, courtesans, warriors, physicians, women poets, musicians, traders (of commodities), artisans, the Saurāshtras, Kurus, Magadha country, Dashārṇa region and the Matsyas.
>
> The fire circle (Agni Manḍala) consists of the seven asterisms—Pushya, Krttika, Vishākhā, Bharaṇi, Magha, Pūrvābhādra and Pūrvāphalguṇi. It reveals its symptoms a week in advance in the following manner. The sky will be filled with falling stars and meteors and will appear aglow as a result of the fire in the horizon; and fire aggravated by the wind will rage over the land. During an earthquake of the Fire Circle, clouds will be destroyed; lakes and tanks will dry up; kings will be at loggerheads with one another; herpes, scab, fever, erysipelas and jaundice will break out; and men of great valour, hot tempered persons, the Ashmakas, Angas, Bāhlikas, Tanganas, Kalingas, Vangas, Dravidas and hillmen of various tribes will be troubled.
>
> The seven asterisms, Abhijit, Śravaṇa, Dhanishtha, Rohini, Jyeshtha, Uttarabhādra and Anurādha, constitute

Indra's Circle. Its symptoms are the following. The clouds looking like moving mountains, sending forth loud peals of thunder, containing flashes of lightning and resembling in colour buffaloes' horn, swarms of bees and serpents, will pour down rains. An earthquake occurring in Indra's circle will ruin men of celebrated families and castes, famous persons, kings and heads of corporations. It will also produce dysentery, swelling of the throat, facial diseases and severe vomiting. It will cause trouble to the people of Kāśi, Yugandhara, the Pauravas, Kirātas, Kīras, Abhisāras, Halas, Madras, Arbudas, Saurāshtra and Mālava countries. It will however bring good rains.

Varuṇa's Circle is constituted by the seven asterisms, Revati, Pūrvāshāḍha, Ārdra, Āslesha, Mūla, Uttarābhādrapada, and Śatabhisha. Its indications appearing a week before are the following. High clouds resembling blue lily, bees and collyrium in colour, rumbling pleasantly, and shining with flashes of lightning, will pour down slender lines of water resembling sharp sprouts. An earthquake of this circle will kill those that are dependent on the seas and rivers; and will lead to excessive rains. People will also bury the hatchet. It will destroy the Gonardas, Kukuras, Kirātas and the people of Videha.

It is also observed that an earthquake bears fruit in six months and a portentous thunder in two months. The sage Garga is noted to include other portents such as eclipses and fall of meteors.

Varāhamihira is noted to have observed that the fruition of an earthquake of Wind Circle takes two months, the Fire Circle takes three fortnights, Indra's Circle takes seven days and Varuṇa's Circle takes immediate effect.

The other portents included by Varāhamihira in his book

Samāsasaṁhitā is given by Bhat (1986) as follows:

> Meteors, serial city, dust, portentous thunder, earthquake, fires in the quarters, furious winds, eclipses of the luminaries, unnatural phenomena in the case of any star or group of stars,rain without clouds, anything unnatural in the sky, excessive rain (or stormy rain), smoke without fire, flames without sparks, entry of wild animals into a village, sight of rainbow at night, unnatural phenomena at the junctures, broken halos round the Sun or the Moon, contrary flow of rivers, and sounds of musical instruments in the heaven. The effect of any other phenomenon which is unnatural should be predicted on the basis of the above Manḍalas or Circles.

Most important is the following observation:

> If there be an earthquake in the Fire Circle and wind period or vice-versa (i.e. Fire period and Wind Circle) there will be calamities or death of celebrated monarchs; and people would be tortured by the dread of famine, mortality and drought. . . . Should an earthquake occur in the Varuṇa Circle and Indra Period or vice-versa, there would be plenty of food crops, prosperity, rain and joy and contentment in the world. Cows would yield milk in abundance and kings settle their differences.

It is also observed by Bhat (1986),

> An earthquake occurring in the Manḍala of Wind shakes the earth to an extent of 200 yojanas; one of the Fire Circle, 110 yojanas; one of Varuna's, 180 yojanas; and one of Indra's, 160 yojanas.

The foundation of the modern theory of earthquakes on scientific terms came into existence in 1897 when Oldham made a thorough study of the Assam earthquakes in the Geological Survey of India. From then onwards the science of seismology has advanced very much; yet there is hardly any theory for predicting earthquakes. In the context of the above, it is worth attempting to examine the theory of earthquakes put forth by the Vedic sages and Varāhamihira for their veracity and to formulate an integrated theory for predicting earthquakes.

All these observations are noted here because they are essentially connected with Indra, i.e., the geomagnetic field, the influence of which is no less in causing earthquakes. The portents listed by Varāhamihira include geo-magnetic storms causing arial city, auroras, etc. The intensity of the earthquake given in *yojanas* may be taken as 8 km per *yojana* and calculated.

Since all the geological changes, especially the geo-morphological ones, including the climate and environment, are due to the precession of the equinoxes under the general force of universal gravitation, it may be possible to consider formulating a theory of predicting earthquakes based on the disposition of major planets which have considerable angular momenta. One may find out the centre of the total angular momenta of the solar system at the deep focus earthquakes in the past and determine the positions of fluctuation in the path of the total angular momenta arrived at by finding out the advanced positions of major planets.

It must be possible for students of earth science to examine the issues connected with the term, Indra — a Sanskrit term for a natural geophysical phenomena — in the *Ṛgveda*, especially by applying Indian logic. There is not much difference in the concept of Indra as given by the sages, and all appear to extend the same idea regarding the concept of Indra. But later, due to the interrelationship of Indra and other geological agencies, concepts like Indrāgni, Indrāmarutaha, etc. came into existence. By the time of the Kṛṣṇayajurvedic Rudra Camaka Praśna, the concept of Indra must have been much diluted, for Indra is mentioned there along with Agni, Soma, Savitā, Sarasvatī, Pūṣa, Bṛhaspati, Mitra, Varuṇa, Tvaṣṭā, Dhātā, Viṣṇu, Aświnau, Marutahaha, Viśvedevāha, Pṛthvī, Antarikṣa, Dyau, Dīśāha, Mūrdhā, Prajāpati. According to Sāyaṇa, it is with the intention of *samāna dharma* or equal identity that the various Vedic deities have been invited along with Indra — that is to say, the multipotency of Indra in encompassing all these deities. This would lead us to recognise the fact of the universal influence that the geomagnetic field has with all these aspects.

Having identified so many geological agencies like Agni, Varuṇa, Maruts, etc. and praising them individually, the Vedic Āryans finally observed that all such forces had equal identity. Then they observed that all forces are the different aspects of one and the same fundamental force. In the *Ṛgveda*, it is observed, according to Bose (1970, p. 318):

> They speak of Indra, Mitra, Varuṇa, Agni and there is the Divine, winged Suparṇa.
> The one being the wise call by many names as Agni, Yama, Mātariśvan.
>
> (*ṚV*, I.164.49)

Here the ultimate reality is arrived at and this possibly identifies the *Brahman*. All such field forces like Indra, Agni, Mitra, Varuṇa, Vāyu, etc. described individually by many Vedic sages in different hymns finally boil down to a single field force out of which they originate and into which they dissolve or merge. This single, all-unified force is called *Brahman* in Indian philosophy. It underlies the natural world with all its multiplicity of a fundamental unity under the cover of general diversity.

This truth of natural philosophy is being realised slowly by modern scientific philosophy in arriving at a unified theory. But it must be observed that the modern scientific philosophy is bereft of the living universe. The 'living' universe has been taken into consideration by the Vedic sages in their perception of geological and other natural agencies as personified forces. Thus, the Indian thinking appears to be wholesome in its approach to the universe which is living as well as non-living. A philosophy which leaves out the living world and examines the issues of the non-living world alone cannot be complete. All this shows the relevance of Indian philosophy.

In this sense, the distinct quality of the Vedic literature as the most fundamental data of natural philosophy cannot be over-exaggerated. There is no other single text in any language under the Sun as the *Vedas* which help a student to understand nature in its varied aspects and know about the most fundamental of all such aspects. The indebtedness of a student to the Vedic sages is something stupendous and the world as a whole stands greatly indebted to Vedic literature for ever.

With regard to the rain-clouds and their dissolution as the first principle of Indra which is so highly praised in the Vedic hymns, the *ṛṣis* later realised that it was just a nature-principle of order. They appear to have abandoned this concept of Indra and their observations have been the great foundations of Indian meteorology from a very long time. In the absence of texts earlier to *Bṛhatsaṁhitā* of Varāhamihira, it has not been possible to trace the ideas of the sages who abandoned the concept of Indra on meteorology. Varāhamihira (Jha, 1959, p. 636) in his monumental text deals with the subject of rains and its prediction in about eight chapters as given below:

21. Garbhalakṣaṇa
22. Garbhadhāraṇa
23. Pravarṣaṇa
24. Rohiṇīyoga
25. Swātiyoga
26. Āṣāḍhiyoga

27. Vātacakra and
28. Sadyovarṣaṇa

In the Garbhalakṣaṇa, i.e., pregnancy of clouds, Varāhamihira mentions that food forms the very life of living beings and it is dependent upon the rains. Hence, the subject of cloud formation, rains, etc. must be thoroughly investigated. He never brings in the 'Indra' concept which perhaps paved the way for pragmatic reasoning. He then makes references to the observations made by Parāśara, Garga, Kaśyapa and Vajra, ('Vajra' is meant by Bādarāyaṇa, Asita and Devala). There must have been some extensive literature pertaining to the aspect of rain and its annual prediction attributed to these sages in the post-Vedic period. This clearly suggests that during the post-Vedic period sages had abandoned the concept of Indra to whom the first attribute of rains was referred to by the *Vedas*. These sages through their reasoning and detailed study have been the originators of Indian meteorology.

While the first attribute of Indra was thus studied in depth for the development of Indian meteorology in the earliest period, study of the second attribute of Indra — Indra as the fixer of the shaky earth and his role in early seismology — was not pursued with similar zeal.

Thus, the concept of Indra in the Vedic literature has been connected to early Indian meteorology and seismology but couched in story form and personification with metaphors. The scientific aspects of this natural agency has not been clearly revealed. Whether one may call it the earliest principle of dissolution of clouds by thunderstorm or the cause of earthquake, the concept of Indra being directly indicative of the geomagnetic field is clear from these facts especially to a student of earth studies.

Agni

Even though maximum attention was given to Indra in the

Ṛgveda, the sages had realised that even Indra was approachable only through Agni, the divine fire. The concept of divinity was associated with the fire in Vyāsa's edition of the *Ṛgveda*. The pride of place was given to Agni, as the very first hymn of the *Ṛgveda* is a song to the divine fire. He is described in the hymn as the chief priest (*ṛtvik*) of *yajña* or sacrifice. *Hotṛ* is the *Ṛg* priest and this position is offered to Agni, the divine fire. According to Macdonell (1976),

> As the personification of the sacrificial fire, Agni is of second importance to Indra only, being addressed in at least 200 hymns. The anthropomorphism of his physical appearance is only rudimentary, and is connected chiefly with the sacrificial aspect of fire. Thus he is butterbacked, flame haired, and has a tawny beard, sharp jaws and golden teeth. Mention is often made of his tongue, through which the gods eat the oblations. With a burning head he faces in all directions.

Agni is compared with the bull with sharpened horns that bellows. At birth he is compared with a calf. He is kindled like a horse who brings gods and yoked to convey the sacrifice to them. He is also described as a divine bird, as eagle of the sky and as a goose dwelling in the waters. He has wood or *ghī* as food; melted butter as beverage. His flames are described as spoons with which he sprinkles the *havis* to gods. He is mostly invited with other gods to drink *soma*.

He is noted to shine like the sun with a lustre resembling that of the dawn and the lightning of the rain-cloud. (In this, he may be compared with the concept of Indra especially as he is depicted as the twin brother of Indra). Agni shines even in the night and dispels darkness. He has a dark-path (*kṛṣṇavartmā*) left after burning of the forests and he is described as one who shaves the earth as a barber. His flames are described as roaring like ocean waves and he sounds like thunder. He is smoke-bannered and his smoke raises up to the heaven.

He has a shining golden car which is sometimes compared to lightning and is drawn by ruddy and tawny horses. He is called Yajñasārathī and is described as the one who brings the gods to a sacrifice on his chariot. Agni is described as the child of the heaven and is often addressed as the *Dyāvā-Pr̥thivī*. He is also described as the progeny of the waters. He is the god who mostly dwells with mortals.

Since he is generated out of the friction of two twigs by force, Agni is addressed as the son of strength. He is noted to devour his parents soon after his birth (the twigs as parents). Since he is generated daily, he is described as young; (hence, no sacrifice could be older than him). Agni is supposed to reside in the embryo of waters. He is also described as having originated in the heavens and brought to earth by Mātariśvan. The sun is noted to be a form of Agni. Hence, Agni has a triple origin — on earth, in waters and in the sky. He is described as the father, brother or the son of his worshippers. He is the messenger of gods and men for he is the 'oblation-bearer'. He is known to have all the knowledge of the sacrifice (*jātavedas*). His greatness is described in superlative terms and it is supposed to surpass that of all other gods. His cosmic and creative powers have been described very well. He is also described as one who devours the dead body and dispels evil spirits and hostile magic.

Agni is synonymous with Vaiśvānara, Vahni, Vītihotra, Dhanañjaya, Kr̥pītayoṇi, Jvalana, Jātaveda, Tanūnapāt, Burhiśuṣmā, Kr̥ṣṇvartmā, Śociśkeśa, Uṣarbudha, Āśrayāśa, Br̥hadbhānu, Kr̥ṣāṇu, Pāvaka, Anala, Rohitāśva, Vāyusakhā, Śikhāvān, Āśuśūkṣaṇi, Hiraṇyaretha, Hutabhuk, Dahana, Havyavāhana, Saptārci, Damunā, Śukra, Citrabhānu, Vibhāvasu, Śūci, Appittam, Ourva, Bādaba and Baḍavānala. He is also described as the semen of god Śiva who is described as 'Kr̥ṣāṇuretha.' Agni is described as having four horns, three feet, two heads, seven hands.* In iconography he is visualised as bearded, with four fangs protruding from his mouth; a third on his forehead; carrying flames, trident, rosary and benediction in his four arms; and is supposed to have two wives, viz., Svāhā and Svadhā. He rides the ram, and his chariot is drawn by four parrots and driven by the wind. By Agni is meant one who has upward movement. He is also described as the son of Kaśyapa and Aditi, and so addressed as 'Āditya'. He is also called the son of Āṅgiras and Brahmā. He is the lord of the south-eastern direction. His eyes are coloured yellow and his robes are black. His helmet is said to be smoky. He is seen as carrying rosary, burning javeline, a water-filled pot, sacrificial laddle, sprinkler lotus and flaming spear in his seven hands.

Agni is described as 'Ratnadhātamā' in the first hymn of the *Ṛgveda*. According to Macdonell (1976), "Ratna never means jewel in the *Ṛgveda*." According to Sāyaṇa (Sontakke, 1972) *ratnadhātamam yāgaphalarūpāṇām ratnānām atiśayeṇa dhāryitāram vā*, meaning, one who possesses the jewels (of deeds?) in fruition of performed sacrifices is Agni. It is not known why the word *ratna* in the *Ṛgveda* does not mean 'jewel'. It was but natural for Sāyaṇācārya to have interpreted so since he was writing a commentary which was purely religious on the *Vedas*. But a scientific commentary need not have attached such a sectarian interpretation. The word *ratna* has an etymology as follows:

> *ramnīyataram yasmāt ramante asmin atīva vā*
> *tasmād ratnamīti khyātam śabdaśāstraviśārdaihi.*
>
> That one item which excels in qualities with all others of the same class, is called 'Ratna' for example Striratna, Pumratna, Gajaratna, Aśvaratna, Maṇiratna, etc.

---

* This is noted by Frawley (1992, p. 342) to indicate the number 4,320,000.000 years constituting a *Kalpa*.

The importance of Agni in bringing 'form' to an idea or concept is very well-known. According to *Taittirīya Upaniṣad* (Achyuta Krishnananda, 1913, p. 267), Ākāśa is qualified with sound, Vāyu is qualified with touch, Agni is qualified with form, Āpas is qualified with taste and Pṛthvī is qualified with smell. In this sense, Agni gives form to all things in nature. The best forms may be called *ratna* as per the above definition. Agni can be interpreted as the creator of all best forms and hence of *ratnadhātama* as well, which includes gemstones. In this sense, the description of Agni as the producer of best of gemstones is certainly commendable as the agency of heat or temperature is one of the factors or the main factor in the production of gemstones in particular which are exceptional minerals formed in the earth. They are *maṇiratna*s and there should not be any objection from critics to this effect since Agni is the major geological agent which has played a very important role in the origin and evolution of the Earth. Minerals being definite physico-chemical entities, the role of temperature and pressure in the formation of gemstones cannot be overemphasised.

While Indra has not been considered as a *pañcamahābhūta* in the *Upaniṣads*, Agni has been considered so. This is one of the most important points to be pondered upon. As mentioned earlier, Indra meant geomagnetic field and thus could not be a member of the *pañcamahābhūtas*. Rightly, Agni is a very important member of the five *bhūtas* along with space, air, water and earth, and the central one of that after space and air. The fire is an agent like the sun in generating heat. Thus, the terrestrial fire, the oceanic fire and fire in the sun all appear to be different aspects of one and the same phenomenon. This is universal heat which manifests itself as geothermal heat in the earth.

AGNI AND THE GEOTHERMAL FIELD

The geothermal field is manifested in the earth since its beginning from the sun. After the formation of oceans, the geothermal field was manifested underneath the oceans. The terrestrial fire and the oceanic fire originate from the sun. Extensive studies have been carried out on the behaviour of the geothermal field. It is a field concept of Agni derived from the statements pertaining to its origin in the heaven and its manifestation on the earth and also in the Sun. In this way, the worshipping of Agni to invest divinity in a sacrifice would mean the charging of powerful sound vibrations into the geothermal field which has contact with all other kinds of field forces and the distribution of the sacrificial *havis* by the divine fire. The instantaneous dissolving of *havis* in fire is unlike what is seen in other mediums. Therefore, fire has been employed for transporting the *havis* to various field forces.

The relationship of the geothermal field with the fields of atmosphere, hydrosphere and lithosphere is clear. Its relationship with the solar and lunar fields through the geomagnetic field is also evident. All these fields exist within the earth simultaneously and influence each other. The many hymns in the *Ṛgveda* concerning any two field forces like Indra-Agni, Agni-Vāyu, or Agni-Marut, Mitra-Varuṇa, Indra-Soma, etc. show us the relationship that exists between these fields. The geomagnetic field influencing the geothermal field, hydrological field, atmospheric field etc. is known. The identity of the geomagnetic and geoelectric fields is also known and their interconvertibility is clear. From all these things, it can be stated that the geothermal field is the only one which has a quick reaction of assimilating things and transferring them to various other fields. Hence, the importance of Agni as the divine fire who is the chief diety of all sacrifices. It can be seen that fire is the middle agent of the pañcamahābhūtas with sky and air on one side, and water and earth on the other side. Agni is perhaps the balancing member of the bhūtagrāma. He can stretch to the sky through air and he can stretch to the earth through water. In this way, he is known to have contact with all the gods and he is the best messenger of the gods to carry havis. That is why Agni is described as the knower or followr of eternal law, i.e., *ṛta.*

Since he is the one who gives a manifested form, the whole visible universe has originated from him. All the solid, liquid and gaseous manifestations are due to him. He is capable of creating the manifest universe as also destroying the same — for which he is addressed as Rudra.

In order to emphasise that the light of the sun and that of Agni are one and the same, the following Ṛgvedic hymns can be cited (Griffiths, 1986):

> Swift and all beautiful art thou, O Sūrya
> maker of the light,
> Illumining all the radiant realm,
>
> (*ṚV*, I.50.4)

> He who like thought goes swiftly on his
> journey, the Sun, alone is ever Lord
> of riches.
>
> (*ṚV*, I.7.9)

The first part is attributed to the sun. It is by Praskaṇvaṛṣi and is set to *gāyatrī* metre. The second is attributed to Agni. It is attributed to Parāśara and is set to *triṣṭubh* metre.

In the commentary by Sāyaṇa one finds a *śloka* to explain the word *taraṇī* in the first part and *sadyaha* in the second reference. It is as follows:

> *yojanānām sahasre dve dve śate dve ca yojane*
> *ekena nimiṣārdhena kramamāṇa namostu te*

According to Raghava Rao (1949, p. 135), these words describe the velocity of light. He observes that Sāyaṇācārya in his commentary on the *Ṛgveda* I.50.4 gives us the wonderfully definite figure regarding the velocity of light in half-*nimeṣa*. Sunlight travels 2,202 *yojanas* in half-*nimeṣa*. What is a *nimeṣa*? . . . This is clearly and unequivocally defined for us in several works. Sage Maitreya gives a correct table of time units:

2	*paramāṇus*	of time one *aṇu*	with 2	*paramāṇus*
3	*aṇus*	of time one *trasareṇu*	with 6	*paramāṇus*
3	*trasareṇus*	of time one *truṭi*	with 18	*paramāṇus*
100	*truṭis*	of time one *vedha*	with 1,800	*paramāṇus*
3	*vedha*	of time one *lava*	with 5,400	*paramāṇus*
3	*lavas*	of time one *nimeṣa*	with 16,200	*paramāṇus*
15	*nimeṣas*	of time one *kāṣṭa*		
30	*kāṣṭa*	of time one *kalā*		
30	*kalās*	of time one *muhūrta*		
30	*muhūrtas*	of time one *diva-rātri* of 24 hours		

24 60 x 60 seconds

Therefore, 15 x 30 x 30 x 30 *nimeṣas* = 24 x 60 x 60 seconds

Therefore, 1 *nimeṣa* $= \frac{24 \times 60 \times 60}{15 \times 30 \times 30 \times 30}$ seconds or $\frac{16th}{75}$ second

In 1/2 *nimeṣa*, i.e., 1/2 of $\frac{16}{75}$ seconds, i.e., $\frac{8}{75}$ seconds,

light travels 2,202 *yojanas*.

1 *yojana* is made up of 4 *krośas*

1 *krośa* is made up of 2000 *daṇḍas* or fathoms

1 *daṇḍa* or fathom is exactly 2 English Yards

1 *krośa* contains 2000 x 2, i.e., 4000 English Yards

1 *yojana* = 4 *krośas* = 4 x 2000 x 2 English Yards

Therefore *yojanas* $\frac{4 \times 2000 \times 2}{1760} = \frac{100}{11}$ i.e.,

$9\frac{1}{11}$ English miles.

In $\frac{8}{75}$ fraction of a second, light travels 2202 *yojanas*.

This means $\frac{2202 \times 100}{11} \times \frac{75}{8} = 1{,}87{,}670$ miles/second

Thus the modern value of 1,86,000 miles per second for the velocity of light is close to the above value. It was about AD 1887 that Michelson and Morley conducted experiments to determine the absolute velocity of the earth through the hypothetical 'ether' which helped determine the velocity of light.

Then the question arises as to why this fact was not brought to light even though it was commented upon by Sāyanācārya as early as the thirteenth century AD. Probably nobody bothered about such data in the long past or the discipline of *Bhauta Śāstra* was not pursued as a science with all its applications in those days in India. In any case, the existence of such a text itself is a testimony for the scholarship of Indian thinkers of yore while there is nothing of this kind in the contemporary world.

The geothermal field aspect of the divine fire is evident from many of the Ṛgvedic hymns. They are all suggestive and do not claim to have developed the concept already. If only these facts had been discussed thoroughly by the application of Indian logic, it would have been possible by now to establish a geophysical phenomenon and understand its application and use. In spite of the existence of both the concept and the means to develop the nature of phenomenon, they just did not apply the mind to an analytical procedure by which they would have been the oldest students of such disciplines of modern science.

Agni is described in many hymns of *Ṛgveda* and some of them are noted below (Griffiths, 1986):

> Agni, thou madest heaven to thunder . . .
>
> (*ṚV*, I. 21.4)

> Thee the Omniscient.
>
> (*ṚV*, I.36.3)

> The flames of Agni full of splendour and of
> might are fearful, not to be approached.
>
> (*ṚV*, I.36.20)

> Smoke-bannered spreader of light
>
> (*ṚV*, I.44.3)

> Deathless nourisher of the world, Immortal
>
> (*ṚV*, I.44.5)

> Thou shonest forth, O Agni, after former dawns, all visible, O rich in light.
>
> (*ṚV*, I.44.10)

> The forehead of the sky, Earth's centre, Agni
> become the messenger of Earth and heaven
>
> (*ṚV*, I.59.2)

> As in the Sun firm rays are set for ever,
> treasures are in Vaisvānara, in Agni.
> Of all the riches in the hills, the waters,
> the herbs among mankind, thou art the .
> Soveran. (*ṚV*, I.59.3)

When through the forest, urged by wind,
he spreads, verily Agni shears the hair
of the Earth. (*Ṛ̣V*, I.65.4)

Bright, splendid, like Dawn's lover, he
hath filled the two joined worlds as
with the light of heaven.
(*ṚV*, I.69.1)

He who is germ of waters, germ of woods,
germs of all things that move not and
move. (*ṚV*, I.70.21)

They made the Night and Dawn of different
colours, and set the black and purple
hues together.
(*ṚV*, I.83.7)

Thine is the task of Cleanser and Presenter.
(*ṚV*, I.76.4)

He with his shining glory blazing far and wide . . .
At whose close touch things solids shake,
and what stable yields like trees
(*ṚV*, I.127.3)

He, roaring very loudly he the Maruts' host.
(*ṚV*, I.127.6)

In ordered course forthwith he traverses the Earth
(*ṚV*, I.128.3)

I laud the seven-rayed, the triple headed,
Agni all-perfect . . . .
Sunk in the lap of all that moves and
moves not, him who hath filled all
luminous realms of heaven
(*ṚV*, I.146.1)

Thou, Agni, shining in thy glory through
the days, art brought to life from out
the waters, from the stone;

(*Ṛ*V, II.1.1)

Around, consuming the broad Earth.

(*Ṛ*V, II.4.7)

bring us O Agni, beauteous Earth and Heaven

(*RV*, III.15.5)

True, circumambient? what to Earth, OAgni.

(*Ṛ*V, IV.3.6)

Similarly many hymns can be cited with reference to the geothermal concept.

Descriptions like 'omniscient', 'forehead of the sky', 'centre of the Earth', 'whose close touch things solid shake', 'in order forthwith he traverses the Earth', 'consuming the broad Earth', etc. clearly indicate the fire or heat as a field force and direct our attention to the geothermal field. The importance of the geothermal field as a principle geological agent in bringing the rock to molten lava condition and solidifying them, in making igneous rocks, and hardening the sediments into rocks as well as causing metamorphic rocks is very well-known in modern petrology—the study of rocks. The effect of the geothermal field in causing volcanoes, thermal springs, and convection currents which move the continental landmasses is also known. The influences of the solar wind on the geothermal field is clear. Where geological agents turning the chemical compounds into minerals by the application of certain temperature and pressure are concerned, the geothermal field is the most important geological agent which was conceived by the great sages as 'divine fire' in the *Ṛgveda.*

That the geothermal field co-exists with the gravitational field, field of pressure due to overburden and atmosphere, the magnetic and the electrical fields should not cause any trouble to us since all of them amount to a single field in the final analysis even from the modern scientific point of view. That such a concept has been covered with highly pregnant meaning in the *Ṛgveda* is to be greatly appreciated. One does not find similar views in any other contemporary world literature. Investing fire with divinity and realising its manifold existence has been the prime factor in the *Ṛgveda*. If the word 'divinity' is divested of its religious meaning and substituted by the scientific concept of field force, it stands to reason that the Ṛgvedic sages were no less scientists in those days.

The cause of earthquakes in the *Agni Maṇḍala* has been detailed earlier. The constellations of this *Maṇḍala* are generally described as fiery. Symptoms of *Agni Maṇḍala* earthquakes have been indicated by the sky filled with falling stars and meteors and appearing with a glow, and fire, aggravated by the wind, raging over the land. These earthquakes are said to destroy clouds and dry up lakes and tanks. People are noted to suffer from heat ailments.

Though the various geological forces exist simultaneously in the earth, it is very difficult to distinguish the activities of the individual agents. This has been accomplished by the Ṛgvedic sages as a first observation. Thus the theory needs to be examined for its veracity and developed further for what it is worth. This, at present, is one of the major problems in the field of earth sciences.

Maruts and Vāyu

While there are 33 hymns attributed to the Maruts, there are only four hymns to Vāyu in the *Ṛgveda*. Some seven hymns, in addition, are attributed to Maruts with Indra and one each with Agni and Pūṣan. There are several hymns to Vāyu in combination with others.

According to Macdonell (1976),

> They form a troop being mentioned in the plural only.

> Their number is thrice sixty or thrice seven. They are the sons of Rudra and of Pṛ̥ṣṇi . . . They are further said to have been generated by Vāyu, the god of Wind. The goddess Rodasi is said to be their bride. They have been described as golden coloured, ruddy, shining like fire, and are associated with lightning. They are sometimes described to have bows and arrows and wear golden mantles, ornaments and helmets. Their car gleans with lightning drawn by tawny, spotted and swift mares. They are great, mighty, young and unageing, fierce, terrible, playful and child like. They make thunder noise and cause mountains to quake. They rend trees and devour forests. They shed rains covering the Sun causing darkness. They are also said to remove heat and dispel darkness preparing a path for the Sun. They are noted to be the singers of heaven. By their association with the thunder and storm, they are related to Indra. Indra is noted to have the Maruts as his allies in all his exploits. They exhibit maleficent traits as their father Rudra occasionally, but they also supply healing remedies in the form of rains.

The story is that Diti, the wife of Kaśyapa, angered by the destruction of her sons by Indra and other Ādityas, resorted to serious penance for begetting a son who would kill Indra by constantly uttering *indraśatrurvardhaśva* but spelt it *indra-śatrurvardhaśva* which meant "O Indra, an enemy is prospering (in me)." It is noted that hearing this, Indra went inside Diti and cut the foetus into seven pieces when it started crying. Indra pacified the crying foetus by telling *Mā Ruda* (Don't cry). When Diti came to know about this, she asked Indra for its protection. The latter is supposed to have given them the status of Maruts who are seven in number. Thus the origin of the Maruts has been explained.

The references to the Maruts and Vāyu in the Ṛgvedic hymns

make it clear that the Ṛgvedic sages worshipped the atmospheric winds as divine Marut or divine Vāyu. The wind as a powerful geological agent is well-known in physical geology. The dynamic activity involved in the process of natural weathering, denudation and transportation is vividly described in physical geology (Holmes 1964). In association with the heat (Agni), and thunder and lightning (Indra) causing a heavy downpour of rains, the destructive activity of the winds can be seen affecting the surface of the earth. Rocks breaking into pieces, and transportation of large-scale earthy material to distant places by wind and the torrential waters of streams and rivers is noted in dynamical geology. All these facts have been mentioned by the Ṛgvedic sages in hymns to the Maruts.

The origin and devastating effects of hurricanes, cyclones, tornadoes, etc. are very well-known. The movement of winds from hot regions to the cold regions affected by a special force called the coriolis force has been well-understood and the formation of NE (north-east) and SW (south-west) trade winds and their utility in the sea-voyages of early ages are also known. The wind erosion, development of different kinds of deserts, and transportation of dust, sand, etc. across large distances are well-recorded by students of geology (Holmes, 1964, pp. 743-81).

In spite of considerable advancement in modern meteorology and the development of sophisticated instruments and detailed observations over several years, it has been observed (Feynman, 1986, pp. 3, 7-8) that

> the theory of meteorology has never been satisfactorily worked out by the physicist. 'Well', you say, 'there is nothing but air, and we know the equations of the motions of air.' 'Yes we do.' 'So if we know the equations and the motions of air, why can't we figure out the conditions of the air tomorrow?' First, we do not really know what the condition is today, because the air is swirling and

twisting everywhere. It turns out to be very sensitive, and even unstable.

In the context of the above it will be interesting to know what were the ideas that the earliest Āryans had about the geological agent when they had their first interactions with nature.

The following references from the *Ṛgveda* on the Maruts will be interesting as these consider the Maruts and winds as one of the most powerful agents of geology (Griffiths, 1986 and Macdonell, 1976 — for *ṚV*, I.85.10):

Shakers of the Earth and heaven.
(*ṚV*, I.37.6)

The rugged-joined mountain yields
(*ṚV*, I.37.7)

They at whose racings forth the Earth
like and age-weakened lord of men,
trembles in terror on their ways.
(*ṚV*, I.37.8)

O Maruts, as your strength is great . . .
so have ye made the mountains fall.
(*ṚV*, I.37.12)

Heroes, your course is through the forest
trees of Earth, and through the fissures
of the rocks.
(*ṚV*, I.39.3)

They make the mountains rock reel,
they rend the forest-kings apart.
(*ṚV*, I.39.5)

Forth rush the torrents of the dark-red stormy
cloud and moisten, like a skin, the

Earth with water-floods.
(*Ṛ*V, I.85.5)

They have split even the firm mountains.
(*ṚV*, I.85.10)

Earth trembles at their racings as if weak and worn . . . shakers of all . . .
(*ṚV*, I.88.3)

Brilliant like gold is he who holds the thunder. Earth have they smitten with the chariot's folly.
(*ṚV*, I.88.2)

For your sake, O ye Maruts very mighty and well-born, have they set the stone, in motion. (*ṚV*, I.88.3)

They cleave the rock asunder in their might (*ṚV*, V.52.9)

They set the storm-cloud free to stream through both the worlds, and rainfloods flow over desert spots.
(*ṚV*, I.53.6)

They gleam with lightning, Heroes, Casters of the Stone, wind-rapid Maruts, Overthrowers of the hills.
Often through desire to rain coming with storm of hail roaring in onset, violent and exceeding strong.
(*ṚV*, V.54.3)

they roar they inundate the Earth with floods of pleasant meath
(*ṚV*, V.54.8)

The paths of air's mid-regions are precipitous
precipitous the mountains with
their running stream

(*Ṛ*V, V.54.9)

O Maruts, from the Ocean ye uplift the
rain, and fraught with vaporous moisture
pour the torrents down.

(*Ṛ*V, V.55.5)

Neither the mountain nor the rivers keep
you back. (*Ṛ*V, V.55.7)

Shaked the rocky mountains as they race along.

(*Ṛ*V, V.56.4)

Bright with the blasts of wind wrapped in their
robes of rain . . .

(*Ṛ*V, V.57.4)

Before you, fierce Ones! woods bow down
in terror; Earth, even the mountains,
trembles at your coming.

(*Ṛ*V, V.60.2)

Halting not, reinless, through the air it
travels, speeding alone its paths through
Earth and heaven.

(*Ṛ*V, VI.66.7)

Earth shakes in terror at their wars.

(*Ṛ*V, VI.66.9)

They make the world-halves tremble with
their greatness; from depths of Earth
and sky they reach to heaven

(*Ṛ*V, VII.63.1)

Even things immovable shake and reel,

> the mountains and the forest trees at
> your approach.
>
> (*Ṛ*V, VIII.60.5)

It is observed for Vāyu :

> It makes the regions red and touches heaven, and as it moves the dust of Earth is scattered.
>
> (*ṚV*, X.168.1)

Thus most of the *r̥ṣi*s have described the actions of winds in their hymns. It is pure geological denudation observed by the sages in their earliest quest to understand nature. In the first interaction itself they have been able to evaluate the action of wind on the dusty earth, the cleaving of rocks, the transportation of dust and sand to far-off places and the influence of the wind in rains and floods.

The wind is also described as spreading its path through the earth. As in the case of other geological agents like Indra and Agni, Maruts and Vāyu have been through the earth simultaneously with other geological field forces. The universality of Maruts and Vāyu has been proclaimed by many and the *Taittirīya Upaniṣad* has observed.

> *namaste vāyu, tvameva pratyakṣam brahmāsi*
> *tvameva pratyakṣam brahma vadiśyāmi* (*Śikṣāvallī*)

meaning "Vāyu or wind you are verily the Brahman", by which it is meant one with all qualifications of the *Brahman*. Without breathing, no life can live even for a moment. Life is what is between the first breath and the last breath. Hence, the importance of air or atmosphere.

Rudra is often associated with the Maruts and the Maruts are said to be his offspring through Pr̥ṣṇi. Etymologically, Rudra means 'howler' and he is known for his destructive aspect. But he is also called 'Śiva', meaning auspicious. His beneficial aspects include his healing powers and he is supposed to be the physician of physicians. The Rudras are mentioned to be eleven in number. They are said to be the 10 *prāṇas* in the body and the *ātmā*—the eleventh. The ten *prāṇas* in the body are given below:

prāṇa	residing in heart
apāna	residing in anus
samāna	residing in naval
udāna	residing in neck
vyāna	residing all through the body
nāga	residing in mouth
kūrma	residing in opening of eye
kṛkara	residing in the eyes
devadatta	residing in yawning
dhanañjaya	residing all through the body

These ten kinds of Vāyus are parts of Maruts. *Ātmā* is the reflection of *Brahman*.

The Maruts have synonyms like Śvasana, Sparśana, Vāyu, Mātariśva, Sadāgati, Pṛśādaśva, Gandhavaha, Gandhavāha, Anila, Āśuga, Samīra, Māruta, Marut, Jagatrāṇa, Samīraṇa, Nabhaśvat, Vāta, Pavana, Pavamāna, Prabhañjana, Prakampana, Atibala, Jañjhāvāta, etc.

Of the 33 gods mentioned by commentators as those belonging to the *Ṛgveda*, ten are the Maruts. Vāyu is also one of the 33 gods. Hence, the Maruts and Vāyu account for one-third of the Ṛgvedic gods. It is not clear whether hymns were devoted separately to each of the Maruts in early Vedic literature. If so, it is not clear whether they were actually omitted by Vyāsa. There are only three hymns to Rudra and four to Vāyu in the *Ṛgveda* edited by Vyāsa. The reason for such unequal treatment is not known. However, these kinds of Maruts are not known to modern science and so, they open up a fascinating field of study.

The capacity of the Maruts and Vāyu to transport clouds has been brought out in a number of hymns. Their contribution as allies of Indra in causing rains is also brought out. Some common aspects like thunder-holding have been given for the Maruts as well as Indra. These aspects seem to have overlapped in the Vedic sages' attempt to identify various natural geological agencies. There are hymns to show the combined effect of the Maruts with Indra, Agni and Pūṣan. The influence of the sun and geothermal heat on the Maruts and Vāyu in causing their movement is well-known. Perhaps these hymns justify such an association.

Later, Vāyu is represented as a *dikpāla* or lord over the directions. He rules the north-western regions. In iconography, he is represented with two heads and as carrying a flag and stick in his hands. He is said to ride the stag. He is open-mouthed with dishevelled hair and his garments are disturbed by breeze or wind.

According to the Beaufort scale of wind force, the calm air has a speed of less than a mile per hour (mph). The gales have speeds ranging from 22 mph to 63 mph. A wind with the speed of 64 to 75 mph is noted to be addressed as storm while the wind moving with a speed of over 75 mph is called a hurricane.

The effect of an earthquake of the *Vāyu Maṇḍala* has already been described. The role of wind in causing earthquakes has also been given earlier. According to Vasiṣṭha, the earthquakes are caused by atmospheric winds colliding with each other and striking the earth with a terrific sound. The 'Wind-Circle' is associated with seven constellations and any earthquake that occurs in these constellations are considered as those caused by wind. Whether the wind under these constellations is heated up by the sun and causes the winds held up within the earth to escape is to be studied. In case there are pockets of wind in the interior of the earth, such pockets have to be identified. The active volcanoes release a tremendous amount of smoke associated with wind held under pressure. Whether the volcanic regions are also regions of air pockets held under great pressure is to be examined. Under such conditions, the ground-wind which gets heated up along with the atmospheric wind as it is a field force is likely to find ways to expand and escape to the freer zones causing earthquakes.

The literature on the Martus and Vāyu in the *Vedas* is far less compared to that on Agni or Indra. But the role of the Maruts and Vāyu in the world environment is simply tremendous. Fresh air is a must for the living beings and the Upaniṣadic sages were not exaggerating when they addressed wind as *Brahman*. Its universality is very well-known and the role of atmosphere as a measure of air navigation is also clear. Its effect on human environment is salutary and its role as a powerful geological agent has been most vividly described. Yet, prediction of weather is a subject of great speculation even to this day.

Varuṇa

According to Macdonell (1976, p. 263), "Besides Indra, Varuṇa is the greatest of the gods of the ṚgVeda, though the number of the hymns in which he is celebrated alone is small, numbering hardly a dozen." His personification in the *Ṛg veda* is perfect since his eyes, face, hands, arms, feet etc. have been praised. His eye is given to be the Sun. He is the upholder of righteousness and he will ruin the wicked. Varuṇa, it is said. sits in his mansion and observes the deeds of all. The fathers are noted to look at him in the heaven. Varuṇa is called a king but he is also addressed as super-king or universal monarch — *samrāṭ*. He is also called *māyin* (crafty). Macdonell also observes:

> Varuṇa is mainly lauded as upholder of physical and moral order. He is a great lord of the law of nature. He established heaven and Earth, and by his law heaven and Earth are held apart. He made the golden swing (the Sun) to shine in heaven; he has made a wide path for the Sun; he placed fire in the waters, the Sun in the sky, Soma in the rock. The wind which resounds through the air is Varuṇa's breath. By his ordinances the Moon shining brightly moves at night and the stars placed upon high are seen at night, but disappear by day. Thus Varuṇa is lord of light both by day and by night. He is also a regulator of waters. He caused the rivers to flow; by his occult power they pour swiftly into the ocean without filling it.

These observations make it clear that Varuṇa is a personification of the law of nature, i.e., gravitation. All the gods are said to follow his order. He is said to embrace the universe and he is the abode of all beings. His omniscience is described. No creature is known to escape his attention.

Varuṇa is noted to be the moral governor. Thus, he is superior to all other deities. He is said to free people of their sins as if he were untying a rope, when approached; but he is a severe master for sinners.

The concept of Varuṇa is that of one encompassing the sky. It is noted to be older than the present texts of *Ṛgveda*.

Varuṇa is noted to be the ruler of the Western direction. However, he is not included in the 33 gods. He is noted to be essentially the god of rivers. In iconography, Varuṇa is noted to have four arms carrying a lotus, lasso, conch and a pot of jewels. He is described as one having a protruding stomach and riding a chariot drawn by seven swans. The seven swans are noted to represent seven oceans — probably based on the original concept of Saptadvīpa-Vasumatī — an idea post-dating the four oceans, Catudvīpa-Vasumatī. But in *Śilpa-śāstra*, Varuṇa is noted to be in a standing posture on a crocodile. He is accompanied by his consort, Gaurī and the river goddesses, Gangā and Yamunā.

This concept of Varuṇa is a late one as he is not associated with Sarasvatī, Dṛśadvatī or Ilā or any such rivers of the Vedic times. That he represents the seven seas makes it clear that he is the god of waters. In other words, he is the lord of hydrosphere. He is also described in the *Amarakośa* as Praceta, Varuṇa, Pāśī, Yādasampāti and Appati.

One of the four *maṇḍalas* to which the earthquakes belong has been noted earlier as that of Varuṇa; therefore, it stands to reason that some earthquakes are caused due to the action of the hydrosphere. Though the maximum depth noted in the Pacific Ocean is nearly 10 km, molten rock material with picrite compositions is noted at depths greater than 400 km from the surface of the earth, suggesting the presence of water to such levels amidst rocks. In the absence of clear knowledge about the interiors of the earth, it is not unjustified to presume that the liquid medium of the earth exists in its great depths and subscribe to the idea that water or hydrosphere simultaneously exists along with geothermal and gravitational fields within the earth.

There is a certain confusion in the concept of Varuṇa as the god of water and also as the upholder of the law which is followed by all gods. The former suggests that Varuṇa indicates the hydrosphere and the latter is suggestive of the Universal Law of Gravitation. That the quality of water is taste as per the *pañcamahābhūta* concept is mentioned earlier; now, we shall examine some of the Ṛgvedic statements supporting these views.

ṚGVEDIC CONCEPT OF VARUṆA

Varuṇa as god of water can be described as the most powerful geological agent that is working incessantly on the earth and changing its scenery. Not only is Varuṇa the lord of the oceans, but he is also the law-maker who is governing all gods. This law is called as *ṛta* in the *Ṛgveda* and described in very beautiful hymns. This *ṛta* is the Law of the Universe or the great cosmic order by which the whole of the manifest Universe is working. This, in other words, appears to be the law of gravitation in simple terms. The recognition of this law-order gave the Vedic Āryans a great satisfaction. They attributed to this law or universal order the term *dharma* from a religious point of view. Varuṇa is regarded as the Lord of this Law as is shown below (Griffiths, 1986):

> True to his holy law, he knows the twelve
> Moons with their progeny:
> He knows the Moon of later birth.
>
> (*ṚV*, I.25.8)

> He knows the pathway of wind, the
> spreading, high, and mighty wind.
>
> (*ṚV*, I.25.9)

According to Griffiths (1986), "Varuṇa is king of the air and of the sea, the latter being often regarded as identical with the former". The twelve Moons are the Moons of the 12 months and 'Moon of later birth' is the 13th Moon of *adhimāsa*. By then the Ṛgvedic sages had developed a lunar calendar to measure the time of a year and this statement supports the identification of the cycle and its repetition. The cycle due to the law of universal gravitation has been known to scientists. Let us study a few more Ṛgvedic verses with reference to Varuṇa :

> He made them flow, the Āditya, the Sustainer
> the rivers run by Varuṇa's commandment
> These feel no weariness, not cease from flowing;
> swift have they flown . . . . .
>
> (*ṚV*, II.28.4)

Who hath struck out, . . . Earth as a skin to
spread in front of Sūrya.

(*Ṛ̣V*, V.85.1)

Set intellect in hearts, fire in the waters,
Sūrya in heaven and Soma on the mountain.

(*Ṛ̣V*, V.85.2)

Varuṇa let the big cask, opening downward,
flow through the heaven and
Earth, and air's mid region.
Therewith the Universe's Sovern waters
Earth as the shower of rain bedews the
barley. (*Ṛ̣V*, V.85.3)

When Varuṇa is fain for milk he moistens
the sky, the land, and the Earth to
her foundations.
Then straight the mountains clothe them
in the rain-cloud;

(*Ṛ̣V*, V.85.4)

I will declare this mighty deed of magic,
of glorious Varuṇa the Lord immortal
who standing in the firmament hath meted
the Earth out with the Sun as with a measure.

(*Ṛ̣V*, V.85.5)

Whereby with all their flood, the lucid
rivers fill not one sea wherein they pour
their waters.

(*Ṛ̣V*, V.85.6)

Who urged the high and mighty sky to
motion, the star of old, and spread the
Earth before him.

(*Ṛ̣V*, VII.86.1)

The wise king Varuṇa hath made in
heaven than Golden swing to cover it
with glory.

(*RV*, VII.86.5)

Ruling in depths and meting out the
region, great saving power hath he,
this world's controller.

(*RV*, VII.86.6)

Varuṇa cut a pathway out for Sūrya
and lead the watery floods of rivers onwards.

(*RV*, VII.87.1)

Before the home of Varuṇa all the Gods
follow his decree.

(*RV*, VIII.41.7)

Thus, the concept of Varuṇa is essentially that of governing the world and keeping it in order rather than one of causing rains and floods and owning oceans. The Vedic Āryans understood that despite several rivers flowing into the oceans, they had not been filled. This brings out the role of Varuṇa as controller of the Universe. It is evidently a suggestion that the universal order forming the path of the Sun and the Moon is gravitation or the General Theory of Relativity, which is addressed by the term Varuṇa in the *Ṛgveda.* The action of waters (*āp*), the rains (*parjanya*), rivers (*nadyaḥ*) and seas (*samudra*) is also brought out in describing the concept of Varuṇa. However, his power to control the gods to keep them in their path including his power to keep the luminaries, the earth and heaven in their assigned positions etc. has been essentially brought out, making Varuṇa a universal force that has set an order. This order can only be the Law of Gravitation or the General Theory of Relativity. According to the latter, the paths of celestial bodies have been known as geodesics as a consequence of space-time continuum. This aspect of the concept of Varuṇa by the Ṛgvedic sages appears to be a long-time precursor of the 'Theory of Relativity' and of the 'Law of Universal Gravitation'. In spite of the existence of such a concept, the post-Vedic scholars did not discuss this matter on Varuṇa by the application of Indian logic as a result of which they did not establish these principles. However, even now, there is lot of scope for any refinement of these theories for understanding the universal laws.

Dyāvāpṛthvī and Bhūmi

The concept of the earth in the *Ṛgveda* is fascinating. It is mostly addressed along with the heaven. There is only one *sūkta* on *pṛthvī* in the *Ṛgveda* while there are six or seven addressed to the *dyāvāpṛthivī*. However, there is an exhaustive hymn in the *Atharvaveda* on *bhūmi*. According to Macdonell (1976) "Heaven and Earth are the most frequently named pair of deities in the Ṛg Veda. They are so closely associated that they are invoked as a pair in six hymns." Further, he observes, "They are great parents being often called pitara, mātara, janitāra besides being separately addressed as 'father', and 'mother'. They have made and sustained all creatures; they are also the parents of gods. They never grow old. They are great and wide-extended; they are broad and vast abodes."

While *pṛthvī*, *bhūmi* and *janitri* terms have been used in the *Vedas* to address the Earth, some 28 names of the earth appear in the literature by the time of Amarasiṁha (Murthy, 1987, p. 127). The Ṛgvedic sages believed that the heaven was wrapped up by the earth and they are held apart by Varuṇa. By the time of the *Taittirīya Upaniṣad* (*Śikṣāvallī*, third *anuvāka*) the Earth is stated to be the earlier form, heaven the later form, and the space is noted to be their junction negotiated by air or atmosphere. In *Ānandavallī* or *Bhṛguvallī*, the evolution of the *pañcabhūtas* has been described in simple terms. The field of *Brahman* appears as *ātmā* in the space; from space evolves Vāyu; from Vāyu evolves Agni; from Agni evolves Āpas; from Āpas evolves Pṛthvī. This theory of evolution of the earth has been largely adopted by almost all the post-Vedic literature. It is a fact that modern science also supports the view that from space originates all celestial bodies. Thus the origin of the earth has been understood in the Vedic and the Upaniṣadic literature.

While space is endowed with the quality of sound, air is endowed with the quality of touch, fire with form, water with taste, and the earth with all these mixed in it and smell. The earth is the grossest form of matter that has evolved out of space.

THE EARTH IN THE RGVEDA

The following ṛks in the *Ṛgveda* need in-depth study (Griffiths, 1986):

> I praise mighty Heaven and Earth. . .the Strengthners of Law.
>
> (*ṚV*, I.159.1)

> Two bowls of noble kind; between these Goddesses and the God, the fulgent Sun, travels by fixed decree.
>
> (*ṚV*, I.160.1)

> Whether of these is elder, whether later? How were they born? Who knoweth it, ye sages?
>
> (*ṚV*, I.185.1)

This may be considered the first inquiry into the origin of the Earth.

> The Twain uphold, though motionless and footless, . . . (*ṚV*, I.185.2)

In this statement they have understood that the Earth and the heaven have no support. Of course, the term motionless is incorrect; but for local observations the Earth 'appears', for all purposes, motionless. This has been rectified in *Aitareya Brāhmaṇa* later. Thus their concepts changed with regard to the earth. A similar idea is expressed in the following hymn:

> Sure in the worlds he was a skilful Craftsman,
> he who produced these Twain,
> the Earth and Heaven.
> Wise, with his power he brought both realms,
> together spacious and deep,
> well fashioned and unsupported.
>
> (*ṚV*, IV.56.3)

> Ye sanctify each other's form, by your
> proper might ye rule.
> And from of old observe the Law.
>
> (*ṚV*, IV 56.6)

THE EARTH IN THE ATHARVAVEDA

By the time of the *Atharvaveda*, the sages appear to have advanced in their understanding of the earth. They were able to measure the time in terms of 12 suns in a year, and some 37 moons in three years. They realised that the day and night might happen due to the movement of the earth about its axis. A full *sūkta* is devoted to *bhūmi* in this *Veda*. In *kāṇḍa* 12, the first *sūkta* is *Bhūmi Sūkta* consisting of 63 *ṛ*ks.

In this context consider the following verse from the *Ṛgveda* (Griffiths, 1986):

> Truth is the base that bears the Earth;
> By Sūrya are the heavens sustained.
>
> By law the Ādityas stand secure, and
> Soma holds his place in heaven.
>
> (*ṚV*, X.85.1)

Ṛta, *Satya*, *Param-Brahman* are all synonyms and by *ṛta* is meant the law of gravitation. The Earth is held in its position by gravitation.

The *Bhūmi Sūkta* of the *Atharvaveda* (Satvalekar, 1944, p. 597) also commences with the same idea. Let that Earth bless us with plenty, it is observed. The Earth supporting varieties of herbs shall protect us. That Earth which is containing the oceans and rivers and by which is food grown shall protect us. By then, the Āryan sages had classified the directions into eight and so they prayed that the Earth with all her eight directions protect them. They had probably spread to the east and south of the Indian mainland. The Earth is addressed as *Viśvambharā*, meaning that she is the representative of the Universe. She is called *Vasudhā* for she contained all the 8 *vasus* mentioned earlier. The Earth is also addressed as *Hiraṇyavakṣā* meaning that the Earth has a gold bosom. The Earth is praised as *jagato niveśanī* — one in whom the Whole Universe is present. She is described as holding Agni — which has already been described as the geothermal field. She is also described as holding Indra, i.e., the geomagnetic field. The Earth is described then as being present in the middle of the oceans (sedimentary rocks) and as one having magical movements. She is one enveloped by the sky or space and causing the force of gravitation. She is stated to be like ambrosia. An earth with so much of strength is praised for making the nation strong. That Earth which is being served day and night by rivers is requested to bless them. That earth mothered by Aśvins and tread upon by Viṣṇu and possessed of Indra is requested to pour water on the worshipper.

The Earth is then described as wide, supporting forests, hills and mountains. The Earth is said to be, at places, white, dark, tawny and of variegated colour. The Earth is then described as raised at some places and lowered at other places. The sages, it is said, have treated them as the children of the Earth and worship the Earth for rains.

The Earth is described as the progenitor of the people and

animals with two or four feet. The people have been identified as of five types.

The divine fire is noted to be in the earth and in herbs, waters and rocks. The divine fire is also noted in all life. The divine fire causes heat in the daytime from the sky. The Earth with such divine fire is asked to give a long life and children. The Earth is noted to have a smell which is in the herbs also. The Earth is made up of rocks and dust as stated in the given statement:

śilā bhūmiraśmā pāmsuhu sā bhūmihi sandhṛtā dhṛtā

Then the Earth is described as enjoying the six *ṛtus*, like *grīṣma, varṣā, śarad, hemanta, śiśira* and *vasanta.* The earth is also described as the wife of rains,

nidhim bibhratī bahudhā guhā vasu
manim hiraṇyam pṛthivī dadātu me

meaning, the Earth contains wealth and she is requested to give the worshipper golden gems.

These statements indicate that the Vedic Āryans had close interaction with the earth and knew that the earth was fully responsible for their food and prosperity. They had recognised the changes in terrestrial scenery during the period of every two months — described by them as *ṛtus* — in a yearly cycle. They could realise that the *ṛtus* were repeated once every year. They knew how to measure the year. They counted days against the movements of the luminaries.

In the iconographic description of the Earth, she is shown as the consort of Mahāviṣṇu, the other consort being Śrī Devī. She is described as having various colours in different texts. A text mentions her in white colour, another in slightly bluish dark colour and yet another in the colour of sprouts of plants. It will be interesting to see what was the colour of the earth noted by Edgar Mitchell on his way to the moon in the 14th Apollo mission.

He has described the earth as a splendid blue jewel suspended against a velvet black sky (Murthy, 1992, p. 118).

The Earth is described as a beautiful goddess bedecked with ornaments who has a pleasant countenance. She is described as having four arms and carrying a jewel pot, a pot filled with plants, a vessel filled with medicinal herbs and a lotus in her hands. She is described to be seated on four elephants of the four quarters. A different description of the earth is available in other texts. She is described as one wearing a *karaṇḍa-mukuṭa* type of crown, and red or yellow garments. Her eyes are compared to that of the lotus flower and her forehead is decorated with curly hairs. She is said to ride on the Cāṭaka bird. She is sometimes described as golden-coloured and sitting under the *kalpa*-tree.

The above concept of the earth is rather restricted. The beauty of the earth is indescribable — in the words of E. Mitchell (Murthy, 1992). The beauty of the earth with her forest-clad mountains and on the banks of wide-flowing rivers, the high seas and mid-oceans, the top of the hills and mountain peaks, the beaches, the confluences of rivers, the river mouths joining or pouring into the seas and oceans, the plains and mountain slopes etc. cannot be described in words. To confine such a source of beauty in a figure of a small goddess with four hands is something improbable. She must be, for all purposes, described in her entirety — a globe. Nothing short of such a thing is capable of bringing the qualities of the Earth. She is a representative of the universe; she is the only planet directly available for the study of the universe and to realise the underlying truth. Thus, the earth holds almost all secrets of nature the unravelling of which will help us in understanding the universe.

THE EARTH IN THE YAJURVEDA

There are few references to the earth in the *Yajurveda* (Satavalekar, 1990, p. 397); however they are important as they show the advancement made over the Ṛgvedic period. In *kāṇḍa* 4, *anuvāka* 5, it is observed that the sage makes a request that inorganic material like rocks, soil, mountains, hills, sands, vegetation, gold, silver, iron, lead, tin, copper and steel be made available to him for the performance of sacrifices. In the same *kāṇḍa* and 6th *anuvāka*, it is stated that the earth which is also Indra be available to the sages for carrying out the sacrifices.

The above statements have great significance in that the rocks, soils, hills and mountains as well as the metals as parts of the earth were well-known to the Yajurvedic sages. The examination of the ground of mountains and hills as well as of the soil, especially for the metallic ores of gold, silver, iron, lead, copper and steel, has been stressed. They must have located the ores of all these metals and also their metallurgical properties; otherwise they would not have been able to mention the metals by name. From the above it is evident that zinc metallurgy was not known to the Yajurvedic sages. Zinc metallurgy happens to be a little difficult. This science has been propounded by one Śākala as mentioned by Kauṭilya in his *Arthaśāstra*, but his treatise is not available to us today. As a result, the metallurgical skill of the Yajurvedic sages has not been fully understood. The most astonishing factor is that the area occupied by the Yajurvedic sages must have been the marginal parts of the Indian Peninsula comprising the Punjab, the plains of the Himachal Pradesh, and Jammu and Kashmir hill areas of the Ṛgvedic times. In the marginal parts of the Indian Peninsula as far interior as Zawar in Rajasthan, very old workings for metallic ores are known. Gold appears to have been obtained by panning the alluvial sands of the Śiwālik foothills of the Himālayas, whose 'pepper and salt' sandstones contain one to two grammes of it per ton of material. They got silver possibly as a byproduct of lead in the Zawar area. The iron amphibolite rocks found in these regions would have served them as iron ores. Some haematitic ores also served their purpose. They would have known steel-making from wrought iron by introducing carbon on second heating in kilns, as has been found out in the manufacturing of wootz steel in Karnataka in the recent past. Copper metallurgy in the ores of Khetri in Rajasthan was also known to them. Bronze and brass alloys have not been mentioned in the *Yajurveda*; probably they are later to the Yajurvedic period.

Almost all rivers originating in the Himālayas and drain the Śiwālik hills carry minute amounts of gold and this allu gold has been very much praised in the Vedic literature. Ever the pan-Indian area, gold was a rare commodity but its praise a utility surpassed that of almost all other metals. Similarly, Mercury, in *Āyurveda-Rasaśāstra*, has found maximum use in Indian medicine though its occurence in the country is almost nil, and it was obtained by barter from abroad. Similarly, gold is another commodity which was found in meagre quantities in India from the ancient times. The Hutti and Kolar mines in Karnataka have been identified as the suppliers of gold for the Harappan and Mohenjo-Daro civilisations. But all put together, indigenous supply of gold even when India was producing maximum of it was but negligible as compared to world production.

These facts suggest that the Vedic sages were good ore hunters and metallurgists at a very early period in human history. No text of any comparative period — for the *Veda*s are the oldest in the library of mankind — could inform us about metallurgical skills as those of the Āryan sages. In later periods, they tried to produce imitations of metallic gold with an alloy of zinc and lead (brass) with 10 to 12 per cent of zinc — when the alloy gets a golden yellow colour (Hegde, 1991, p. 86). This alloy probably accounted for the 'fabulous gold' of the country in the early and middle ages which invited invasions.

The most important issue is the availability of tin ore, cassiterite (called *kastīra*) in Sanskrit. It is suggested by the author that the Tosham hill deposit might have accounted for a small quantity of alluvial tin in the area of Āryan origin. But the pan-Indian civilisation might have accounted for tin from Burma (now Myānmār), Malāyā, Sumātrā and other places in the east and Afghanistan, Baluchistan in the mid-east. India within her present territory has very little quantity of tin ore (Murthy, 1991, p. 106).

The Earth is also Indra, as has already been explained, as Indra meant the geomagnetic-electrical field encompassing the whole earth. Thus, the Vedic sages had mastered many a field of study including hunting, mining, metallurgy. etc.

THE EARTH IS CALLED VASUNDHARĀ

Of the 33 gods (*trayastriṁśaddevāḥ*), the vasus constitute eight. These *aṣṭa* vasus are said to be Agni, Pṛthvī, Vāyu, Antarikṣa, Āditya, Dyau, Candramā and Nakṣatras. As such, the Earth is one of the *aṣṭa* vasus. But as She bears all the other vasus mentioned above, She is addressed as *Vasundharā*. The terrestrial fire, a face of the divine fire, which is also in the sun, and hence Āditya, and all the *devas* are noted to reside within the Earth as Vāyu, Dyau etc. and they include the moon and stars. The Earth is formed of *antarikṣa* i.e., space. As such no other member of this group has the honour of being addressed as *Vasundharā*, except the Earth. It has been explained earlier that the other gods including the 11 Rudras and the 12 Ādiyas, Indra and Prajāpati are parts or specialities of Vāyu; the Sun is in different sections of the zodiac; and Indra is the Earth. That Prajāpati or *Brahman* is enclosing all these or is present in all these objects is known. Hence, all the gods of the *Ṛgveda* reside in the Earth. The earth, therefore, enjoys a unique position in the *Vedas*.

One of the most important aspects of these hymns is investing the earth with divinity. The earth is elevated to the position of a goddess. This is the most important distinction between the modern view in the study of the earth sciences and the Vedic view. In the modern study of the earth, the earth is treated as a lifeless planet showing various movements around the sun along with other planets. But in the Vedic view, the earth is not lifeless. It is invested with the divinity of Indra, Agni, Varuṇa, Vāyu etc. All the planets, the moon and the sun are invested with divinity. Not only are they considered to be divine manifestations but also that the supreme subtle spirit called the *Brahman* is seen as residing in all these celestial and terrestrial objects. Herein lies the difference in the conception of the universal objects as reflected in the philosophies of the East and the West. The Western philosophy has, as a result of the non-living conditions of all objects analysed by scientific acumen, arrived at the final 'space-time continuum' as the truth of the universe. But cracks have developed in that philosophy and they are in search of some other principle which can satisfy all these observations. But where Indian philosophy is concerned, the grounding in the Vedic deities made the people find the universal spirit in all the universal manifestations, both living and non-living. Hence, their final conclusion is that the field of *Brahman* is in existence in the whole 'universe', both living and non-living. The first data for both these kinds of philosophies is the same: a detailed study of the natural geological agencies and the planets, luminaries, stars etc. But while Indian philosophy has taken a course of lively discussions, the Western — which has come to be called scientific — philosophy has taken a dreary course and ended in a universe without life, with only an abstract 'space-time continuum'.

It is rather difficult to reconcile these two dimensions of philosophy. It is not possible to think of the existence of life-force within the material world. At no stretch of imagination is it possible to feel the existence of life in natural forces like geothermal, geomagnetic, electrical and other fields. Similarly, it has been difficult to arrive at the idea of a 'living Earth' with all the numerous forms of life on its surface. It would be rather difficult to substantiate the destructive activity of the earth through its storms, heavy rains, volcanoes, earthquakes etc.

Similarly, where its constructive activities are concerned, it is uncertain whether they are done intentionally by the earth or the activities occur subject to some unknown principle, which has not yet been understood by the geoscientists. The earth has a life-field within it; it must also have a field of mind — however subtle it may be. But it has not been proved; there is no means to prove it, except by way of certain inferences like the life supporting capacity of the earth. But there are certain other celestial objects — the other planets, for instance — which have no trace of life in them. Hence, they may be devoid of even the life-supporting capacity of the Earth. How then can divinity be invested in them?

These are very tricky and, at the same time highly reasonable questions to be answered by students studying the earth. That such a thing is mentioned in the *Vedas* cannot be considered as evidence. All these aspects cannot be proved by physical experiments. Hence, the direct observations as well as empirical data have not been considered by Sāyaṇa as the substratum of the *Vedas* for he observes that:

pratyakṣoṇānumityāvā yastūpāyo na budhyate

But then it is the aim of modern students of the earth to reconciliate the concepts of the living and non-living universe.

Though the geological agencies like the geothermal field, the hydrosphere, atmosphere etc. could be considered in the references to the Vedic deities and the prevalance of field of *Brahman* — which defies all kinds of description — as the living–non-living universe, there still appears to be something lacking in the oriental philosophy. The absence of such a complete understanding is declared as *māyā* or ignorance. It is also said that by the realisation of the *Brahman*, nothing is left to know. Most of the *ṛṣis* of the Vedic school have been known to be *brahmarṣis* i.e., one who has realised the *Brahman*. Even they have not been able to solve many of the seemingly contradictory factors happening on the surface of the earth, for example, the human misery due to the destructive activity of the various geological agencies. They have their 'Theory of *Karma*' which does not have a strong base. And they also insist that the *Brahman* has nothing to do with the activities of the *bhūtagrāma*. It is just like any field force which has nothing to do with human values. Proving such a thing and realising such a fact does not lead anywhere. Hence, there is the need to combine the Eastern and the Western philosophical ideas especially in the context of life on the earth. Such a philosophy may appeal to the human mind and may be practicable as well. There is scope for a psycho-spiritual-material philosophy, considering all aspects of the Universe.

It is noted in the *Taittirīya Upaniṣad* that the *Brahman* is the concept of *satyam-jñānam-anantam*, meaning that the eternal truth of knowledge is *Brahman*. It includes the human psyche also when it describes the *manomaya* shell. The *Brahman* is still subtler, it is observed, and is beyond *vijñānamaya* shell, i.e., even transcending the scientific perceptions. Even then the field of *Brahman* is noted to be not responsible in any way for the worldly activities. 'Worldly' is taken as ignorance. Transcending the level of ignorance and realising *Brahman* takes one beyond time and space. Hence, no scope for any other philosophy is mentioned. Thus, the Earth is the basis of all realisations.

One of the most important or the most important hymn in the *Ṛgveda* which considers the earth as the foundation to discuss the nature of the Creator is given below (Griffiths, 1986):

> Who hath beheld him as he sprang to
> being, seen how the boneless one
> supports the bony?
> Where is the blood of Earth, the life, the
> spirit? who may approach the man
> who knows, to ask it?
> Formed with twelve spokes, by length of

time, unweakened, rolls round the
heaven this wheel of during Order.
Herein established, joined in pairs together
seven hundred sons and twenty
stand, O Agni.

(*ṚV*, I.164.4-11)

The boneless one is the unsubstantiated, i.e., the *prakṛti* or the Nature and the bony is the substantiated one — the visible universe, the representative of which is the earth. In these hymns, Ṛṣi Dīrghatamas question as to how life on the earth originated with blood and spirit and who knows the truth of it. Not only is the question concerned with the manifest universal origin but it also enquiries about life on earth. This question was not asked in the Western world nor even thought of earlier than the nineteenth century and the answer was obtained only in the early part of this century. The same was accomplished by the Upaniṣadic sages eons ago in India. They arrived at conclusions in line with those of the West but these were substantiated by the concept of the life-spirit leading to the *Brahman*.

The life-supporting capacity of the earth cannot be substantiated if we do not consider that life exists in the earth. This does not mean that life does not exist in other planets where life has not been reported. Life exists in them also but the necessary conditions for its manifestation might be absent in them or life in some other form may exist in those bodies. In any case, the Vedic students of the earth rightly consider the earth as being governed by a field of life.

The concept of 'divine earth' is due to the Ṛgvedic sages. That the earth represents a tiny form of the vast universe is also due to them. These are absolutely new to modern science studies of the Earth which have accepted the latter observation but not the former.

The Ṛgvedic hymn given above is important from the view of

measurement of time. Earlier, they noted six *ṛtus*; now they note 12 months of the year called spokes of the wheel. Further, the day and night in pairs are described herein as seven hundred and twenty sons, meaning 360 days and nights pairs. Perhaps this is the first measure of time of a year found in any literature. They have scrupulously, in ascertaining the time for their sacrifices, maintained a correct measure of time. The early lunar calendar was slowly blended into a later solar calender for a still later luni-solar calendar, the measure of which made them keep perfect time for their sacrifices. The naming of the solar months in Vedic period as Madhu, Mādhava etc. appears to be an extended observation on the terrestrial scene from the *ṛtus*. And the nomenclature of the lunar months is found based on the star during which the full moon appeared, e.g. Āśwayuja, Kārttika etc. Thus, according to Shamasastry (1936, p. 61), "The mean periods of the *Vedāṅgajyotiṣa*, thus adjusted, are so perfect that they could have been observed for 10,000 years without an year going wrong by a single day". Thus, the movements of the Earth helped the Vedic students form a perfect calendar.

The solar sweep of the earth has been described as seven houses and they are named as the seven metres of the Vedic *mantras* including the *Gāyatrī* which could be substantiated by the shadow of gnoman. That such an earth protects us is the meaning of *ṛk*. no. 16 of hymn 22 in *Maṇḍala* I. The *ṛk* no. 15 of the same hymn describes the earth as a vast spread and the dwelling place that affords no botheration. Such an Earth is requested to bestow peace on the sage. The 13th *ṛk* of the same hymn also makes an observation on the Earth. She is requested to help the sage in performing the sacrifice with her products, by which the sage can get plenty. Similarly, there are numerous *ṛks* which describe the earth in many terms and the meanings of such terms make us believe that the Vedic bards had a very close and highly appreciative tone in their compositions on the earth. They even went to the extent of questioning the Creator who made mountains like the Himālayas, the rivers and the watersheet of the earth, and presented their respectful oblations (as in *ṛk* no. 4, Hymn 121, *Maṇḍala* X).

It is difficult to estimate the sea change in the concepts of the *Ṛgveda* and the *Upaniṣads*. Though there are the *Brāhmaṇas* and the *Āraṇyakas* to bridge the gap, it is hardly enough to trace the most fascinating evolution of ideas during the conceptual renaissance in the later Vedic and post-Vedic periods. A considerable amount of literature must have been in existence which have been omitted by later authorities or destroyed. The concept of the 33 gods has been done away with and the five most important of them came to be recognised in later times. Of the 33 gods, Agni, Pṛthvī and Vāyu were considered the most important, as also Antarikṣa. To this group, Āpas was also added. They abandoned the concept of Indra, Rudras and Ādityas in favour of the above. What prompted them to do so and why they abandoned the others is a matter of serious concern and we do not have any literature to enlighten us on the subject.

Antarikṣa

In the earlier chapters it has been shown that the *Ṛgveda* essentially deals with poetry of physical geology. The Ṛgvedic hymns are the earliest compositions of the Āryans and they are concerned with the physical-geological agencies that the Āryans came across in the lap of the western Himālayas, especially in present-day Punjab, Himachal Pradesh and Jammu and Kashmir. The early Āryanisation of India extended the observations of the Āryans to the mainland of India. Later literature could claim to be Vedic and post-Vedic literature consisting of the main aspects of the physical geology of India in prose and poetry.

Modern geological observations, especially physical geology dealing with the origin, evolution and denudation of the surface of the earth, do not include a discussion on the space aspects of the earth. This was accomplished by the Vedic bards. The Vedic bards considered the duo of the earth and sky when they spoke of *Dyāvā-Pṛthvī* in many *sūktas*. From the beginning of the Vedic thought, the Āryans related the earth with the space or sky.

According to Amarasiṁha (Lewis Rice, 1970, p. 407) there are 21 synonyms for the sky in *Vyomavarga.* They are Dyo, Divau, Abhram, Vyoma, Puṣkaram, Amabaram, Nabhaḥ, Antarikṣam, Gaganam, Anantam, Suravartma, Kham, Viyat, Viṣṇupadam, Ākāśa, Vihāyasi, Vihāyasa, Nāka, Tārāpatha, Śabdaguṇaḥ, Meghadvāram and Mahābilam.

In the *Ṛgveda* the heaven and earth are called 'father' and 'mother' who never grow old. They have been described as great; they are broad and vast abodes, according to Macdonell (1976). They have been described as divine bowls.

The same idea is taken by the *Taittirīya Upaniṣad* in the *Śikṣāvallī,* third *anuvāka.* Discussing the *Adhilokam,* the earth is noted as the earlier form and the sky as the later form, and connected by space they are inducted by air or atmosphere.

A discussion on space or sky is very terse. What is space? It is that medium which accommodates the manifest universe. It is characterised by the quality of sound according to *Taittirīya Upaniṣad.* It is noted to give rise to the earth through Vāyu, Agni and Āpas. The concept of space and time in Indian philosophy has been discussed by Pandurangi (1988, pp. 244-47). Indian logic applied to the discussion on space has many interesting results. The *Nyāyavaiśeṣika* school considers both space and time as primary and separate categories of being. These are treated as eternal entities. Space and time are all-pervasive in the sense that they are co-extensive with the entire matter, all events and actions, and a new word *vibhu* is employed to describe it. The term *dik* is used to indicate space while *ākāśa* is used for a substance that is the locus of sound. In *Pūrvamīmāṁsā,* space is used in the sense of a substance that is an evolute of sound.

The term *ākāśa* is not used in the sense of space in both these systems. While *Nyāyavaiśeṣika* considers both space and time as inferred, *Mīmāṁsā* states that both space and time are perceived according to the senses along with the objects. *Sāṁkhya* holds two views about space and time. One view is that there are no space and time either as separate entities or aspects of matter. The primordial matter (*prakṛti*) evolves with objects, events and activities which cause the notions of extention and duration. The other view is that there are two levels of space and time, viz., *akhaṇḍa* and *sakhaṇḍa*. The *akhaṇḍa* is one continuous block of time and space while the *sakhaṇḍa* is the divisible space and time. The first is an aspect of *prakṛti* while the second is the comprehension of *ākāśa* under certain conditions. The first view that there is no space and time is akin to the Advaitic view. The *Sāṁkhya* school relates space and time to the process of evolution of primordial matter. Hence, the need to consider them as separate entities. *Dvaita* and *Viśiṣṭādvaita* schools consider the primordial matter as the basic category of being; while the former school considers space as separate entity and time as derived of it, the latter holds the just opposite view. The space is called *avyākṛtākāśa* and *dik* is a natural division of it. The *Dvaita* school does not accept the *akhaṇḍakāla*. Each moment is all-pervasive but not eternal. Every moment perishes to make room for the next moment. Time is envisaged as a close associate of continuous evolution of matter and is known intuitively.

According to the *Advaita* school, the concept of space and time are the effects or aspects of *avidyā*. The space itself is the reflection of *Brahman*. Since *avidyā* and its effects are not real, space and time are not real.

There is another dimension of the concept of *ākāśa*. In the sixth *anuvāka* of *Śkṣāvallī* of the *Taittirīya Upaniṣad*, it is observed that *ākāśa* is *hṛdaya* or *manas*, i.e., mind. It is noted that the internal mind is *ākāśa sa ya eśontarhṛdaya ākāśaḥ* — that the internal mind is recognised as *ātman*, a reflection of the *Brahman* as per the *Advaita* school. It means that the internal mind of a person is a common field for all living beings. It speaks the truth of universal nature — that is, the universal mind forms the internal mind and the universal mind is nothing but *ākāśa.*

According to modern science, space — which is a medium for light to propagate — bends near celestial objects (Hawking, 1994, p. 198). Hence, the space-time continuum is a most fundamental object which generates and destroys the material or visible universe. The *Sāṁkhya* school which noted the primordial matter as fundamental differs from the modern scientific ideas. So do the *Dvaita* and *Viśiṣṭādvaita* schools which consider the primordial matter as a basic category. The *Nyāyavaiśeṣika* school considers both space and time as primary and hence, it is nearer or closer to the modern scientific view; however, it differs in its assertion that they are separate entities.

Applications of modern technology to the theory of space has brought about a revolution in modern science. By the advancement in space science it has been possible to study the planetary bodies of the solar family and the moon in great detail. Space navigation is becoming real and the 21st century may witness space travel as a common affair, a routine matter.

In spite of spectacular advancements in space science, there is much to be understood about space. No or little advancement has been made in modern science regarding the direction of origin of space and its nature. What is it that we call *antarikṣa* or space is not yet certain. Its subtlety necessitates a very deep study. Is there any fundamental or subtle medium other than space out of which space originates? This is to be examined. In any case, this has posed a challenge to modern science. But in Indian philosophy, the field of the *Brahman* is noted to be the real and the most fundamental thing, the reflection of which is space. A discussion on the field of the *Brahman* as per the Advaitic school of Indian philosophy is beyond the scope of the present work. Modern science may need some more time before it finally realises the field of the *Brahman*.

Āpaḥ

Natural waters including the rains, rivers and oceans fascinated the Āryan sages very much. They have described them in their *Ab sūktas*, *Parjanya sūkta*, *Nadyaḥ sūkta* etc. All these divisions of hydrosphere have been elevated to the level of Goddesses and Gods. They have been described as mother and recognised as celestial as well as terrestrial. They have the sea as their goal. Varuṇa is supposed to move amidst them and the divine fire is called the son of waters. They are supposed to bestow remedies for ill-health, and wealth, strength, long-life and immortality.

In modern geology the hydrosphere is known to occupy two-thirds of the surface of the earth and it acts as a powerful geological agent in the process of weathering and transportation and in the development of sedimentary rocks. The action of each form of water like the rain, the rivers, glaciers, oceans, dew, fog, ice etc. has been detailed. The cycle of water in the form of evaporation from the sheet of water and from the oceans, formation of clouds, rains from clouds, and rivers and streams again joining the oceans has been well brought out in the Vedic compositions along with the copious description of the vivid rain clouds discharging the waters attended by thunder and lightning in terms of god Indra. Though the Vedic bards recognised the various manifestations of water on the surface of the earth, the present version of the *Ṛgveda* does not bring out the action or effects of dew, fog, ice, glaciers etc. [Iyer's (1911, p. 199) description of glaciers as Indra is untenable]. It is confined to the rains, rivers, streams and oceans. The occurrence of floods and innumerable streams soon after a heavy downpour, which is common in *varṣā-rtu* or the rainy season even to this day, is noticed. But the Vedic compositions do not give a detailed description of the geological activity of the various manifestations of water as known to physical geology today. Nevertheless, by instilling divinity in them and extolling their universal properties, the Vedic literature bring before our eyes the action-packed, forceful, living nature of these manifestations.

PARJANYA

There is a full *sūkta* describing the rains. Therein, the sage invites rains for the growth of crops (Griffiths, 1986).

> The bull (cloud) roaring loud, swift to send his bounty
> lays in the plants the seed for
> germination (*ṚV*, V.83.1)
>
> He smites the trees apart, . . .
> all life fears who wields the mighty
> weapon. (*ṚV*, V.83.2)
>
> Like a car-driver whipping on his horses,
> he makes the messengers of rain spring
> forward
> Far off resounds the roaring of the lion,
> what time Parjanya fill the sky with
> rain-cloud (*ṚV*, V.83.3)
>
> Forth burst the winds, down come the
> lightning flashes: the plants shoot up,
> the realm of is streaming.
> Food springs abundant for all living creatures,
> What time Parjanya quickens earth
> with moisture (*ṚV*, V.83.4)
>
> Thou at whose bidding earth bows low
> before thee . . .
> At whose behest the plants assume all

colours . . .

(*Ṛ*V, V.83.5)

Send down for us the rain of heaven, ye
Maruts, and let the Stallion's flood
descent in torrents
Come hither with this thunder while thou
pourest the waters down . . . .

(*Ṛ*V, V.83.6)

Thunder and roar: the gem of life deposit. . . . .
Thine opened water-skin draw with thee
downward, and let the follows and the
heights be level.

(*Ṛ*V, V.83.7)

Lift up the mighty vessel, pour down water,
and let the liberated streams rush
forward.
Saturate both the earth and heaven with
fatness and for the cows let there be
drink abundant . . . .

(*Ṛ*V, V.83.8)

Thou hast poured down the rain flood,
now withhold it. Thou hast made desert
place fit for travel.
Thou hast made herbs to grow for our enjoyment;
ye, . . .

(*Ṛ*V, V.83.10)

Thus a vivid description is provided of the torrential rains attended by their roaring thunder and forming numerous streams, elevating the low ground and lowering the high ground to keep a levelled ground. The direct relation between the vegetation and the rains has been noted. Similarly, a *ṛk.* describes the waters of rain treated by the sun as ambrosia and full of healing powers.

I call the waters, Goddesses, wherein our
cattle quench their thirst

(*Ṛ*V, I.23.18)

Amrit is in the waters; in the waters
there is healing balm.

(*Ṛ*V, I.23.19)

RIVERS

There are several compositions in the *Ṛgveda* describing the rivers as directly connected with the rains (Griffiths, 1986).

From her descend in streams the seas of
water: thereby the world's four regions
have their being
Thence flows the imperishable flood
and thence the universe hath life.

(*Ṛ*V, I.164.42)

Further, it is mentioned that the river Sarasvatī brings prosperity due to rains.

Wealth-giver, treasure-finder, free bestower:
bring that Saraswati, that we may drain it.

(*Ṛ*V, I.164.49)

Numerous streams are referred to —

Of ninety rivers and of nine . . . . . (*Ṛ*V, I.191.13)

The incessant activity of the streams is described:

The streams unceasing flow . . . . .
Day after day goes on the sheen of waters.
What time hath past since they were
first set flowing?

(*Ṛ*V, II.30.1)

Cutting their path . . . .

day after day flow to their goal
the rivers. (*Ṛ*V, II.30.2)

The association of wind with rain and rivers is brought out:

Saraswati . . . with the Maruts allied . . .

(*Ṛ*V, II.30.8)

and the river Sarasvatī has been described in superlative terms:

Forth from the bosom of the mountains
eager as two swift mares with loosened
rein contending
Like two bright mother cows who lick
their youngling, Vipāsha and Sutudri
speed down their waters.
Flowing together, swelling with your billows,
O lucid streams, each of you seeks
the other.

(*Ṛ*V, III.33.1)

There is a complete hymn to the river Sarasvatī.

She (Saraswati) with her might . . . . .
hath burst with her strong
waves the ridges of the hills

(*Ṛ*V, VI.61.2)

Whose limitless unbroken flood, swift
moving with a rapid rush,
Comes onward with tempestuous roar

(*Ṛ*V, VI.61.8)

Yea, she most dear amid dear streams,
Seven-sistered . . . . .

(*Ṛ*V, VI.61.10)

Marked out by majesty among the Mighty
ones, in glory swifter than the other

rapid streams.

(*Ṛ**V*, VI.61.13)

The river Sarasvatī is described as an iron fort in another hymn:

The stream Saraswati with fostering current
comes forth, our sure defence,
our fort of iron,
As on a car, the flood flows on, surpassing
in majesty and might all other waters.

(*ṚV*, VII.45.1)

The purity of the waters of Sarasvatī is described thus:

Pure in her course from mountain to
the ocean, alone of streams Saraswati
hath listened.

(*ṚV*, VII.45.2)

The cleansing nature of the rivers has been noted as:

Forth from the middle of the flood the
Waters — their chief the Sea-flow
Cleansing, never sleeping.

(*ṚV*, VII.49.1)

Waters which come from heaven, or those
that wander dug from the earth, or
flowing free by nature
Bright, purifying, speeding to the Ocean . . .

(*ṚV*, VII.49.2)

The river Sindhu and others have been described in another *sūkta* thus:

The rivers have come forward triply, seven
and seven. Sindhu in might surpasses
all the streams that flow.

(*ṚV*, X.85.1)

Varuna cut the channels for thy forward
course, O Sindhu, when thou rannest on
to win the race
Thou speedest over precipitous ridges of
the earth, when thou art Lord and Leader
of these maving floods.

(*ṚV*, X.85.2)

His roar is lifted up to heaven above the
earth: he puts forth endless vigour with
a flash of light
Light floods of rain that fall in thunder
from the cloud, so Sindhu rushes on
bellowing like a bull.

(*ṚV*, X.85.3)

O Śutudri, Parushṇi, and Saraswati:
With Asikni, Vitastā, O Marudvridhā, O
Ārjikīya with Suṣoma . . . . . .

(*ṚV*, X.85.5)

First with Trsṭāma thou art eager to flow
forth, with Rasā, and Suśartu, and with
Svetyā here
With Kubha: and with these, Sindhu!
and Mehatnu, thou seekest in thy course
Krumu and Gomati

(*ṚV*, X.85.6)

Flashing and whitely-gleaning in her
mightiness, she moves along her ample
volumes through the realms
Most active of the active, Sindhu unrestrained
. . . . beautiful, fair to see.

(*ṚV*, X.85.7)

Thus, most of the rivers flowing in the region of Brahmāvartta have been described by the Āryans in their first understanding of the rivers. A modern critic of geology may find many details missing in these descriptions. But it must be remembered that these hymns are the oldest of their kind and the earliest human-river interactions. They may well be considered as the first lessons in physical geology of the Brahmāvartta area. They are the most beautiful versions of any physical geo-poetic literature found on the earth.

The above facts suggest that there must have been many other compositions by other sages who lived amidst the natural beauty but they are not available to us today. They might have been excluded by Bādarāyaṇa during his editing to retain only those useful for performing sacrifices. In any case, they might have been lost for ever.

SEA WATERS

The cleansing and active nature of the sea waters have been described by the sages thus (Griffiths, 1986):

> Forth from the middle of the flood the
> Waters — their chief the Sea-flow
> cleansing, never sleeping.
>
> (*Ṛ**V*, VII.49.1)

> Waters which come from heaven, or those
> that wander dug from the earth,
> or flowing free by nature,
> Bright, purifying, speeding to the Ocean.
>
> (*ṚV*, VII.49.2)

The importance of waters in the development of crops and growth of vegetation was recognised by the Vedic sages. Their ability to cure sickness and diseases was also recognised. The various rivers of the Brahmāvartta and their flooding nature, roaring movement, thunderful rains, confluences, the effect of erosion of the banks and mountains etc. have been vividly described. The destructive activities of the rains and rivers assisted by the wind have been brought out. The sea as their receptacle has been defined.

More than all, the cleansing effect of the rivers has been recognised. The importance of water, i.e., pure water, for human health and environment is a matter to be appreciated. The water-cycle was known to them. Located in Brahmāvartta, the wide, flowing rivers acted as a fort or a barrier for outsiders in case of an entry into their land. They were not satisfied in their prayer to the rivers in an ordinary sense hence, they elevated the river Sarasvatī to godhood and as the best of mothers. Such a concept in respect of a river is not found in modern science in spite of these rivers acting as the nerve centres of nations. Modern science is, of late, beginning to understand the environmental importance of the rivers and other manifestations of waters. There is hardly any substitute for pure, sparkling water. Its importance in maintaining human and animal health has been only recently understood by modern science. But this was realised way back by the Vedic sages. One of the Vedic statements daily used in prayer is the following (Griffiths, 1986):

> The waters have their healing powers, the
> waters drive diseases away.
> The waters have a balm for all; let them
> make medicine for thee.
>
> (*Ṛ̣V*, X.137.6)

Another of the hymn observes that these waters are the most benevolent and they are able to cure all diseases; they are also the agents to bring prosperity to the nation and they flow as national ambrosia.

These facts by the sages reveal that they had a profound understanding of the value of these geological agencies. They did not treat them only as geological agencies which result in geological changes in the long time. But the sages gave an importance to them that even modern science did not accord them till recently. Environmental science is an area of study of very recent origin. Till the recent development of this field, the importance of these geological agents in keeping the land clean and maintaining public health was not much appreciated. But the Vedic sages accorded them importance a long time ago.

That the three rivers, Gaṅgā, Yamunā and Sarasvatī meet at Allahabad (Triveṇī or Prayāga) was and is an idea among the Hindus who believe that if one leaves his mortal body in this *saṅgam* or confluence one will be immortalised. But one finds only the Gaṅgā and Yamunā rivers meeting here. One will, however, be told that the river Sarasvatī is joining them at the bottom as *supta-nadī* or sleeping river. It is well-known that the river Sarasvatī originated in the Western Himālayas and draining the northern districts of Ambālā and flowing through the states of Rajasthan and Gujarat towards the south-west, joined the Arabian Sea at the Prabhāsa Kṣetra (Bhargava, 1864, p. 157). Since the river Sarasvatī is not found today, many believe that it is a myth. But it is not a myth but a geological truth (Murthy, 1980, pp. 189-92). The existence of river Sarasvatī has been very much described in the *Veda*s and Krishnan (1968, pp. 555) has observed that the "withdrawal of the waters from the Sutlej and possibly from Jamuna, dried up the Saraswati".

The river Gaṅgā has been declared the most sacred river in the world. It is worshipped in every Hindu house and a Hindu believes that taking a spoon of Gaṅgā water at the time of death will liberate him from the shackles of life and death. The physics of the waters of the river Gaṅgā is something evasive. The waters of the Gaṅgā is known to be repellent to mosquitoes. The waters kept in copper vessels will not get dry for decades while the waters of Yamunā and other rivers get micro-organisms in a short time and dry up. The Gaṅgā water is antibiotic and dead bodies thrown into it get decomposed and the river water does not get polluted for a long time. The Gaṅgā water has such qualities that it gets purified automatically—most probably due to its calcium-rich condition.

The river Gangā is a recent river compared to the river Sarasvatī described in the *Veda*. All the attributes of the river Sarasvatī are true of the river Gaṅgā also. Its late mention in the Vedic literature appears to coincide with the extinction of the river Sarasvatī. While there are several hymns and *r̥ks* describing the river Sarasvatī in the *Ṛgveda*, only one *r̥k*. (No. 5 of hymn no. 75 in *Maṇḍala* X) mentions the river Gaṅgā by name along with others.

Bhargava recognises four seas in the *Ṛgveda*. They are the Arvāvat, the Pārāvat, the Sārasvat and the Śaraṇyavat to the east, west, south and north respectively. According to him (Bhargava, 1964), there were extensive geological changes towards the end of the Ṛgvedic period that resulted in almost the present-day distribution of land and oceans, rivers and mountains—some events of which have been described in the *Mahābhārata*. the *Ramayaṇa* and the *Puraṇas*. He relates the extinction of several rivers including the river Sarasvatī, some of its tributaries and the seas due to the upliftment of some of the land portions and subsidence of some others. The sinking of the Vindhya mountains connected with the story of the southern march of *r̥ṣi* Agastya and the slow rising of the Himālaya mountains which probably were not so high as they are today are the effects of various geological changes. It will be an exercise to trace these geological changes from the viewpoint of Vedic and post-Vedic literature.

2

Graha Maṇḍala

THE GRAHAS

THE Vedic school believed that the earth is a representative of the universe and named the earth *Viśvambharā*. When once the relationship of the earth to the universe was established, the idea that the earth is a separate entity to be studied exclusively was given up. Even in the *Dyāvāpṛthvī* hymns, the earth is considered along with the heaven. This concept of the earth in relation to the universe is as old as the *Ṛgveda* which paved the way for a geo-cosmic theory in the Orient. The idea of a disc-like earth floating on water is as old as the Babylonian period. It was modified by Homer into a 'spherical universe'. Pythagoras also considered the earth as spherical and this view was accepted by Plato and Aristotle. This paved the way for a scientific cosmogony in the West during the middle of the seventeenth and eighteenth centuries AD. The most important 'Theory of the Earth' in that period was given by Descartes in his *Philosophe Principle* (1644) as per C.A. Ronan (1964, p. 232). He said that the various bodies of planets were originally glowing masses like the sun, the earth being no exception, and they possessed a nucleus of incandescent self-luminous mass of matter of which the middle zone was composed of an opaque solid substance which had initially been liquid in condition and the outer zone was of solid crust (Murthy,

1987). He explained at length the disposition of various planets around the sun and expressed some ideas about volcanoes and the occurrence of earthquakes — as due to the escape of internal heat of the earth along with volatiles. C.A. Ronan (1964) informs us that Leibnitz developed the theory (Acta Eruditarium, 1639). He observed that the mountains were formed by the irregular development of the early crust and the erosion of these parts caused the sedimentary rocks among other things. While no such ideas emerged in the Orient, the Ṛgvedic school made some observations on the celestial bodies, the most important of them being the luminaries. There are a number of hymns to the sun and the moon and a few hymns to the other planetary bodies as well. Here, the concept behind these celestial bodies will be brought out to understand the earth and other universal bodies.

Savitṛ, Āditya, Pūṣan, Viṣṇu

The sun has been one of the most important — rather, the most important — celestial body described in the *Ṛgveda*. Almost all the *kula-maṇḍalas* contain a description of the sun towards which the Ṛgvedic sages seem to have had a special attraction. So much so, the sun is praised in all the three *Vedas*. The *Gāyatrī* — the most fascinating *mantra* or the *ṛk* — is attributed to the sun. This was composed by *ṛṣi* Viśvāmitra and forms the third *Maṇḍala*, 62nd Hymn, 10th *ṛk* of the *Ṛgveda*. The celebrated *Gāyatrī* hymn is employed when initiating a student to Vedic studies with a 'new eye' (*Upanayana*).

According to *Amarakośa*, the following words are synonymous with the sun: Sūra, Sūrya, Aryamā, Āditya, Dvadaśātmā, Divākara, Bhāskara, Ahaskara, Bradhna, Prabhākara, Vibhākara, Bhāsvan, Vivaśvan, Saptāśva, Haridaśva, Uṣṇaraśmi, Vikartana, Araka, Mārtaṇḍa, Mihira, Aruṇa, Pūṣan, Dyumaṇi, Taraṇī, Mitra, Citrabhānu, Virocana, Vibhāvasu, Grahapati, Viśāmpati, Ahaḥpati, Bhānu, Haṁsa, Sahasrāṁśu, Tapana, Savitā, Ravi, Karmasākṣī, Jagatcakṣu, Aṁśumāli, Trayītanu, Pradyotana,

Dinamaṇi, Khadyota, Lokabāndhava, Surottamma, Dāmanidhi, Padminīvallabha and Hari.

It is very difficult to estimate the extent to which the Vedic bards were concerned with this super celestial body which is closer to man. According to Macdonell (1976),

> He is preeminently a golden deity: the epithets golden-eyed, golden-handed and golden tongued are peculiar to him. He has mighty golden splendour which he diffuses, illuminating heaven, earth and air. Shining with the rays of the Sun, yellow-haired, Savitr raises up his light continuously from the east. His ancient paths in the air are dustless and easy to traverse. He observes fixed laws; the waters and the wind are subject to him. The other gods follow his lead; and no being can resist his will.

Further, Macdonell (1976) states that

> Sūrya himself is also often called the eye of Mitra and Varuṇa, as well as of Agni and of the gods. He is the soul of all that moves or is stationary. His car is drawn by seven swift mares called harit bays. His father is Dyaus or Heaven. He is a gem of the sky, or a variegated stone in the midst of heaven. He dispels the darkness. He measures the days and prolongs life. He drives away sickness, diseases and evil dreams. All creatures depend on him.

Many qualities of Pūsan are identical with those of the sun but Macdonell (1976) remarks that his individuality is vague and his anthropomorphic traits are scanty Sūrya is noted to be the husband of Pūsan and he is connected with the marriage-ceremony in the wedding hymn (*Mandala* X, Hymn 85). With the golden aerial ships, Pūsan acts as the messenger of the sun.

Visnu is a subordinate god in the *Ṛgveda*. The central feature of his nature consists in his three steps, two of which are visible and the third is described as an eye fixed in the heaven shining brightly. Macdonell (1976) remarks that there is no doubt that these three steps refer to the course of the Sun and, in all probability, to its passage through the three divisions of the world — earth, air and heaven. Viṣṇu sets in motion, like a revolving wheel, his ninety steeds (days) with their four names (seasons) which is an allusion to the three hundred and sixty days of the solar year. He is the personification of the sun.

The Ṛgvedic references to the above concept are (Griffiths, 1986):

> . . . . . . cloud born god.
>
> (*ṚV*, I.42.1)

> His bright rays bear him up aloft . . . .
>
> (*ṚV*, I.50.1)

> The constellations pass away, like thieves,
> together with their beams,
> Before the all-beholding Sun
>
> (*ṚV*, I.50.2)

> His herald rays are seen afar refulgent
> Like flames of fire that burn and blaze.
>
> (*ṚV*, I.50.3)

> Sūrya hath yoked the pure bright Seven,
> The daughters of the car, with these,
> His own dear team, he goeth forth.
>
> (*ṚV*, I.50.9)

The seven daughers (or mares, steeds) are the seven different colours of the white light which are expressed as the rainbow (the 'VIBGYOR'). The explanation of the rainbow was brought out by Newton in the seventeenth century. It is not known whether such a concept existed in any other literature of the world in the period contemporary to the Vedic times and in later periods.

Sūrya is described as one who cures heart diseases in a hymn. The sun is also requested to cure jaundice.

> Sūrya, remove my heart's disease, take from me
> this yellow hue.
>
> (*ṚV*, I.50.11)

How these diseases are connected to the sun is a very fascinating matter. Whether the climatic changes cause these diseases of which one gets cured when the sun causes further changes in the climate, favourable to man's health, is a matter for research especially from the point of view of environmental sciences.

In another hymn, the Sun is called the eye of Mitra, Varuṇa and Agni.

> The brilliant presence of the Gods hath
> risen, the eye of Mitra, Varuṇa and
> Agni.
> The soul of all that moveth not or moveth,
> the Sun hath filled the air and earth
> and heaven.
>
> (*ṚV*, I.115.1)

Here the Sun is described as the soul of the moving and stationary world, the living and non-living.

The Viṣṇu aspect of the sun who sweeps the earth, heaven and the mid-air by his rays is given:

> I will declare the mighty deeds of
> Vishnu, of him who measured out the
> earthly regions.
> Who propped the highest place of
> congregation, thrice setting down his
> footsteps, widely striding.
>
> (*ṚV*, I.154.1)

His who strodes, widely pacing, with three steppings forth over the realms of earth . . .

(*Ṛ*V, I.155.4)

The sun's control of the weather is mentioned as given below:

who guides the Marut hosts.

(*Ṛ*V, I.156.4)

The might of the sun as a perfect follower of natural law is given in the following *ṛk*.

Mighty through Law, Ādityas, is your greatness . . .

(*Ṛ*V, II.27.8)

There is a *ṛk*. which states that the Law of the Sun is followed by the waters, the winds, and the Sun brings about the seasons.

Even the waters bend them to his service:
Even this wind rests in the circling region.

(*Ṛ*V, II.38.2)

. . . . and parted seasons.

(*Ṛ*V, II.38.4)

Him whose high Law not Varuna nor Indra, nor Mitra, Aryaman, nor Rudra breaketh.

(*Ṛ*V. II.38.9)

This law is the *ṛta* reflected in the cycle of the seasons and it is set by the Sun. This law cannot be broken by any other god.

The control the sun exerts on the formation and movement of clouds of rain is described:

To lofty hills thou sendest those whom

> Indra leads, and gives fixed abodes with
> houses unto these.
> However they may fly and draw themselves
> apart, still Savitr, they stand obeying
> thy behest.
>
> (*Ṛ*V, IV.54.5)

The effect of eclipses caused by Rāhu is described:

> O Sūrya, when the Asura's descendent
> Swarbhānu, pierced thee through and
> through with darkness
> All creatures looked like one who is
> bewildered, who knoweth not the place
> when he is standing.
>
> (*Ṛ*V, V.40.5)

The establishment of the period of time of a year is attributed to Mitra-Varuna:

> They who have established year and month
> and then the day, night . . .
>
> (*Ṛ*V, VII.66.11)

In another hymn, according to *ṛṣi* Hiraṇyastūpa, the Sun is described as the one that sets forth for the dark worlds in his golden chariot, observing the whole universe, to set the immortals and mortals in their respective places.

> Throughout the dusky firmament advancing,
> laying to rest the immortal and the mortal,
> Borne in his golden chariot he cometh,
> Savitr, God who looks on every creature.
>
> (*Ṛ*V, I.35.2)

The solar study which started in this manner in the Ṛgvedic times continued in the Yajurvedic and Atharvavedic times. Through the *saura* and *mahāsaura* hymns, the *Gāyatrī* and *Brahmāstra mantras*, the Āditya Hṛdaya in the Vālmiki *Rāmāyaṇa* etc., solar studies continued; but a positive outlook as the result of a scientific point of view did not come about. Writing about astronomers before the Greeks, C.A. Ronan (1964) observes, "At any rate we can give it a name and we shall call it the 'Sun'. Clearly it is a body of great power; it gives us warmth and provides us with the periods of daylight; and, in addition, it is far and away the brightest of all the bodies which shine on the earth from above. If we take the next step and think of it as a god of life and power, who is to say we are wrong? Who can deny that the sun is not what we claim?" In the above senses the *Ṛgveda* can impart the earliest lessons on the sun.

According to one *ṛk* the sun and the moon move in the heavens like children playing:

> By their own power these Twain in close
> succession move;
> They go as playing children round the sacrifice.
> One of the pair beholdeth all existing
> things; the other orderth seasons and
> is born again.
>
> (*ṚV*, X. 85.18)

Thus the relationship between the earth and the sun has been brought out in the *Ṛgveda*. The sun as the most prominent celestial body responsible for the origin, evolution and destruction of the earth has rightly been described by the sages in the best words. That the waters, winds, etc. are controlled by the sun, and all the moving and non-moving world at once follow his law suggests to us the great force that the sun exerts on the terrestrial scene. The earliest lessons being thus imparted, the solar studies continued in the post-Vedic times in a tremendous manner especially during the Upaniṣadic and Siddhāntic periods. The origin of the sun and the moon in every creation was noted by a Ṛgvedic *mantra* which states:

> *sūryācandramasau dhātā yathā pūrvam akalpayat*

It was believed that all the celestial bodies are created as has been done in this creation or the earlier creations.

The change in the terrestrial scene by the apparent motion of the sun was recognised and the law underlying it sung by many sages Though this law was realised by them, it appears that they did not bring out the reality behind it. The reality they recognised was the *Brahman*, for fear of whom the sun rises and the wind moves. Could it be the harbinger of the 'Theory of Gravitation' which was explained by Isaac Newton in the seventeenth century AD?

The observation that the sun is the soul of the entire moving and non-moving world is pregnant with full meaning. The sun is described as:

sūrya ātmā jagataha tasthuśaśca

meaning, the Sun is the soul of the Universe. It is praiseworthy that the Ṛgvedic sages realised the earth-sun relationship in such beauty. Similarly, the most important effect that the light has on the human mind in influencing it was realised by them in the celebrated *Gāyatrī* hymn attributed to *ṛṣi* Viśvāmitra. It is most appropriate that a detailed study be undertaken by modern psychologists in unravelling this influence in order to help mankind by the application of light therapy. While the most theoretical foundations were laid in the *Ṛgveda*, the quantitative aspects of the celestial bodies and the earth were undertaken for study by the students of Vedic and post-Vedic astronomy.

Soma

The next important object after the sun is the moon. Almost the whole of the IXth *maṇḍala* of the *Ṛgveda* and many hymns in other *maṇḍalas* are attributed to Soma. According to Macdonell (1976), Soma's anthropomorphism is less developed. He is much associated with Indra, Agni, Pūṣan and Rudra. His car is drawn by the Maruts and he is noted to wield sharp weapons.

According to *Amarakośa*, Soma is synonymous with terms like Vidhu, Sudhāṁśu, Śubhrāṁśu, Oṣadhīśa, Niśāpati, Abjaha, Jaivātrkaḥa, Glauhu, Mr̥gānkaḥ, Kalānidhi, Dvijarāja, Śaśadhara, Nakṣatreśa, Kṣapākara etc. Soma's association with water is brought out in many *r̥ks*. According to Macdonell (1976), "Owing to his yellow colour, Soma's brilliance is the physical aspect most dwelt upon by poets. He is then often likened to or associated with the Sun." He is said to dwell on the mountains where he is usually seen but his real abode is the heaven. He is described as the child or milk purified of heaven. He is noted to be the lord of wood and the important herbs (*oṣadhīśa*). Further Macdonell (1976) states, "In a few of the later hymns of the *Ṛgveda*, Soma begins to be mystically identified with the Moon; in the *Atharvaveda*, Soma several times means Moon; and in the *Brāhmaṇas* this identification has already become commonplace." Much of the earlier Ṛgvedic literature mean by 'Soma' an intoxicating drink produced out of a special herb of the same name that has a pink colour, which is said to be very much liked by all gods and used as *havis*. The transformation of the term 'Soma' to mean the Moon is significant especially as the moon was identified as the lord of herbs.

That the moon as the lord of herbs and vegetation was extended to cover all *rasas* or liquids shows an extension of their thought. As lord of all liquids, he became the lord of *Rasa-śāstra* in later times. This means chemistry in modern science though the term *rasa-śāstra* was given to the mineral medicines of *Āyurveda*.

THE ṚGVEDIC SOMA

A description of Soma is given in the following hymns (Griffiths, 1986):

> He shines in splendour like the Sun, refulgent as bright gold is he.
>
> (*ṚV*, I.43.5)

> Soma . . . central point . . . at the highest of holy law.
> (*ṚV*, I.43.9)

> These herbs . . . and these running waters, all these O Soma thou hast generated.
> The Spacious firmament hast thou expanded and with the light thou hast dispelled the darkness.
> (*ṚV*, I.91.22)

The moon and the sun measuring the region are described in a hymn:

> Soma and Pushan, urge your chariot hither, the seven-wheeled car that measures out the region
> suggesting the time reckoning by the luminaries.
> (*ṚV*, II.40.3)

The moon is addressed as a god and compared to a bird flying in the sky. Such comparisons are many in the later texts such as Vālmīki's *Rāmāyaṇa.*

> Here present this Immortal God flies, like a bird upon her wings,
> (*ṚV*, IX.3.1)

> This God . . .
> runs swiftly through the winding ways Inviolable as he flows.
> (*ṚV*, IX.3.2)

The movement of the moon with the sun is described in a hymn as given below:

> Soma thou shinest mounting heaven as 'twere above light's triple realm. And moving seem'st to speed the Sun.
> (*ṚV*, IX.17.5)

Some of the *ṛk*s suggest that the Moon is under eclipse as, for example,

They being young at first showed visibly
distinct the Creature that is half-
concealed and half-exposed

(*RV*, IX.68.5)

The moon is asked to flow onwards from the clutches of the ecliptic demon:

Flow onward Soma . . .

(*ṚV*, IX.59.1)

Flow onward from the waters,

(*ṚV*, IX.59.2)

Soma, as Pavamāna, pass over all trouble
and distress

(*ṚV*, IX.59.3)

There are references to sages offering food during eclipses:

Flow onward, Indu, with this food for him
who in thy wild delight
Battered the nine-and-ninety down

(*ṚV*, IX.61.1)

Smote swiftly forts . . . .

(*ṚV*, IX.61.2)

The moon, freed from the eclipse, is noted to shine brightly:

O thou who seest all things, Sovern as
thou art and passing strong, thy rays
encompass all abodes

(*ṚV*, IX.86.5)

The beams of Pavamāna, sent from earth and heaven,
his ensigns who is ever steadfast,
travel round
When on the seive the Golden-hued is

cleansed . . .

(*ṚV*, IX.86.6)

He hath assumed the rays of Sūrya for
his robe . . . .

(*ṚV*, IX.86.32)

The moon is described as the measurer of days.

Dweller in floods, King, Foremost, he
displays his might, set among living
things as measurer of days.

(*ṚV*, IX.86.45)

The moon is described as the father and the *Brahman*.

Father of holy hymns, Soma flows onward,
the Father of the earth, Father of heaven
Father of Agni, Sūrya's generator, the
Father who beget Indra and Vishnu
Brahman of Gods, the leader of the posts,
Rsi of sages, Bull of savage creature
Falcon amid the vultures, Axe of forests,
over the cleansing sieve goes Soma singing.

(*ṚV*, IX.96.5-6)

The moon's origin out of the ocean is described:

Far-seeing, lively, guided by the men, the
God whose home is in the sea.

(*RV*, IX.107.16)

This reminds us of the Darwinian theory of the origin of the moon according to which the moon originated out of the earth leaving behind a scar which is the Pacific Ocean (Giekie, 1903, p. 702).

The moon is also described as the guardian of law:

Guardian of Law . . . . .

(*ṚV*, IX.73.8)

In one of the most important hymns, the Moon is described as having originated out of the mind of the cosmic *puruṣa.*

> The Moon was gendered from his (Cosmic Puruṣa's) mind.
>
> (*Ṛ*V, IX.73.8)

Thus, the moon was the centre of attraction for the Ṛgvedic sages whose hymns for the moon fill almost a full *maṇḍala*, i.e., no. IX called the Soma-Pavamāna. Most of these hymns describe the fairness of the moon and his adventures and under the spell of these *ṛk*s the moon was to pass through the eclipse, becoming brighter to present a soothing look over the world with his ambrosia-like rays.

One of the most important aspects explained by Shamasastry (1938) is that a major portion of the *Ṛgveda* was composed by various sages with the intention of releasing the luminaries out of the dark field of eclipses. According to him, "The *Veda*s are nothing but a record of the religious spells performed and the prayers sung to help the gods free themselves from the demon of eclipses." Further, he states that

> Soma, the Moon, is regarded as the father and the Sun, as the mother. Their union on the day of the new Moon is believed to be the cause of productivity of the world . . the Vedic poets feared that in the solar eclipse a new beast or demon might outrage the Savitri and become the cause of mixed blood. This they could not avert and the only course left for them was to make an oblation into the fire with prayers to Agni to cut off the second seed . . . The lunar eclipse is sometimes regarded as the capture of Soma while hunting in distant forests by wild tribes . . . Hence Soma-krayaṇa or geurdon is symbolically paid to the Soma-seller for the restoration of the Moon. As there are only seven lunar eclipses in each of three divisions of the cycle (thrissapta) with seven more in what is called

the head of the cycle, the geurdons are also only seven. As there are, however, eleven lunar eclipses forming part of eleven Rudra eclipses, there may likewise be eleven or ten Soma-krayaṇas corresponding to the eleven Gandharvas or Soma captors. Sometimes a solar eclipse is also spoken of as a battle between Indra and Vṛtra or Śambara for Soma liquor. At other times it is spoken of as an act of snatching off the Soma food of the gods and departed souls by a Kravyāda or a flesh eating demon. On other occasions the Moon is regarded as a woman or a she goat and the lunar eclipse is described as an attack of the she goat by another male goat of a demon. The captors are either seven hunters in the country of the Dasārṇas; or they are seven wild beasts in the mountain regions of Kālānjana; or they are the Chakravāka birds sucking the Moon in the Sar island; or they are seven swans eating the lotus like Moon in the Mānasa lake. Thus numberless are the stories devised to account for the phenomena of eclipse.

Role of the Luminaries in the Vedic Calendar

Among the cosmic aspects of geology, the most important is the origin and development of a method of time by the Vedic Āryans. The calendar that developed was a result of many years of close observation of the movements of these luminaries. While in the Ṛgvedic text itself there is nothing about this calendar, it was already a fact then to study the time calculations separately for the benefit of performing sacrifices. This subject of time calculation was called the science of time, *Jyotiṣa*. Thus *Ṛgvedāṅga Jyotiṣa* is an adjunct of the *Ṛgveda* and it is by Lagadha. It is in 36 verses. Since it was to be committed to memory the verses are crisp and full of meaning, as is usual in Sanskrit.

Comparing the Vedic calendar to the modern Indian calendar, Shamasastry (1936, p. 61) notes,

> *The working of the Vedāngajyoutisha calendar was very much like the working of the modern Indian calendar* in that during the currency of a normal *Yuga* of five years i.e. a *Yuga* beginning *when the Sun as well as the Moon were in Dhanishṭah Nakṣatra on Māgha Sukla 1*, the lunar month Māgha might begin any time from 0 to 29.5 days before the Sun had reached Dhanishtadi (293^0). Just as the modern lunar year (Chaitra Pratipad) begins at intervals varying from 0 to 29.5 days before the Sun reaches the Āshwinādi or Meshādi (0^0); but after the expiry of the first normal Yuga, the month of Māgha would begin at varying intervals, from 4-1/2 to 29-1/2 days after the Sun had reached Dhaniṣṭhā Nakshatra.

This itself is a grand testimony to the astronomical acumen of Ṛgvedic bards which has sustained time calculations in India for more than six thousand years. Not that there was no later improvement over this calendar but the applicability or the utility of a calendar of such remote past testifies to the sound observations of the Vedic Āryans regarding the movements of luminaries and their skill in utilising these observations to formulate a calendar.

The moon has been referred to as the measurer of time and he is also called *Māsakṛt*— one who makes *māsa*. According to *Kṛṣṇa Yajurveda* (Satavalekar, 1990, p. 397), the annual months were called by different names in the Vedic period. They are as follows (I.4, 14):

Vedic Names	*Later Names*
Madhu	Caitra
Mādhava	Vaiśākha
Śukra	Jyeṣṭha
Śuci	Aṣāḍha

Nabha	Śrāvaṇa
Nabhasya	Bhādrapada
Īśaśca	Āśvayuja
Ūrjaśca	Kārttīka
Sahaśca	Mārgaśīrṣa
Sahasya	Puṣya
Tapaśca	Māgha
Tapasya	Phālguna

It can be seen that the names of the Vedic months just express the seasons or the scenery on the earth. There was the excess period over the lunar months in the year which was called either Saṁsarpa or Aṁhaspati and the accumulation of this period caused a third month in the course of three years, accounting for an *adhikamāsa* or *kṣayamāsa* in a longer period. This thirteenth month was referred to in the *Ṛgveda* (Shamasastry, 1938):

> He, who, accepting the rites knows the twelve months and their productions, and that which is supplimentarily engendered.
>
> (*ṚV*, I.25.8)

This suggests that the Ṛgvedic sages had already understood the luni-solar movements and were aware of the excess period of the solar cycle over that of the lunar which they called *adhimāsa*.

The same idea is expressed in the *Atharvaveda* (Shamasastry, 1990)

> Weakling by name art thou, the thirteenth month, Indra's house.
>
> (*ṚV*, 5.6.4)

The five-year cycle that was adopted during the Vedic period had the following names: 1. *Samvatsara*, 2. *Parivatsara*, 3. *Idāvatsara*, 4. *Anuvatsara*, and 5. *Idvatsara*.

The Vedic sacrificial performances appear to be a great exercise in the formulation and refinement of a calendar to account for a correct time. The whole of the *Kṛṣṇa Yajurveda*, the *Brāhmaṇas*, the *Atharvaveda* hymns go to show that the Vedic sages were involved in an exercise for the development of a calendar. According to Shamasastry (1938),

> But it should be borne in mind that the various systems of calendar described in the Sūtras are not the result of an observation of the heavens in a day, but are the outcome of the experience gained and adjustments made by many successive calculators of time. Nor are allusions to a calendar altogether wanting even in the Vedas.

That is why the Ṛgvedic observations were dynastic. The *kula-maṇḍalas* are the result of such continued observations over several generations kept secret by each of the institutions.

During the *Sūtra* period, the consideration of the *Ekāṣṭaka* day (the eighth day of the dark half of Māgha) as the beginning of a new year was in vogue. This has been discussed by Shamasastry (1938). According to him,

> The description of the New Year's Day was occurring on the Ekāshtaka day, i.e. the eighth day of the dark half of the month of Māgha (corresponding to December-January) in the times with which we are dealing, as well as the distinct references to a thirteenth month which must necessarily have been an additional month intercalated for the purpose of keeping the beginning of the year more or less close to its natural time, go a long way to prove that the Vedic poets kept a systematic calendar based upon scientific principles.

Then, Shamasastry (1938) brings out references from the *Atharvaveda* to describe the *Ekāṣṭaka* day also supported by *Tāṇḍya Mahābrāhmaṇa, Kṛṣṇa Yajurveda* and *Sāmaveda.* These facts suggest that the task of making a perfect calendar was going on since the beginning of the Ṛgvedic times in India.

The season-based nomenclature of the months in the Vedic period was then changed to the *nakṣatra*-based nomenclature during the later Vedic and *Siddhāntik* periods. The names of the lunar months were given based on the name of the *nakṣatra* in which the full moon occurred. The identification of stars of the ecliptic and their utility in the establishment of a calendar was, though not of early Vedic, probably of later Vedic origin. The extensive literature on astronomical information and the formulation of calendars is not available to us today. The only text that is available to us today is the *Vedāṅga Jyotiṣa* of Lagadha. The luni-solar movements and their relationship with the starry zodiac and the concerned literature, though of a considerable nature, is not perhaps the only such material that would have prevailed during the early Vedic period. It would be worthwhile to trace the development of systematic studies of the luminaries in the Vedic period in the establishment of a fundamental calendar.

The twelve divisions of the zodiac is as old as the *Ṛgveda* (Griffiths, 1986):

> Formed with twelve spokes, by length of time,
> unweakened, rolls round the heaven
> this wheel of during order.
> Herein established, joined in pairs together,
> seven hundred sons and twenty
> stand, O Agni.
>
> (*ṚV*, I.164.11)

Here the twelve spokes indicate the 12 divisions of the zodiac and the 720 children stand for the nights and days in a year. This is supported in another instance.

> Twelve are the fellies, and the wheel is single, three are the naves, what man hath understood it?
> Therein are set together spokes three hundred and sixty, which in nowise can be loosened.
>
> (*ṚV*, I.164.18)

The 12 fellies indicate the 12 months of a year and three naves refer to the three *Cāturmāsyas* of the year. The 360 spokes indicate the days of the year.

While there are references to the 12 solar mansions and 360 days of a year in the *Ṛgveda*, it is recorded that except for the names of Tiṣyā, Maghā and Citrā stars, the names of all the other stars of the zodiac have not been given in the text of the *Ṛgveda* (The Calendar Reform Committee, 1973, p. 263). However, the names of all the stars have been given along with their respective deities in the *Vedāṅga Jyotiṣa* of the Ṛgvedic period. Thus, it should not be said that because the names of the 27/28 stars have not been found in the Ṛgvedic edition prepared by Bādarāyaṇa such a system did not exist. This is far from the truth. It must be made clear that the *Ṛgveda* was chiefly edited to be used for prayers of various gods and it does not contain the full astronomy of that period. We do not know how many other texts like that of Lagadha existed and were destroyed or are not yet available. According to Subbarayappa *et al.* (1985),

> The Vedānga-Jyoutisha conceived of a cycle of five years — a luni-solar cycle called the Yuga, at the beginning of which the Sun and the Moon would lie at the starting point of the nakshatra, Dhanishṭha. During this period, there would be 5 revolutions of the Sun, Moon's 67 sidereal and 62 synodic months; 1830 sāvana or civil

> days; 1835 sidereal days, 1800 solar days and 1860 lunar days or tithis. The civil day was divided into 30 muhūrtas; 1 *muhūtra* into 2 nādikas; 1 *nāḍika* into 10.1/20 kalas; 1 kala into 124 kāshṭhas and 1 kāshṭha into 5 aksharas. The text, in a succinct manner, mentions the 27 nakshatras, 10 ayanas and vishuvana, and 30 ṛtus all in archaic, aphoristic language. The object of dividing the day into 124 parts was to have the ending movements of the tithis in whole units; likewise of the nakshatras. Each nakshatra was conceived in terms of 124 parts. Since there are 1830 civil days in a five year period, the year would consist of 366 days each; the ṛtus (when divided by 6) would have 61 days, and each ayana, 183 days. The intercalary months were thought of, one at the end of the fifth ayana and the other at the end of the 10th, for luni-solar adjustments. To make the calendrical computation more accurate, the day-length was considered to change by 6 muhūrtas, in one ayana i.e. the daily change would be 6/183 or 2/61 muhūrtas.

According to David Pingree (1981),

> At present there exist in India and outside of it some 1,00,000 manuscripts on the various aspects of Jyoutishshāstra. The great majority of these were copied within the sevententh, eighteenth and nineteenth centuries; for manuscripts cannot survive long in India except under exceptional circumstances. We have, therefore, essentially those texts selected for study or composed by the scholars of the Mughal and British rajyas. Since the copying of the manuscripts is virtually dead in modern India, many of these estimated 1,00,000 manuscripts will soon disappear, and the possibility of our achieving a reasonably accurate assessment of the continuity, development, and transformation of the astral mathematical sciences in India, will be correspondingly

> diminished. But even without the appalling prospect, we must be constantly aware of the arbitrary way in which was made the selection of texts and commentaries preserved in today's libraries.

This is the latest survey of an ancient discipline in the light of Yāskācārya's statement that 13 or 14 contributions on the subject of *Nirukta* had been lost prior to his time. There is hardly any doubt that many texts on *Vedāṅga Jyotiṣa* also would have met with a similar fate. In the absence of many such texts, the available Sanskrit works are just the tip of the iceberg on the subject. From these works alone, it cannot be argued that the study of the Vedic people was restricted to them.

On the same subject, David Pingree (1981) further observed the following:

> Though the fundamental approach and many of the models and parameters of each period were determined by the foreign sources, the basic traditions of Indian astronomy imposed on these external systems its peculiar stamp, and transformed the Science of Mesopotamia, Greece or Iran into something unique to India.

Pingree has divided Indian Astronomy into the following five periods.

1. Vedic — 1000 to 400 BC
2. Babylonian — 400 to AD 200
3. Graeco-Babylonian — AD 200 to AD 400
4. Greek — AD 400 to AD 1600
5. Islamic — AD 1600 to AD 1800

From this classification itself it is clear that Vedic astronomy is quite old although the dates mentioned against it are questionable.

Though it has been influenced from outside, it has nevertheless retained its originality.

Different systems of measurement of time in Vedic times has resulted in different nomenclatures. The names of the 13 months of the lunar measure of a year are mentioned in *Taittirīya Brāhmaṇa* as Aruṇa, Arunarajas, Pundarīka, Viśvajit, Abhijit, Ārdrā, Pinvamāna, Annavān, Rasavān, Iravān, Sarvasudhā, Śambhara and Mahāsvān. And so are the names of the 24 half-months of a year different in their nomenclature from the ones followed at present. The given names are Pavitra, Paviṣyan, Puta, Medhya, Yaśas, Yaśasvin, Āyus, Amṛta, Jīva, Jīvisyam, Sarga, Loka, Sahasvān, Sahiyan, Ojasvan, Sahamāna, Jayan, Abhijayan, Sūdravida, Dravinodas, Ārdrapavitra, Harikeśa, Moda and Pramoda.

The Vedic people had developed their own nomenclature for the day-time and night-time of the bright and dark fortnights separately. Samjñāna, Vijñāna, Prajñāna, Janad, Abhijanad, Samkalpamāna, Prakalpamāna, Upakalpamāna, Upaklptamāna, Klpta, Śraya, Vasiya, Āyat, Sambhūta and Bhūta are the 15 names referring to day-time of the bright fortnight. Darśa, Drsta, Darśata, Viśvarūpa, Sudarśana, Āpyāyamāna, Pyāyamāna, Pyāya, Sūnrta, Ira, Apūryamana, Pūryamana, Pūrayanti, Pūrna, and Pūrṇamāsī are the 15 names of night-time of the bright fortnight. Where the dark fortnight is concerned Prastuta, Vistuta, Saṁstuta, Kalyāṇa, Viśvarūpa, Śukra, Amṛta, Tejasvī, Tejas, Samiddha, Aruṇa, Bhānumat, Marīcimat, Abhitapat and Tapasvat are the 15 names of day-time, and Sūtra, Sunvati, Prasūta, Sūyamana, Abhisūyamana, Pītī, Prapā, Saṁpa, Tṛpti, Tarpayantī, Kānta, Kāmya, Kāmajata, Āyuśmati, and Kāmadugha are the 15 names of night-time.

Similarly, the *muhūrtas* of day-time in the bright fortnight were named Citta, Ketu, Prabhā, Nabhān, Saṁbhān, Jyotiṣmān, Tejaśvan, Ātapan, Tapan, Abhitapan, Rocana, Rocāmāna,

Śobhana, Śobhamāna, and Kalyāṇa. The *muhūrtas* of the night-time in the bright fortnight are Savitā, Prasavitā, Dīpta, Dīpayan, Dīpayamāna, Jvalan, Jvalita, Tapan, Vitapan, Saṁtapan, Rocana, Rocamāna, Sambhu, Sambhumāna and Vāma. Dātā, Pradātā, Ānanda, Moda, Pramoda, Aveśayan, Niveśayan, Samveśana, Saṁśānta, Śānta, Abhavan, Prabhavan, Saṁbhavan, Sambhūta and Bhūta are the 15 names of the *muhūrtas* in day-time of the dark fortnight. Abhiśaśta, Anumanta, Ānanda, Moda, Pramoda, Asadayan, Nisādayan, Samsādana, Samsanna, Sanna, Ābhu, Vibhu, Prabhu, Śambhu and Bhuva are the 15 names of the *muhūrtas* of the night-time in the dark fortnight.

The *muhūrta* is divided into 15 *pratimuhūrtas* according to *Taittirīya Brāhmaṇa*. They are Idānīm, Tadānīm, Étarhi, Kṣipram, Ajiram, Āsu, Nimesa, Phaṇa, Dravan, Atidravan, Tvaran, Tvaramāna, Āsu, Asiyan and Java.

According to *Aitareya Brāhmaṇa*, a *thithi* is the period of time during which the moon sets and rises.

According to *Yajurveda Vedāṅga Jyotiṣa*, 366 days form a solar year. In a year there are six *ṛtus* and two *ayanas*. Madhu and Mādhava form *Vasanta-ṛtu;* Śukra and Śuci form *Grīsma-ṛtu*; Nabha and Nabhasya form *Varṣā-ṛtu*; Īśa and Ūrja form *Śarada-ṛtu*; Sahas and Sahasya form *Hemanta-ṛtu*; and Tapas and Tapsya form *Śiśira-ṛtu*.

Further it states that when the sun and the moon occupy the same position in the zodiac together with the asterism of Dhanistha, then is the beginning of the *Yuga*, the synodic month of Māgha, the solar month of Tapas, the bright fortnight of Māgha, and the Uttarāyana. When the Sun moves from Āśleṣā, it is Daksināyana. In a *yuga* of 5 years, the number of risings of Jyeṣthā and other stars is the same as the number of days i.e., 1830 + 5 = 1835. The number of risings of the moon is 62 less than this number that is, 1835 – 62 = 1768. Various other details of the observations are also enumerated. The system of measurement of time in terms of Āḍhaka *pramāṇa* is also found in *Yajurveda Vedāṅga Jyotiṣa.*

It can be observed that the system of nomenclature where the days form a week was not in vogue during the Vedic period. To perform their sacrifices, the Vedic sages relied on a perfect calendar which was based on the movements of the earth. This is something superb, the like of which is not seen in any other literature of the time.

Pañcagrahas

The other five planets (other than the luminaries) have been recorded in the following *ṛk* of the *Ṛgveda.* (Subbarayappa, 1985)

> These five mighty gods were seen on the vast expanse of the sky. Even though they were seen coming together when I composed the hymns in honour of the gods, they have all gone away today.

Griffiths translates the same *ṛk* as given below:

> May those five Bulls which stand on high
> full in the midst of mighty heaven
> Having together swiftly borne my praises
> to the Gods, return. Mark this my woe,
> ye Earth and Heaven. (*ṚV*, I.105.10)

According to Sāyaṇa these five have been stated to be Indra, Varuṇa, Agni, Aryaman and Sāvitrī or Fire, Wind, Sun, Moon and Lightning respectively. But the five gods described in the hymn appear to be the five planets, leaving out the luminaries. These five are Mars, Mercury, Jupiter, Venus and Saturn.

In the worship of the luminaries and the planets, several *ṛks* are employed even to this day and they are drawn essentially from the *Ṛgveda.* It is difficult to establish the relationship between a celestial body and a Ṛgvedic ṛk. However, interesting information can be culled out with reference to the origin of the celestial bodies etc. The luminaries and the five planets and the two sensitive points on the ecliptic, Rāhu and Ketu, are the nine *grahas* worshipped traditionally as per the Vedic injunctions. Each of the *grahas* is given to have one *Adhidevatā* and another *Pratyādhidevatā*, the concept of which is not very clear. However, in this chapter, the Ṛgvedic hymnal *ṛk* chanted for the *grahas* will be presented along with a discussion on the *grahas* and their implications *vis-a-vis* the terrestrial changes which may be hinted or suggested by the *ṛk*. The origin of these planets in the respective arcs of the zodiac indicated in the ritual portion will be discussed but its source is uncertain. It is evident that the *Vedāṅga Jyotiṣa* deals only with the luminaries and stars and does not make any reference to these five planets. But many contend that certain *ṛks* describe the planets Jupiter, Venus and Mercury. However, the identification of the *ṛks* with specific *grahas* in the *Graha-Yajña*, as it is called, needs a thorough examination.

GRAHA-YAJÑA

In the *Graha-Yajña* section of the text *Āśvalāyana Pūrva Prayoga* (Josyer, 1950, p. 284) the following *ṛks* have been employed in the worship and *homa* of *grahas*.

PRAKĀŚAKA GRAHAS

The Sun

The following praising the sun is attributed to Hiraṇyastūparṣi and set to *triṣṭubh* metre (Griffiths, 1986):

> Throughout the dusky firmament advancing
> laying to rest the immortal and
> the mortal

Borne in his golden chariot he cometh
Sāvitrī, God who looks on every creature.

(*ṚV*, I.35.2)

AGNI-ADHIDEVATA

We choose Agni the messenger, the herald,
master of all wealth,
Well skilled in this our sacrifice.

(*ṚV*, I.12.1)

This is in praise of the divine fire, a face of the Sun. It is attributed to Hiraṇyastūparṣi and set to *jagatī* metre.

RUDRA-PRATYĀDHIDEVATĀ

What shall we sing to Rudra, strong,
most bounteous, excellently wise,
That shall be dearest to his heart.

(*RV*, I.43.1)

This is in praise of Rudra, another face of the Sun. It is attributed to Kaṇvarṣi and set to *gāyatrī* metre.

The Sun is given to rule the Kaliṅga land (Orissa) and belongs to Kāśyapa *gotra* being born on Prabhava Saṁvatsara, Māgha *Śukla Saptamī* in Kṛttikā Star. He is the lord of the Leo section of the Zodiac and the lord of Sunday. His symbol is a circle. and he is seated in the centre of the worshipping *Vedī* (Shastry, Laxminarasimha, 1991).

According to Dayānanda Sarasvatī (1976, p. 361), the first of the above *ṛk*s suggests the attraction of the sun instead of the dusky firmament. He observes that the word *Ākṛṣṇena* means that the sun moves in the heaven with his rays of golden splendour over looking all the worlds and dragging or attracting them. This kind of an interpretation appears to be more in line with the scientific thinking than that of Sāyaṇa who interprets that the sun moves in the heaven removing the dark worlds or darkness of the worlds. The chief aim of the star-like sun is its motion in the heaven attracting those celestial bodies which come within its ambit and dispelling darkness. He is round or with a circular face which itself has been considered as his symbol. Probably the invention of zero was owing to his symbol.

There are umpteen hymns in the *Ṛgveda* which bring out the attributes of the sun, and the pride of place among them is given to the Viśvāmitra-Savitā-Gāyatrī. But the purpose of it is different and so, as such that *ṛk* has not been employed here. Its meaning, in effect, pertains to the attractive nature of the sun dragging all other celestial bodies within its ambit, its universal nature, and its secular outlook.

It is possible that the positive role of the sun is described in the *Adhidevatā* divine fire while the destructive face is praised in its *Pratyādhidevatā* Rudra. We are acquainted with the sun ruling the Leo arc of the zodiac or the most powerful influence exercised when the Sun transits this arc. His origin in the Kṛttikā star on the seventh day of the bright half of the Māgha month in *Prabhava Saṁvatsara* is interesting. It is a mystery as to how the sages came to the conclusion that the Sun was born on that specific day in the Kṛttikā arc. It is also debatable whether this is a conclusion original to the Vedic school or one drawn by the *Siddhānta* school later on. However, modern astronomers can ponder over this theory of the origin or the formation of the Sun within the arc of Kṛttikā star.

The central position of the sun in *Navagraha Vedī* is very important. The heliocentric concept is evident here, though no theory to that effect was propounded by anybody during the Vedic period. Though the Indian astronomers employed the geocentric theory for astronomical and calendrical purposes, the heliocentric concept was known to them from the Vedic times.

The solar observations in the *Ṛgveda* are considerable in number. It would call for a separate project to evaluate these observations on the sun and its relationship with the Maruts and Parjanya, storms and quake-causing phenomena and many other features especially from the point of view of modern science of meteorology. Though the various kinds of terrestrial changes resulting from the movement of the sun through the starry path have been gathered by later astronomers and presented by Varāhamihira in his monumental text *Bṛhatsaṁhitā* under the head 'Ādityacāra' — which is a superb chapter in the 'Theory of the Earth' (Murthy 1987), similar studies have not been carried out in modern science in spite of spectacular advancement in heliology and instrumentation.

The Vedic heliology is a fascinating subject. The simple commentaries that are available on the *Saura Sūktas* do not do justice to these concepts. The sun directly influences the earth and various terrestrial activities. The slightest change in temperature, for instance, will affect the people to an enormous extent. Actually, almost all chemical, physical and biological changes that are taking place on the surface of the earth can directly be related to the solar influence. On the basis of the information available from the Vedic past to the recent times on the influence of the sun on the earth, students can formulate sound principles for the future interpretation of the terrestrial changes, a foundation aspect of the 'Theory of the Earth'. Thus, the Vedic study of heliology can be of utmost importance as the greatest contribution from the oldest school of thought on the earth.

It is my fervent desire that an integrated study of the ancient Indian and modern contributions in heliology pave way for a fruitful interpretation of the earth's surface changes as well as the changes in its interior. It is only the surface changes that are well-known; the internal changes caused by the heliological influence on the geomagnetic storms and convection currents, etc. are not yet known. In the formulation of such theories, the ancient Indian concepts may help, if not in a ready-made way then at least in a suggestive manner.

The Moon

The essential ṛks to the moon are given below (Griffiths, 1986):

> Soma wax great, From every side may vigorous powers unite in thee
> Be in the gathering-place of strength.
>
> (*Ṛ*V, I.91.16 and IX.31.4)

This ṛk is attributed to Gautamaṛṣi and set to *gāyatrī* metre.

AP-ADHIDEVATĀ

> Within the Waters-Soma thus hath told me dwell all balms that heal,
> And Agni, he who blesseth all. The waters hold all medicines.
>
> (*Ṛ*V, I.23.20 and X.9.6)

This *mantra* is attributed to Medhātithi Kaṇvaṛṣi and set to *anuṣṭubh* metre.

GAURĪ OR VĀK-PRATYĀDHIDEVATĀ

> Forming the water-floods, the buffalo (*vāk*) hath lowed. one-footed-or two-footed or four-footed, she,
> Who hath become eight-footed or hath got nine feet, the thousand-syllabled in the sublimest heaven.
>
> (*Ṛ*V, I.23.41)

This is attributed to Dīrghatamasaṛṣi and set to *jagatī* metre. According to Sāyaṇa, one-footed is sounding from cloud; two-footed sounding from cloud and sky; four-footed from the four cardinal points; eight-footed from the four directions and four intermediate directions; and nine-footed, from the eight points mentioned and the zenith. Gaurī is the *vāk* or the speech of the sky.

It is difficult to relate these ṛks with lunar worshipping. The first of the above hymns is a hymn of general praise to the Moon. In the second, the healing powers of the waters are indicated. The *ṛṣi* observes that Soma had said this to him. Possibly in the third, the sounding of the water-bearing clouds is described. In that case, the last mentioned *ṛk* may have some astronomical significance as well.

Then, the Moon is noted to rule the land of Yamunā and the arc of Cancer in the zodiac. He is said to belong to Atri *gotra*, having been born in *Saumya Saṁvatsara*, Kārttika *Śukla daśamī* in Uttarābhādrā star, or its arc in the zodiac.

The Vedic selenological studies, just as the Vedic heliological studies, are very interesting. The influence of the moon on the terrestrial changes is as important as the influence of the sun on the earth. The lunar influences on the earth observed from the Vedic times to that of Varāhamihira have been presented by him in his *Bṛhatsaṁhitā* (Murthy, 1987). Though the lunar influence on the earth may be lesser than the influence of the sun on the earth, the luni-solar influence is most important. This is because the combined influence is responsible for much of the changing scenery on the earth, that is, the environmental changes on it. The sociological influences of the moon are also very important. How the influence of the moon is actually related to social problems may be taken up as a multidisciplinary study involving social scientists, astronomers and medicos.

Apart from these, the interaction among the bary-centre (the centre of the earth-moon system), the magnetic centre of the earth and the gravity centre of the earth causes many important geological changes. Modern selenological studies have brought a wealth of data on the origin and evolution of the moon. The absence of a strong seleno-magnetic field and a low intensity gravity field on the moon have resulted in the absence of any life on it similar to that on the Earth. The evolution of rocks on the moon also stopped some time after its origin.

A study of the lunar cycle and the hydrological cycle, and the relationship that may exist between the lunar cycle and the terrestrial vegetation cycle may be an interesting proposition. A study of the crop pattern and the lunar cycle may help in understanding the world's agricultural pattern and problems.

In the *Graha-Yajña*, moon is placed to the south-east of the Sun and his symbol is a square or *caturasra*.

Mars

Mars is worshipped in the following *ṛk*. Though the subject-matter is Agni, it is employed here to instal Mars on *Yajñavedī*.

> Agni is head and height of heaven, the master of the earth is he.
>
> He quickeneth the water's seed.
>
> (*ṚV*, VIII.44.16)

This *ṛk* is attributed to Virūparṣi and is set to *gāyatrī* metre.

According to Sāyaṇa, he (Agni) is the best of gods and is the lord of the earth. He radiates into the moving and the stationary world.

PṚTHVĪ IS ADHIDEVATĀ

> Thornless be thou, O Earth, spread wide before us for a dwelling-place.
>
> Vouchsafe us shelter broad and sure.
>
> (*ṚV*, I.22.15)

This is attributed to Medhātithirṣi and set to *gāyatrī* metre.

KUMĀRA-PRATYĀDHIDEVATĀ

> The youthful Mother keeps the Boy in secret pressed to her close, not yields him to the Father.

> But, when he lies upon the arc, the people see his unfading countenance before them.
>
> (*ṚV*, V.2.1)

This *ṛk* is attributed to Skandarṣi and set to *triṣṭubh* metre.

It is commented by Griffiths (1986) that the kindling of the fire is figuratively described here.

Mars is called Kuja in Sanskrit and it is synonymous with Bhauma, Lohitāṅga and Mahīsuta. Mars is noted to be the son of the earth and red in colour, or the colour of the fire. Mars is said to rule Avantīdeśa and belong to Bhārdvāja *gotra*. He governs the Aries and Scorpio sections of the zodiac and is stated to have been born (formed) in *Rākṣasa Saṁvatsara*, Āsādha *Kṛṣṇa Caturdaśī* in Mṛgaśirā star. He is triangular, symbolic and is placed to the south of the sun in *Graha-Yajña*.

It appears that Mars was not studied much in the Rgvedic period. However, Mars with a ruddy look was always known to be related to fire; hence, it was Aṅgāraka. As such, Mars was worshipped in the form of Agni with the Earth and Kumāra as subordinate deities.

The absence of any study on Mars in the *Ṛgveda* is glaring. This is true of the other *Veda*s also. It may not be a fact that the Vedic astronomers neglected this study; actually, it is difficult to believe that such a vast literature as the *Veda*s which existed before Vyāsa and which have been described as *ananta* (endless) did not include the study of the *graha*s. It is possible that the Vedic version edited by Vyāsa did not include the then existing literature on the study of the *graha*s. In that case, one wonders why the Vyāsa-edited *Veda*s did not include a study of the *graha*s.

*Rsi*s like Āśvalāyana, Baudhāyana and others who mastered the sixteen *samskāra*s and instituted their own schools were not Vedic sages but later *rsi*s who employed Vedic *ṛk*s for propitiating the *grahas* in *Graha-Yajñas*. But if the Vedic *ṛṣis* did not know the existence of the *grahas*, how could the *Prayoga-kartās* have included the *ṛks*, praising them in their schools of *samskāras*? It is possible that some texts which are not available to us now to fill the gap between the time of the Vedic sages and *Prayoga- kārakas* may be discovered to throw light on this field. As of now, the evidence from texts like the *Pūrva-Prayoga* of Āśvalāyana is just sufficient proof to state that some of these *ṛks* describe the nature and aspects of the *grahas* as known by the Vedic sages.

This situation can also be viewed from another angle. After the *Vedāṅga-Jyotiṣa* (*Ṛg*, *Yajus*, *Sāman* and *Atharvan*) period, it is the sixth century AD that provides us a text of astronomical importance, namely, the *Pañcasiddhāntikā* of Varāhamihira. The time gap is vast and has accounted for 5 *Siddhāntas*, that is, the Sūrya (old), Pitāmaha, Romaka, Pauliṣa and Vasiṣṭha (Thibaut, 1968). The full extent of these five *siddhāntas* is not available to us today; what is available is the section edited by Varāhamihira who states that his chief reason or special cause for editing this text was to rationalise the eclipses of the luminaries — identified as the main problem in the Vedic literature by Shamasastry (1938).

According to Varāhamihira (Thibaut, 1968), the order of importance of these five *Siddhāntas* is Sūrya followed by Romaka, and Pauliṣa (as about equally correct) *Siddhāntas*. He has paid little attention to Pitāmaha and Vasiṣṭha *Siddhāntas*. According to Thibaut (*ibid.*), "The Pitāmaha Siddhānta, in the first place, is the representative of the pre-scientific stage of astronomical knowledge, the other sources of which are the Jyotisha Vedānga, the Garga-Samhita, the astronomical books of the Jainas, and a number of quotations from various old authors as, for example, Parāśara." He further states about the Vasiṣṭha *Siddhānta* summarised by Varāhamihira that "while apparently more advanced than the Pitāmaha Siddhānta, it yet seems to have been decidedly inferior to the scientific Siddhāntas. We therefore shall most probably not be mistaken in assigning it to the period marking the transition from the old, purely indigenous systems. . ." meaning that the two *Siddhāntas* fill the gap between the Vedic period and the Siddhāntic period though the latter may overlap the former. The other three *Siddhāntas*, namely the Sūrya, Pauliṣa and Romaka, are noted to be later *Siddhāntas*, that is, later to the influence of Greek astronomy from the time of Ptolemy (AD 127-151). But it is not clear which texts influenced Indian astronomy especially from the West.

In any case, the old *Sūrya Siddhānta* has the credit of presenting the mean motion of the planets. According to Thibaut (*ibid.*) ". . . the merit of originality as far as it goes, would most probably belong to the unknown author of the old Sūrya Siddhānta." The old *Sūrya Siddhānta* says, "In the Samhita, in the beginning of the chapter on Rāhu's course, I have fully explained to what causes, apart from Rāhu, solar and lunar eclipses are due" (verse 10, chapter XV, *Pañcasiddhāntikā* of Varāhamihira, Thibaut, 1986). All the while explaining Drapsa, Shamasastry (1938) states that most of the Vedic literature contained spells to be employed to take out the luminaries from the clutches of Rāhu during eclipses. This fear, however, must have faded when the old *Sūrya Siddhānta* explained the scientific cause of the eclipses.

The institution of week-days also owes its origin to the old *Sūrya Siddhānta*. The global concept of the earth is given by the verses 22 and 23 of chapter XV as follows:

> 22. The Sun, when rising in the Bhāratavarsha, at the same time makes midday in the region of the Bhadrāśavarsha, sunset in that of Kurus, midnight in Ketumāla.
>
> 23. What is sunrise in Lanka is sunset in Siddhapura, midday in Yamakoti, midnight in Romaka country.

Thus the old *Sūrya Siddhānta* had some understanding about the major regions of the world.

The most important point to observe in the old *Sūrya Siddhānta* is its mention of the number of revolutions of the planets in a cycle of *Mahāyuga*—the concept of which is original to this text. It is known that in a *Mahāyuga*, there will be 4.32 million solar years or 1577917800 days. They are:

Planets	*Cycles in a Mahāyuga*
Saturn	146564
Jupiter	364220
Mars	2296824
Venus	7022388
Mercury	17937000

This is the first time in post-Vedic literature that a text says something about the *grahas* from the available literature. It is to be observed that knowledge about the *grahas*, though not found in the Vedic literature, was first reported in a Sanskrit text of the Siddhāntic period. This does not mean that the observations about the *grahas* were there prior to the old *Sūrya Siddhānta* text; it must have taken a considerable time for the post-Vedic astronomers to arrive at this data, but they finally did calculate the grand scale of time of a *yuga* and the number of revolutions of the *grahas* in one *mahāyuga*.

It would have been a herculean task for the post-Vedic astronomers to give a scientific explanation for the eclipses of the luminaries and initiate a scientific study of the *grahas*. This exercise would have filled the gap of time from the *Vedāṅga*

Jyotiṣa to the old *Sūrya Siddhānta*. Such an attempt to understand the relationship of the earth with the luminaries and *graha*s cannot be seen in any contemporary literature the worldover, and this is a matter to be emphasised.

Mercury

Mercury is propitiated by the following *ṛk*s:

> Wake with one mind, my friends, and kindle Agni.
> ye who are many and who dwell together.
> Agni and Dadhikras and Dawn the goddess, you gods with
> Indra, I call down to help us.
>
> (*ṚV*, X.101.1)

This is attributed to Budharṣi and set to *triṣṭubh* metre.

VIṢṆU-ADHIDEVATĀ

> Through all this world strode Vishnu;
> thrice his foot he planted, and the whole was gathered
> in his footstep's dust.
>
> (*ṚV*, I.22.17)

This *ṛk* is attributed to Medhātithirṣi and set to *gāyatrī* metre.

PURUṢA-PRATYĀDHIDEVATĀ

> A thousand heads hath Purusha, a thousand eyes, a
> thousand feet
> on every side pervading earth he fills a space ten fingers
> wide.
>
> (*ṚV*, X.90.1)

This *ṛk* is attributed to Nārāyaṇarṣi, and set to *anuṣṭubh* metre.

Mercury is said to rule the Magadha land and it governs the Gemini and Virgo sectors of the zodiac. He is noted to belong to Ātreya *gotra*, having been born in Pūrvabhādrā star in Mārgaśirā

Suddha Saptamī in Āṅgirasa year.

Here again, the basis of the selection of the *ṛk*s in order to propitiate the planet Mercury by Asvalāyanarsi is not clear. The first *rk* of the three given above is addressed to Viśvedavas and, according to Sāyaṇa, it is addressed to Ṛtvik friends who were enkindling divine fire to become single-minded and to pursue their respective works with intelligence. The second *ṛk* is attributed to Viṣṇu and, according to Sāyaṇa, Viṣṇu intended to transgress the whole world and strode with his three feet or the worlds gathered as dust at his feet. He also observes that Yāska commented that because he is capable of entering all places, he is called Viṣṇu — who stepped the sky, the heaven and the earth (at Gayā). Perhaps the hottest spot was Gayā and they meant that Viṣṇu (actually, the sun) strode upon all the three worlds. Mercury is located to the north-east of the sun and his symbol is given to be an arrow, on *graha-vedī*. In the third *ṛk* it is intended to describe the Virāṭa Puruṣa who is mentioned as governing the earth in all directions. It is again the sun who governs the earth in all directions who is meant here. Hence, in all the above *rk*s the sun is described as propitiating the closest of all the planets to the sun, Mercury. From the first *rk* it is also clear that the planet Mercury is a planet of thought and intelligence. How they arrived at such a concept is, however, debatable.

According to Āśvalāyanaṛṣi, there is the concept of the theory that Mars in the form of fire, Mercury in the form of the earth, Jupiter in the form of space, Venus in the form of water, Saturn in the form of air, Moon in the form of mind, the Sun in the form of soul and the zodiacal sensitive points, Rāhu and Ketu are present in the body of the living and the non-living world. These planets when in adverse dispositions create imbalances in the body. In order to set them to balance, one should undertake *Graha-yajña*. This theory makes it clear that in the living body and also in the natural environment, changes take place due to the motion of the planets producing helpful or adverse vibrations affecting both the living and non-living world in respect of these five elements (*pañcabhūtas*), mind and soul. The adverse vibrations include imbalance in the activity of digestive fire due to Mars, the earthly elements due to Mercury, the sound element due to Jupiter, the element of water due to Venus, the element of air due to Saturn, the mind due to the moon, and tensions due to the sun. The element of mind and soul are present in the non-living world also though in a gross form. As the living body is sensitive, the feel is very effective. Since all these elements originate from space which is characterised by the quality of sound, the changes due to adverse vibrations of these *grahas* can, to an extent, be balanced by the application of sound of the *ṛks*. That is noted to be appeasement of the *grahas* or *graha-śānti* by *mantra-japa*. The same school of thought is extended to worshipping (*arcanā*), sacrifice (*homa*) and parting with things (*dāna*). There appears to be nothing unscientific about this theory. All the *saṁskāras* are preambled with *Graha-yajña* for the single, simple reason of having the adverse vibrations converted to sympathetic ones favouring the specific aspect of the *samskaras*.

Jupiter

Jupiter is propitiated in the following *ṛks*:

> Bṛhaspati, that which the foe deserves not which shines among the folk effectual splendid,
> That, Son of Law which is with might refulgent — that treasure wonderful bestow them on us.
>
> (*ṚV*, II.23.15)

This is attributed to Ghṛtsamadṛṣi and set to *triṣṭubh* metre.

INDRA-ADHIDEVATA

> Indra we laud thy great deeds wrought aforetime, we laud thy exploits later of achievements;

We laud the bolt that in thine arms lies eager; we laud thy two Bay Steeds, heralds of Sūrya.

(Ṛ*V*, II.21.6)

This is attributed to Ghṛtsamadarṣi and set to *triṣṭubh* metre.

BRAHMĀ-PRATYĀDHIDEVATĀ

Those who are yoked by prayer I harness, fleet friendly Bays who take their joy together
Mounting thy firm and easy car, O Indra, wise and all-knowing come thou to the Soma.

(Ṛ*V*, III.36.4)

It is attributed to Viśvāmitrarsi and set to *triṣṭubh* metre.

Jupiter is said to rule the region of Sindhudvīpa and govern the sectors of Sagittarius and Pisces in the zodiac. He belongs to Āṅgīrasa *gotra* and is stated to have been born (formed) in the arc of Bharanī star on the fourteenth day of the dark half of Vaiśākha month in *Dhātṛ Samvatsara*. However, *Taittirīya Brāhmana*, 3.1.5 (Subbarayappa, *et al.*, 1985) mentions that Jupiter was born in Puṣyā star. Juptier is located to the north of the Sun on *Graha-Vedī* and is represented by a *dīrgha-caturasra* (rectangle) symbol.

There are five full hymns and several *ṛk*s in more than 10 hymns in the *Ṛgveda* with regard to Bṛhaspati or Bṛhamanaspati. He is described as the friend of Indra (I.18.6) and addressed as the lord of assemblies. He is the priest of gods. According to the following *ṛk*, the great distance of Jupiter from the earth is evident:

Brhaspati, from thy remotest distance have they sat down who love the law eternal.
For thee were dug wells springing from the mountain, which murmuring round about pour streams of sweetness.

(Ṛ*V*, IV.50.3)

During the interval of time between the Vedic period of these preliminary observations and the old *Sūrya Siddhanta* period, considerable amount of data appears to have been collected. Similarly, during the period of the old *Sūrya Siddhanta* and that of the *Bṛhatsaṁhitā* of Varāhamihira in the sixth century AD, much more data was collected. The Jovian reckoning of time of a cycle of 60 years of 12 divisions each of five years reminds us of the five-year cycle of the *Vedāṅga-Jyotiṣa.*

The influence of Jupiter on the earth was considered salutary. Jupiter was referred to by the name *guru* meaning the 'heaviest' amongst all the planets. The various terrestrial changes that attended upon the Jovian movement of the 60-year cycle have been presented by the author elsewhere (Murthy, 1978). Though all such data are of post-Vedic Siddhāntic period, it must be remembered that the foundations for such a study was laid during the Vedic period.

In spite of spectacular developments in modern planetology by employing satellite-studies, observations with regard to the Jovian influence on the Earth in respect of changes in weather, rainfall, climate, environment etc. are yet to be gathered. From this point of view, Indian astronomy can contribute valuable information especially in favour of evolving a 'Theory of the Earth'.

Venus

Venus is propitiated by the following *ṛk*s:

> Like heaven art thou; one form is bright
> one holy, like Day and Night dissimilar in colour.
> All magic powers thou aidest, self-dependent auspicious
> by thy bounty here, O Pūṣan.
>
> (*RV*, VI.58.1)

This is attributed to Bharadvājarṣi and set to *tristubh* metre.

This hymn is in praise of Pūṣan and not Venus Śukra here

means brightness. But Āśvalāyanarṣi appears to have instituted this *rk* as one in praise of Venus. How Pūṣan is going to exercise magic powers is not clear here. However, Jupiter is said to be essentially Ṛgvedic while Mars is of *Sāmaveda*; similarly, Venus is of *Yajurveda* and Mercury is of *Atharvaveda*. The magic powers belong to the school of *Atharvaveda*. Even then, this *ṛk* must have been appropriate to propitiate Mercury; but the word *Śukra* was perhaps considered as referring to Venus by Ācārya Āśvalāyana.

INDRĀṆĪ-ADHIDEVATĀ

> So have I heard Indrāni called most fortunate among these Dames,
> For never shall her Consort die in future time through length of days. Supreme is Indra overall.
>
> (*ṚV*, X.86.11)

This is attributed to Vṛṣākapirṣi and is set to *paṅkti* metre.

Again, the selection of the *ṛk* of Indrāṇī to worship Venus is not clear. But it may have been employed for the female deity controlling wealth — coming under the purview of Venus.

INDRA-PRATYĀDHIDEVATĀ

> For your sake from each side we call Indra away from other men:
> Ours, and none others, may he be.
>
> (*ṚV*, I.7.10)

This *ṛk* is attributed to Mudhucchandarṣi and set to *gāyatrī* metre.

Description of Indra here is for the wealth which is represented by Venus.

Venus is given to rule Kambodia (Kāmboja) and sometimes

the Mahārāṣṭra region. He governs the Taurus and Librā sections of the zodiac. He belongs to Bhārgava dynāsty. He is said to have born (formed) in Jyeṣṭhā star on a dvādasīday of bright fortnight of Śrāvaṇa *māsa* in *Pārthiva Saṁvatsara*.

The significance of the origin of all these planets (Shastry, 1938) will be explained later. However, it is not yet known how the sages could arrive at such information. It may be recalled that even to this day, modern science in neither astronomy nor planetology has been able to arrive at the point of origin where the genesis of the planets is concerned. It is simply a mystery as to how the sages of the post-Vedic period, especially the Siddhāntic period, could get such important information especially in the absence of scientific disciplines like Celestial Dynamics. In spite of advancements in examination and even mapping the surface of planets and ascertaining their nature, it has not been possible for modern scientists to observe the point or specific arc of origin of these planets in the zodiac. Moreover, such information is absent in works contemporary to the *Veda*s as well as modern works.

One of the most important factors is the sages' conception of these planetary bodies as living manifestations of nature. Even if such a concept is untenable any more, the theory of the enrichment of planets in specific *Pañcabhūta*s mentioned earlier makes this concept most appealing and highlights the effect of the planets on environment due to their motion through space. Such a conceptual prognostication has been the foundation of a theory for the school of Indian Medicine and all other branches of *Śāstras* (Murthy, 1992, p. 118).

Venus is represented by a pentagon symbol and is placed to the east of the Sun in *Graha-Yajña*. He is also addressed as Uṣanā, Bhārgava and Kavi. There is the concept that the Aśvins are twins — identified with the planets Mercury and Venus. There is also the star Aśvini praised in the *Ṛgveda* in more than 50 hymns and in many *ṛks* in numerous hymns. Accordingly, they are described as divine physicians who heal diseases with their remedies, restore sight, and cure the sick and maimed. They appear in the sky after the Usas and shine bright in the evening sky also. Their car is described to be swifter than thought and they go round the Sun. They are addressed as Aśvinau, Dasrau (wonderous), Nāsatyau (true), Svarvaidyau (physicians of gods), Āśvineyau or Āśvinisuthau (children of Aśvini), suggestive of their birth in the star arc of Aśvini, but Venus is born in Jyeṣṭhā star and Mercury in Purvābhādrā star, as mentioned earlier, perhaps a correction due to the Siddhāntic school. Their going round the sun and appearing in sky after dawn and before darkness sets in the evening just suggests that they are morning and evening stars.

The influence of the Venus on the Earth during its sojourn in the sky round the Sun has been summarised by Varāhamihira in his *Bṛhatsaṁhitā* which has data collected from the post-Vedic period till Varāhamihira's time (data woven into a Theory of the Earth in my work, *An Integrated Theory of the Earth*). In spite of much study of the planet Venus by employing satellites etc. its actual influence on the Earth has not been revealed by modern science. The various changes attending on the terrestrial scene — climatic differences, rainfall, crops that prosper due to the influence of Venus on the Earth etc. — have been dealt with by Varāhamihira. But such studies are yet to be undertaken in modern science to evolve a 'Theory of the Earth'. Considerable amount of data is necessary to formulate such a theory and the observational record may have to be extended over several centuries. But not even an attempt is being made in modern science towards this end. The Vedic and post-Vedic studies can, actually, contribute valuable data from an observational record of more than a couple of thousands of years. It may then be possible to even forecast the behaviour of the earth with a certain amount of accuracy.

Saturn

The planet Saturn is propitiated in the following *ṛks*.

> May Agni bless us with his fires, and Sūrya warm us pleasantly:
> May the pure Wind breathe sweet on us,
> and chase our foes.
>
> (*RV*, VIII.18.9)

This *ṛk* is attributed to Ririmbitaṛṣi and set to *uṣṇik* metre.

Once again, it is difficult to explain why a *ṛk* in praise of the divine fire and Sūrya has been put forth to invoke the planet Saturn. Saturn is noted to be the son of the Sun, specifically in the later Siddhāntic period. The Vedic hymns do not indicate this clearly, but in the post-Vedic literature both of them are said to belong to Kāśyapa *gotra*. Hence, this *ṛk* praising Sūrya, Agni (his shadow) and wind (a form of Saturn) is probably used here to propitiate Saturn.

HIRAṆYAGARBHA PRAJĀPATI-ADHIDEVATĀ

> Prajāpati, Thou only comprehendest all these created things, and none beside thee
> Grant us our heart's desire when we invoke thee may we have store of riches in possession.
>
> (*ṚV*, X.121.10)

This *ṛk* is attributed to Prajāpatiṛṣi and set to *triṣṭubh* metre.

YAMA-PRATYĀDHIDEVATĀ

> To Yama pour the Soma, bring to Yama consecrated gifts
> To Yama sacrifice prepared and heralded by Agni goes.
>
> (*ṚV*, X.14.13)

This is attributed of Yamaṛṣi and set to *anuṣṭubh* metre.

Yama, the office or the natural law of *dharma* or *ṛta*, is praised here as the *Pratyādhidevatā* of Saturn, since Saturn is the balancing wheel of the Solar System. This is very symbolic and pregnant with meaning when seen from astronomical point of view.

Although there is no direct link between the above *ṛks* and the planet Saturn, it is to be noted that the planet is being propitiated symbolically. These *rks* recognise Saturn as the son of the Sun (originated of the Sun), windy in nature and the most important balancing wheel of the solar system.

Saturn is represented by the symbol of an arch and placed to the west of the Sun in *Graha-Yajña*. Saturn is supposed to govern Gujarat (Saurāṣṭradeśa). He is the planet with a great influence in the Capricorn and Aquarius sections of the zodiac. Saturn is said to have formed or originated in the arc of Swāti star on a new moon day of the dark half of Pūṣya *māsa* in *Pramodūta Samvatsara*.

It is very well-known that though 99.87 per cent of the mass of the solar system rests with the sun, 98.99 per cent of the aggregate angular momentum of the solar system rests with the planets. Amongst them, Jupiter with 725 units (the unit being of that of the Earth) exerts the greatest influence and next is Saturn with 294 units (Murthy, 1987). Hence, Jupiter and Saturn have a final say in all matters of the terrestrial changes taking place due to the movement of the planets and the sun. Thus, the influence of Saturn is to be reckoned with in all aspects of the earth.

Saturn is called *Śani*, meaning that he is slow-moving and is same as *manda*. He is also called *śauri* (born of the Sun), *paṅgu* (lame), *kālā* (dark), *chāyāputra* (son of shadow), *asīta* (not white) and *arkaja* (born to the Sun).

The terrestrial influence of Saturn, probably recorded in the Vedic times based on these concepts, was later summarised by

Varāhamihira (Murthy, 1987). A considerable amount of data has been and is still being accumulated by modern astronomers since a long time but there is not much information on the influence of the planet Saturn on climate and other changes on the earth. An integrated study needs to be undertaken to evaluate the available data in this area.

APRAKĀŚAKA GRAHAS

Rāhu

Rāhu and Ketu are described as non-shining *graha*s. These two cannot be found in the form of material body in the heavens but they exercise tremendous attraction or force on the ecliptic. *Graha* in Sanskrit means that one which attracts, i.e., *karṣati*. While all the other *graha*s described so far are material bodies in the zodiac belt, these two are only sensitive points; hence, Rāhu and Ketu have been personified and described. That Rāhu has been described in the *Ṛgveda* under the term 'Svarbhānu' is very well-evident. This point on the zodiac is also called Tama, Rāhu, Saimhikeya and Vidhuntuda.

In the *Ṛgveda*, Rāhu is described as one who eats away the Sun and Moon (*rahavati bhuktva candrarkau*, Oka, 1913). This is clear from the following *r̥k*s attributed to Atri Bhaumar̥ṣi and set to *anuṣṭubh* metre. (Subbarayappa, *et al.*, 1985)

> O Sun, when the demon Swarbhānu overspread you with darkness, all the worlds stood as if not knowing where they were.
> O Indra, you destroy the illusions of Swarbhānu which exists under the sky. Sage Atri got back the Sun who was hidden by darkness, by means of the fourth brahma incantations.
> O sage Atri, may that malicious demon, desirous of food, not devour me with that dreadful darkness. You are a

> friend and truth is your wealth. May you and god Varuṇa protect me.
> The sage Atri sent the press-stone, propitiated the gods with prayers and salutations and dispelled Swarbhānu and set his eye on Sun's light.
> Atri and his descendants alone could restore the Sun when the demon had overspread (the Sun) with darkness. None besides them had the power to do so.
> (*Ṛ̣V*, V.40.5-9)

Says Shamasastry (1938),

> I think that these examples referred to in the Atharvaveda and Rigveda are enough to prove that the Vedic poets had a cycle of eclipses and that those eclipses were the measures of their seven Soma sacrifices.

According to him,

> It may, however, be questioned why no commentator either on the Vedas or the Brāhmanas or even on any Tantric work has a word to say connecting the numbers 1000, 72,33,14,7 and the like with any cycle of eclipses or pointing out that the Ashtachakra or Srichakra is a graphic representation of eclipses. So far as the Vedic texts themselves are concerned, there can be no doubt that such Vedic expressions as 'Three Sheep'. 'Five Sheep', 'Cow', 'calf and bulls', and 'he-goat and she-goat' all mean eclipses, as already pointed out. Likewise the word Graha itself is a general name to eclipses, Soma-graha denoting lunar eclipse and Āditya-graha, solar eclipse, the earthly soma-juice being an imitation of the heavenly soma-juice, drunk by gods and departed souls on the occasions of new moons or by demons of eclipses on the days of eclipses. The Vedic poets feared that on occasions of eclipses their fathers in heaven would be

> starved to death on account of the Moon which is believed to be their food on the days of new moons being carried off and devoured by the seven hunters, or seven wild beasts, or seven Chakravāka or moon-light drinking birds, or seven swans living in the Manasa lake. Hence they seem to have thought it necessary to perform a Srāddha rite and offer rice-balls to the fathers on the days of eclipses. These verses are even now recited during the performance of Srāddha rites together with the Vashatkāra formula of 17 syllables.

Further, Shamasastry observes,

> The forms of solar and lunar eclipses seem to have given rise to the twenty-four Mudras of witch-craft. Figures like those of the Sun (Gāyatri, Sāvitri and Saraswati) in the several eclipses of the cycle are formed with two hands and fingers, and the Gāyatri is recited to exorcise evil spirits by all the twice born people in their morning, mid-day and evening prayers.

Shamasastry continues,

> The names of the figures are:
>
> 1. A disc like figure
> 2. The same with fingers not touching each other
> 3. The same with fingers drawn apart from each other
> 4. A figure with two, three, four, five, six heads corresponding to the six solar eclipses in a line in the cycle.

Shamasastry says,

> Figures like an Anjali, like a cart, like a noose, like two things kissing each other, like fish, a tortoise, a boar, a lion, a cow's udder with two or four nipples, like a circle,

> a lotus and like a Linga. I have already pointed out how the gnoman's shadow in various months forms figures like those of fish and other animals. This explains the traditional story that the various incarnations of Viṣṇu were predicted by the sages and they would take place in each Kalpa in their own time to ease the earth from its burden.

Finally, he remarks,

> Whatever might be the reason for the loss of tradition underlying the cult of eclipses which forms the main theme of the Vedas, this much is certain that the Vedas are the attempted explanations of the eclipses and the spells and the charms devised to avert the calamities that would happen to gods, fathers and men from Vritra, Shamabara and other demons of eclipses.

Until the origin of the text of the old *Sūrya Siddhānta* (since nothing about eclipses is evident from the text of *Vedāṅga Jyotiṣa* of Lagadha), it appears that the Vedic sages were under the erroneous assumption that the Rāhu gulped down the luminaries during the eclipses. *Grahaṇa* means the nothingness of *graha* or loss of *graha* (*graha-ṇa*). This theory was well-developed by the astronomers of the post-Vedic period to ascertain the terrestrial changes followed by different types of eclipses which have been summarised by Varāhamihira in his *Bṛhatsaṁhitā*. (Bhat, 1986). The *Siddhāntas* have presented scientific explanations for the cause of eclipses and removed the old Vedic concept of the luminaries being devoured by the demon called Svarbhānu.

This sensitive point of the zodiac has been drawn into *Graha-Yajña* by *Smṛti* - and *Saṁskāra-kāras* who have employed the following ṛks in propitiating him. They are given below.

With what help will he come to us,

Wonderful, ever waxing friend;
With what most mighty company?

(*ṚV*, IV.31.1)

This is attributed to Vāmadevarṣi and is set to *gāyatrī* metre.

This *ṛk* is actually in praise of Indra according to Sāyaṇa and it is not known when this was drawn to describe Svarbhānu. Probably, Ācārya Aśvalāyana proposed this *ṛk* to praise Svarbhānu.

SARPARĀGINĪ-ADHIDEVATĀ

This spotted Bull hath come, and sat before the Mother
in the east,
Advancing to his Father heaven.

(*ṚV*, X.189.1)

This is attributed to Sarparāginīṛṣi and set to *gāyatrī* metre.

This *ṛk* is attributed to Sūrya (or also, Sarparāginī) according to Sāyaṇa. Accordingly, the Sun shining and transiting has transgressed Udayācala in the east along with Mother Earth. He has even transgressed the heaven and *Pitṛ-loka*. This *ṛk* possibly suggests that the Sun has taken the dead elders to the heaven; for the next *ṛk* suggests that the god of death should vacate the path of heaven for the elders to enter.

MṚTYU-PRATYĀDHIDEVATĀ

Go hence, O Death, pursue thy special pathway apart
from that which Gods are wont to travel
To thee I say it who hast eyes and hearest;
Touch not our offspring, injure not our heroes.

(*ṚV*, X.18.1)

This *ṛk* is attributed to Śaṅkuśakoṛṣi and set to *triṣṭubh* metre.

It appears that the same concept of 'devouring' continues with regard to Svarbhānu in the later period of *Graha-Yajña*.

Rāhu is described to be a serpent-head and he is equated with Yama, the god of death; then, he is requested to clear the path for the dead to go to heaven. Rāhu does not harm progeny; he is, thus, being equated with the genitals of the human body while Ketu is equated with the head of the human body.

Rāhu is noted to belong to Pithīnasa *gotra* and he governs the Barbara region. He is described to have been originated from a point in the arc of Hastā star from the fourteenth day of dark-half of Bhādrapada *māsa* in *Rākṣasa Samvatsara.* He is located to the south-west of the Sun on a *śūrpa* symbol in *Graha-Yajna* while Ketu is located to the north-west of the Sun on a *dhvaja* symbol. Rāhu is said to govern the Leo sector of the zodiac though some state it to be Gemini.

In this way, the origin of the two luminaries, five planets and two sensitive points was described probably during the Siddhāntic period, based essentially on the data which had been accumulated from the Ṛgvedic times. It may be mentioned that the *smṛti*-and *saṁskāra-kāras* of later period have, however, drawn their appreciation of these *Nava-grahas* — as they have come to be called — from the Ṛgvedic hymns. Whether they are really appropriate and relevant to the occasion may be examined by the competent. What may be emphasised here is that the Vedic bards were most familiar with the terrestrial nature as well as the celestial objects which attracted their attention by their shining and movements. Moreover, the origin of the planets as described by them can be evaluated from the modern point of view, although they did not describe any theory as to the origin of the members of the solar family. The modern theories on the origin of the planets do not give any data as to the first formation or origin of the members of the solar family in terms as precise as the ones mentioned so far.

Vedic astronomy was far advanced than the data from *Vedāṅga Jyotiṣa, Garga Saṁhita,* similar texts that we have now, and only a part of what was known to the Vedic astronomers is available to us now. The gap between the Vedic astronomy and the old *Sūrya Siddhānta* is very wide and it is difficult to believe that there existed no other text during this period — i.e., the post-Vedic time. While there was the institution of *Śulvasūtras* by the time of *Yajurveda*, it is difficult to understand the absence of texts on geometry and symbology belonging to the Vedic times.

Ketu

Ketu is also noted to be another unseen *graha* at about 180° away from Rāhu. They are usually set at opposite points in the zodiac. Ketu is propitiated by the following *ṛks*.

> Thou making light where no light was and form,
> O men: where form was not,
> Wast born together with the Dawns.
>
> (*ṚV*, I.6.3)

This is attributed to Madhucchandarṣi and set to *gāyatrī* metre.

According to Sāyana, this *rk* is addressed to Indra (in the form of Sūrya) who wakes up persons going to sleep on his setting when no matter can be cited. *Ketum kṛṇvanprajñām kurvan* means that 'enlightening' in the morning.

BṚHASPATI-ADHIDEVATĀ

> Vena, with the first enlightenment of the Brahman through his *ṛks*, through his intelligence could grasp the root of truth and false. (author)
>
> (*ṚV*, III.22.1)

This *ṛk* is attributed to Venarṣi and set to *triṣṭubh* metre.

CITRAGUPTA-PRATYĀDHIDEVATĀ

> Wondrous of wondrous power give to the singer wealth

wonderous, marked, most wonderful, life-giving
Wealth bright, O Bright one, vast with many heros, give
with thy bright flames to the man who lauds, thee.
(*Ṛ*V, VI.6.3)

This is attributed to Bhārdvājaṛṣi and set to *triṣṭubh* metre.

According to Sāyaṇa, this *ṛk* is addressed to Agni. But one may wonder about the commentary by Sāyaṇa and the English rendering by Griffiths (1986). Perhaps it is the variegated colour of the sky (owing to the rising Sun or the Moon) which is described by the *ṛṣi*. The bright light referred to in the *ṛk* suggests that the sky is described as having been carried away by 'Ketus' (*Ṛ*V, I.50.1) 'Ketavaha', according to Sāyaṇa, is *Sūryaraśmayaḥ*, meaning, the sunrays.

Ketu is noted to be a spot or insignia by *Amarakośa*. The words *kalaṅka*, *aṅka*, *lāñchana*, *cinham*, *laxma*, *laksana*, *pāli*, *ketu*, *dhvaja*, *liṅgam*, *nimittam*, *vyañjanam*, *padam*, *prajñānam*, *abhijñānam*, *lalāma*, etc. are synonymous. *Amarakośa* also said *grahabhede dhvajo ketuhu*, meaning, Ketu is a *graha* signified by a flag.

Ketu is said to belong to Jaimini *gotra* and is noted to govern the *Antaravedī* region. He is noted to have formed from the arc of Revatī star on the fourteenth day of dark-half of Caitra *māsa* in *Rāksasa Samvatsara*. He governs the Karkataka sector of the zodiac.

Ketu is described as comets by Bhat (1986, p. 1106). It is described in plural form in the *Ṛgveda* as *Ketavah*. Varāhamihira has described 1020 comets in his *Bṛhatsamhitā*, probably accumulating the data up to his time from the time of the *Ṛgveda*. According to Baker (1965), a comet is characterised by a foggy envelop of the coma with a tail fanning out in a direction away from the sun. Comets revolve around the sun generally in highly eccentric orbits. Compare this description with the

Ṛgvedic statement, *udutyam jātavedasam devam vahanti ketavaḥ*, meaning, the comets carry the rising sun. Meteoritic streams are the products of the disintegrated comets.

It is difficult to make out whether Ketu denotes a non-existing point of attraction (*aprakāśaka graha*) or actually a comet. It is also not known when it started meaning comets or a point of attraction in the zodiac. In any case, it is clear from the texts that the Ṛgvedic Ketu is an astronomical phenomenon. It goes to the credit of the Ṛgvedic sages that they discovered the Ketus and came up with the idea of the sun being carried away by them — an apt description since comets are known to encircle the sun in eccentric orbits.

3

Nakṣatra Maṇḍala

In the earlier chapters, we dealt with the earth in the *Ṛgveda* from the point of view of terrestrial facts and near celestial objects (*grahas*). The next distant objects of the universe which form the background for consideration of the motions of the *grahas*, especially in the celestial zone of the ecliptic (zodiac), happen to be the stars. The Vedic seers did make an attempt to study the stars in their singleness and plurality for their importance in the day-to-day and annual calendar to ascertain the time for sacrifices etc. Though the direct relationship of any of the stars to the earth has not been presented in the Vedic literature, it is discussed that the stars form a permanent path for the motion of the luminaries and the *grahas* to reckon with, thus relating to the earth in the tertiary phase. The Vedic sages made a thorough study of the stellar path forming a background or frame for the *grahas* and recognised some 27 or 28 stars/ groups and gave them names based on certain observations. Thus, the theory of the earth as a representative of the universe is complete only when it is studied in the background of the universal manifestation.

Nakṣatra is defined as the one which is motionless — *nakṣatrati, calayati iti* — and it is synonymous with *ṛkṣa*, *bham*, *tāram*, *tārake*, and *udu*. By the time of the *Ṛgveda*, the seers were well-acquainted with the stars of the zodiac. The establishment of the *Nakṣatra Maṇḍala* made it easy for them to form the earliest Vedic calendar as has been explained earlier. Their five-year calendar began with the luminaries joining in the Dhaniṣṭhā star. Thus, the identification of the starry path helped them to establish their calendar for the purposes of fixing the time for sacrifices etc.

The *Vedāṅga Jyotiṣa* lists the 27 stars and their presiding deities. This is probably the earliest text in Sanskrit literature to list the 27 stars. The stars are mentioned below:

Nakṣatras	*Presiding deities*
Kṛttikā	Agni
Rohiṇī	Prajāpati
Mṛgaśirā	Soma
Ārdrā	Rudra
Punarvasu	Aditi
Puṣyā	Bṛhaspati
Āśleṣā	Serpent
Maghā	Pitṛs
Pūrvāphālgunī	Bhaga
Uttarāphālgunī	Aryamā
Hastā	Sāvitrī
Citrā	Tvaṣṭṛ
Swāti	Vāyu
Viśākhā	Indrāgni
Anurādhā	Mitra
Jyeṣṭhā	Indra

Mūlā	Nirṛti
Pūrvāṣāḍhā	Āpas
Uttarāṣāḍhā	Viśvedevas
Śravaṇā	Viṣṇu
Dhaniṣṭhā	Vasus
Śatabhiṣaj	Varuṇa
Pūrvābhādrā	Ajaikapād
Uttarābhādrā	Ahirbudhnya
Revatī	Pūṣā
Aśvinī	Aśvins
Bharaṇī	Yāma

(*Vedāṅga-Jyotiṣa* of Lagadha by Shamasastry, 1936)

It can be observed that the starry nomenclature has been derived with respect to the most dominant factor — the prominent geological phenomena-terrestrial surface change — and the concerned geological agent is recognised as the presiding deity. Though exceptions are there like in the case of Bharaṇī, Aśvinī etc. the remaining deities, by and large, actually represent the major terrestrial change or the scene called by the name of the respective deity — like Vāyu for Swāti, since wind action will be more efficient during the day or month ruled by Swāti.

According to Subbarayappa *et al.*, (1985, p. 338) the *Atharvaveda Pariśiṣṭa-Nakṣatrakalpa* lists the number of stars in each of the groups identified above. They are as follows: Kṛttikā — 6; Rohiṇī — 1; Mṛgaśirā — 3; Ārdrā — 1; Punarvasu — 2; Puṣyā — 1; Āśleṣā — 6; Maghā — 6; Pūrvāphālgunī — 2; Uttarāphālgunī — 2; Hastā — 5; Citrā — 1; Swāti — 1; Viśākhā — 2; Anūrādhā — 4; Jyeṣṭhā — 1; Mūlā — 7; Purvāṣāḍhā — 7;

Uttarāṣāḍhā — 1; Abhijit — 1 (this is not in the list of stars given above); Śravaṇā — 3; Dhaniṣṭhā — 5; Śatabhiṣaj — 1; (or 100 as some say); Pūrvābhādrā — 2; Uttarābhādrā — 2; Revatī — 1; Aśvinī — 2; and Bharaṇī — 3.

They also named the stars in each of the *Nakṣatras*, for example, in Kṛttikā, the seven stars are named as Ambā, Dulā, Netatni, Abhrayantī, Meghayantī, Varṣayantī and Cupuṇika (*Taittirīya Saṁhitā* quoted by Subbaryappa *et al.*, *ibid.*). The deities given by Lagadha are repeated in the *Yajurveda Taittirīya Saṁhitā* (4.4.10, Satavalekar, 1990, p. 397) and the *Nakṣatra Sūktas* of *Atharvaveda* also list them with a request to confer good on the sages (Satavalekar, 1944). They constitute the 7th and 8th *sūktas* of the 19th *kāṇḍa*. They describe 28 stars instead of 27 in the *Ṛgveda* and are aimed at warding off evils and bad omens. The deity of the Abhijit star (before Śravaṇā) is given as Brahmā.

According to the *Ṛgveda* the stars disappear along with the night when the Sun rises (I.50.2) even as the Moon remains nearer to them (X.85.2), i.e., transiting the stars, describing the motion of the lunar and solar bodies on the starry path. Each of the stars is propitiated by the Ṛgvedic *mantras* in the sacrifice of stars or *Nakṣatreṣṭhī*. Now let us examine the purport of each of the Ṛgvedic *ṛks* describing the stars for their meaning and comprehension. The *Nakṣatreṣṭhī* (Bhatta, 1991), not in vogue today, might have been a very important sacrifice of the period of the *Yajurveda*.

Aśvinī

The star Aśvinī ruled by Aśvinī *devatās* has been propitiated employing the following *mantras* (Griffiths, 1986).

> Aśvins, with truth they call you Twain
> bestowers of felicity;
> At sacrifice most prompt to hear, most

gracious ye at sacrifice.
Most pleasing to the Asvins to these prayers
which magnify their might.
Which we have fashioned, even as cars; high
reverence have we spoken forth.

(*ṚV*, V.73.9-10)

This hymn is attributed to Paurarṣi and set to *anuṣṭubh* metre.

The Aśvins have been described to be twins who are *nāsatyau*, or 'most truthful', and endowed with the power to cure diseases — hence addressed as *svarvaidyau* or 'the divine doctors'. It is difficult to ascertain the purport of the author (Āśvalāyanarṣi) in selecting the above two *ṛk*s from the *Ṛgveda* to propitiate the Aśvins. It would have been better had the *ṛṣi*s selected some meaningful hymns instead of the above two hymns — as, for example, *ṛk* no. 3 of the same hymn which says that the Aśvins had carved their own third path distinct from that of the sun and the moon and other *graha*s:

Another beautious wheel have ye fixed
there to decorate your car
with others through the realms ye roam in
might unto the neighbouring tribes.

Or the *ṛk*. no. 5 of the same hymn which reads:

When Sūrya mounted on your car that
rolls forever rapidly
Birds of red hue were round about
and burning splendours compassed you.

The Aśvins have also been equated with Venus and Mercury (the morning and evening stars) who are equally capable of removing sickness. The Aśvins are said to have rid Cyavana of old age and got him lost eyes according to some *sūkta*s. The Aśvins, it is said, helped Atri, Paura, Saptavadhri and others recover from their difficulties. Their distant path is described and their ability to remove sickness could have been described.

Their astronomical details including their longitude-latitude, motion, brightness etc. were ascertained in the later Siddhāntic period and the Ṛgvedic sages were only concerned with the first interaction of their identification and description. Not only did these sages identify the stars, they conceived — as has been emphasised several times earlier — some superior force in them and saw that as the presiding deity. The characteristic difference in the approach of the modern astronomers and the Ṛgvedic sages lies in this assigning of divinity to the stars.

It may be necessary to examine the Vedic literature to refine the meaning of the ṛks of the *Nakṣatreṣṭhī* especially in the context of their actual power invested as divinity in them. In that sense, the power of the Aśvins is in their capacity to restore the invalid and the sick to their original health. It is difficult to ascertain how the sages came to be aware of the supernatural powers attributable to these twins.

Coming to post-Vedic literature, data accumulated up to the time of Varāhamihira are summarised by him in his *Bṛhatsaṁhitā*. Accordingly, Kṛttikā, Rohiṇī, Mṛgaśirā are said to govern the Central region; Ārdrā, Punarvasu, Puṣyā — the Eastern region; Āśleṣā, Maghā, Pubbā — South-Eastern region; Uttarā, Hastā, Citrā — Southern region; Swāti, Viśākhā, Anūrādhā — South-Western region; Jyeṣṭhā, Mūlā, Purvāṣāḍhā — Western region; Uttarāṣāḍha Śravaṇā, Dhaniṣṭhā — North-Western region; Śatabhiṣā, Purvābhādrā, Uttarābhādrā — Northern region; and Revatī, Aśvinī, Bharaṇī — North-Eastern region. This correlation or identification and its basis is not clear. However, the crop patterns, rains, food etc. observed during the transit of the sun in the arc of each star have been recorded for purposes of future interpretation and they are given in almost all the almanacs in India today. This part of the 'Theory of the Earth' is, however, not included here since the observations are partly of the Vedic though mostly of the post-Vedic period.

Bharaṇī

The star Bharaṇī has been propitiated by employing the following *mantras*. The deity of this star is noted to be Yama, the god of death.

> Offer to Yama holy gifts enriched with
> butter, and draw near;
> So may he grant that we may live long
> days of life among the Gods.
> Offer to Yama, to the King, oblation very
> rich in meath;
> Bow down before the Rshis of the ancient
> times, who made this path in days of
> old
>
> (*RV*, X.14.14-15)

This hymn is attributed to Yamaṛṣi; *ṛk* 14 is set to *anuṣṭubh* metre and15 to *bṛhatī* metre.

It is clear from these *ṛk*s that the *Smṛti-* and *Saṁskāra-kartās* desired to select only such hymns for the religious sacrifices. However, this aspect does not deter us from recognising the actual meaning of the star lore related to the earth in terms of its tertiary influence. For example, the 16th *ṛk* of the above hymn states:

> Into the six expanses flies the Great One
> in Trikadrukas
> The Gayatri, the Trishtub, all metres in
> Yama contained.

It is interpreted to deal with the first three days of the Abhiplava festival; perhaps this refers to an astronomic phenomenon in which the six months of the sun's southern journey (*Dakṣiṇāyana*) is referred to wherein the gnomon of *gāyatrī*, *triṣṭubh* etc. can be deciphered. Since the direction of *dakṣiṇa* is associated with Yama or death, the significance becomes apparent. But it is not very clear exactly how Bharaṇī is connected with Yama as literature on this aspect is not available. The name Bharaṇī is given to the two stars since they make up a small container.

Kṛttikā

The star Kṛttikā is propitiated by the following *ṛks*:

> Help us thou Brahman, best of all invokers
> of the gods in song.
> Beam, friend of Maruts, bliss on us, O
> Agni, a most liberal God.
> Ye grant us treasure thousand fold with children
> and with nourishment.
> And Agni, splendid hero strength, exalted,
> wasting not away.
>
> (RV, III. 13.6-7)

They are attributed to Vaiśvāmitrarṣabharṣi and set to *anuṣṭubh* metre.

The presiding deity of Kṛttikā star is divine fire. Of the 200 and odd hymns attributed to the divine fire in the *Ṛgveda*, it is not known why only these two *ṛks* have been selected to propitiate the star Kṛttikā. The star lore of the *Vedas* also commences with Kṛttikā and ends with Bharaṇī while the present-day list of stars commences from Aśvini ending with Revatī. It is possible that Kṛttikā was the first star by the time of the *Yajurveda* which deals with the performance of sacrifices.

Even to this day, the sun's transit of the arc of Kṛttikā is declared as *Agninakṣatra-doṣa* in the sense that it portends a variety of sickness due to extreme heat. The period is usually a month long — from the solar transit of Bharaṇī III *pāda* and lasting up to the solar transit of Rohiṇī II *pāda*. This period coincides with the month of May all over India and this is a period of abnormal heat. It can be seen that an arc of 6°40' before the entry of the sun to Kṛttikā star and 6°40' after leaving Kṛttikā star is governed by this period, having the star arc of Kṛttikā in the middle. What makes the Sun so hot in this region may be an interesting subject-matter for study. But by direct observation, the Vedic sages have rightly identified the transit of the sun through the arc of Kṛttikā which is the hottest period and named the presiding deity of this star as divine fire. Here, it is a clear case of the tertiary influence of stars on the earth.

Rohiṇī

The presiding deity of the Rohiṇī star, Prajāpati, is propitiated by the following *ṛk*s:

> In his own house he dwells in peace and
> comfort; to him for ever holy food
> flows richly.
> To him the people with freewill pay homage-
> the king with whom the Brahman has
> precedence.
> He, unopposed, is master of the riches of
> his own subjects and of hostile people.
> The gods uphold that King with their protection
> who helps the Brahman when he seeks
> his favour.
>
> (*ṚV*, IV 50.8-9)

These are attributed to Vāmadevaṛṣi and set to *triṣṭubh* metre.

The meaning of some of the *ṛk*s in this hymn clearly indicate worship of Indra in the form of Bṛhaspati. Also, one may note the meaning of the latter half of the *ṛk* no. 3 of this hymn (Griffiths, 1986):

> Or thee were dug wells springing from the
> mountain, which murmuring round about
> pour streams of sweetness.

The term 'Ṙohiṇī' means that which is growing or prosperous, perhaps the chief quality of Bṛhaspati (or *Brahman*?) to evolve into something living. Perhaps the star has been named Rohiṇī after observing this quality during the transit of moon in this arc of the star. It is not that in the other stars, things do not grow; but the process may be more prominent and effective in this star.

In later literature, we find information regarding the different crops which grow profusely in certain stars. According to *Nakṣatra Cūḍāmaṇi of Padmanābha* (Nanjunda Shastry, 1924) sowing in Aśvini will yield very less crop but planting coconut will be beneficial there; rains are abundant and crops prosper in Bharaṇī star, thorny shrubs grow profusely in the arc of Kṛttikā star; paddy, sugarcane etc. grow well when sown in the Rohinī star; and so on.

Mṛgaśirā

The presiding deity of Mṛgaśirā is Soma and he is propitiated by the following *ṛk*s:

> Such of thy glories as with poured oblations
> men honour, may they all invest our
> worship.
> Wealth-giver, furtherer with troops of heroes,
> sparing the brave, come, Soma to our houses.
> To him who worships Soma gives the milch cow, a
> fleet steed and a man of active knowledge
> skilled in home duties, meet for holy synod,
> for council meet, a glory to his father.
>
> (*ṚV*, I.91.19-20)

These are attributed to Gautamarṣi and set to *triṣṭubh* metre.

And *ṛk* no. 22 of the same hymn says:

> These herbs, these milch-kine, and these
> running waters, all these O Soma,
> thou hast generated.
> The spacious firmament hast thou expanded,
> and with the light thou hast
> dispelled the darkness.

The Moon probably shines the best in the arc of this star; for the presiding deity of this star is noted to be Soma or the Moon. This star is noted to be favourable to agriculture.

According to Amarasiṁha (Rice, 1970, p. 407), the star Mṛgaśirā is also called Āgrahāyaṇī. Tilak (1972, p. 342) has made it clear that 'Āgrahāyaṇikā' meant the full moon day in 'Mṛgaśirā' being the first day of the year. He further observes, "The oldest period in the Āryan Civilization may therefore be called the Aditi or the pre-Orion period, and we may roughly assign 6000-4000 BC as its limit. We next come to the Orion period which roughly speaking extended from 4000 BC to 2500 BC . . . The third of the Kṛttikā period commences with the vernal equinox in the asterism of Kṛttikās and extends up to the period recorded in the Vedānga Jyoutisha i.e. from 2500 BC to 1400 BC."

Ārdrā

The presiding deity of the star Ārdrā is Rudra, and he is propitiated by the following *ṛk*s:

> To the strong Rudra bring we these our
> songs of praise, to him the Lord of
> Heros, with the braided hair,
> That it be well with all our cattle and our
> men, that in this village all be healthy
> and well-fed.
> Be gracious unto us, O Rudra, bring to us joy;

thee, Lord of Heroes, thee with
reverence will we serve.
Whatever health and strength our father Manu
won by sacrifice may we, under thy
guidance gain.

(*Ṛ*V, I.114.1-2)

These are attributed to Kutsaṛṣi and set to *jagatī* metre.

In the same hymn, *ṛk* 6, he is referred to in "To him the Maruts' Father"; this indicates that he is the origin of the groups of winds, Maruts. 'May he, his hand filled full of sovran medicines' in *ṛk* 5 of the same hymn suggests his sickness-removing capacity. Ārdrā is said to have a single star. According to Raghavá Rao (1949), "Betelgeaux is Ārdrā . . . and the modern science fully confirms the terrible fiery nature of Rudra as the star Ārdrā". He gives a footnote of an observer's description of Beteleaux: "I saw it blazing. How many millions of Suns rolled into one. I seemed almost to hear the roar of that unbelievable furnace seething across the night, burning forever and ever". Griffiths (1986) in his footnote mentions that Rudra is generally described as 'the Roarer' owing to the sound of stormy winds, 'the God of Tempests' and 'Father of the Maruts'. That Rudra might have drawn his name from the sound of the star which roars and burns has been noted.

According to Padmanabha (Nanjunda Shastry, 1924) if halos and rainbows appear in this star rain is assured. This statement is supported in the *Bṛhatsaṁhitā of Varāhamira* (Bhat, 1991) that describes different kinds of halos and rainbows and their weather indications.

Punarvasu

The presiding deity of Punarvasu is Aditi and he is propitiated by the following *ṛks*.

Earth sprang from the productive power;

the regions from the Earth were born
Daksha was born of Aditi, and Aditi was
Daksha's child
For Aditi, O Daksha, she who is thy daughter,
was brought forth,
After her were the blessed Gods born
sharers of immortal life.

(*RV*, X.72.4-5)

These are attributed to Bṛhaspatirṣi and set to *anuṣṭubh* metre.

This hymn is devoted to many gods. In *ṛk* 1 it is mentioned that the sage will proclaim the origin of these gods. In *ṛk* 2, it is stated that Brahmaṇaspati produced the gods like a smith and the gods sprang from non-existence. Similarly, the Earth sprang from the productive power which helped generate the gods from non-existence or space!

This is a beautiful hymn in which one can see the seeds of Indian philosophy on the question of origin of the earth and the gods — the geological agents, originating from non-existence; extending the meaning of this hymn, we can state that the universe here is said to originate out of space.

As has been described earlier, the Aditi age is the earliest age of the Vedic *ṛk*s that date back to 6000-4000 BC according to B.G. Tilak. All the Vedic compositions from this age to the end of the *Vedāṅga Jyotiṣa* period, that is, 2500-1400 BC, are not available to us today. By the time of Veda-Vyāsa, i.e., about the beginning of the present *kali yuga* said to have commenced from 3102 BC, the *Veda*s had become vast and unwieldy; Veda-Vyāsa edited the *Veda*s so that they could be memorised, and easily used in the sacrifices. That the age of Aditi is *purāṇa* or *pūrvyām* is clear from the 9th *ṛk* of the above hymn which can be translated as follows:

So with her Seven sons Aditi went forth
to meet the earlier age.

Puṣyā

The presiding deity of Puṣyā is Bṛhaspati and he is propitiated by the following hymns:

> Serve we with sacrifices, gifts, and homage
> even thus the Steer of all the Gods, the
> father.
> Bṛhaspati, may we be lords of riches, with noble
> progeny and store of heroes.
> Surely, that king by power and might heroic
> hath made him lord of all his foe's possessions,
> Who cherishes Bṛhaspati well-tended, adorns and
> worships him as foremost sharer.
>
> (*ṚV*, IV.50.6-7)

These are attributed to Vāmadevaṛṣi and set to *triṣṭubh* metre.

While *ṛks* 8-9 were employed for propitiation of Prajāpati, the deity of Rohiṇī star, the above *ṛks* are for worshipping Puṣyā, the presiding deity of which is Bṛhaspati.

The planet Jupiter is said to have been born (or formed) in the arc of this star in the ecliptic. In this sense, Jupiter is also associated with the arc of the star Bharaṇī. It is difficult to find out the actual star arcs in which the planets have taken their shape since the authors have not made any reference to the texts giving the details. The Puṣyā origin of Jupiter is mentioned by Padmanābha in his *Nakṣatra Cūḍāmaṇi* (Nanjunda Sastry, 1924) while Bharaṇī origin of Jupiter is mentioned by Laxminarasimha Shastry in his booklet *Navagraha-Homam, Navagraha-Shanti Vidhānamu* (published in Machlipatnam, 1938). We do not know if other versions of the origin of planets are also there. Though this fact may belong to the Siddhāntic period, none of the well-known *Siddhānta*s have given this detail. Perhaps this data was obtained as the Vedic lore advanced into *Yajña* lore.

Āśleṣā

Serpents are the presiding deity of Āśleṣā star and they are propitiated by *Khila Adhyāya* 2, *Sūkta* 15, *ṛk*s 3-4 (Sontakke, 1983) of the *Ṛgveda*. They are attributed to some *ṛṣi* whose name is not mentioned. The metre is also not stated.

Freely translated, the *ṛk*s mean that *ajagara*, the mighty serpent full with poison, moves in the oceans (*siddhavaḥ*). Kāliya, the serpent with a thousand hoods that originated in the deep waters of Yamunā, formed the vehicle of Nārāyaṇa.

The concept of the serpent-head devouring the luminaries must have come from times earlier to the Aditi age and it has continued since then. According to Raghava Rao (1949),

> Detach Arcturus from the Bootes group. Join together the rest of the Bootes with Serpens. By joining serpens with Ophichus 5 we get the beautiful figure of Ṣesha with his folds of heads. . . . of Sheshashāyi. Of several starry serpents in the sky this is preeminently the Serpent.

Again, the Kāliya is said to form the vehicle of Nārāyaṇa. The verb *vahati* also means 'carrier' or 'holder'. In that sense, the word *nārāyaṇavāhanaḥ* means that Nārāyaṇa is contained by it i.e., Śeṣāśāyī, which suggests the familiar image of Nārāyaṇa sleeping over the coiled serpent. The coiling of the serpent with its hoods opened up may indicate a combined picture of the earth with its rotational and revolutional motion.

Rāhu is noted to govern Gemini and Ketu, Cancer. The picture of Śeṣāśāyī is formed as given above along with the *saptarṣi maṇḍala* in Leo. Governing the head portion of Mahāviṣṇu who is lying down is the thousand hooded serpent — the head portion of the serpent suggestive of Rāhu. The lower portion of the sky picture is the constellation Cancer governed by Ketu, the tail portion of the serpent.

Rāhu is said to have been originated from the Hastā star and Ketu from the Revatī star 180^0 opposite in position. It is possible to relate the motion of the serpent to that of the seismic waves of the earth during its movements. This interesting possibility can be examined in detail.

Maghā

The presiding deity of the Maghā star is Pitr̥ and he is propitiated by the following *r̥ks*:

> Thou, Agni Jātavedas, when entreated, didst
> bear the offerings which thou madest
> fragrant,
> And give them to the Fathers who did eat them
> with Svadhā. Eat, thou God, the gifts
> we bring thee.
> Thou, Jātavedas knowest well the number of
> Fathers who are here and who are absent,
> Of Fathers whom we know and whom we know not;
> accept the sacrifices well prepared
> with portions.
>
> (*R̥V*, X.15.12-13)

These are attributed to Śaṅkhar̥ṣi and are set to *triṣṭubh* metre.

This prayer is to the divine fire for its passing on of the offerings to *pitr̥ devatās*. But how exactly the star Maghā is connected with the *pitr̥ devatās* is uncertain. This star is identified with Alpha, Eta, Gamma, Zeta, Myu and Epsilon Leonis, according to Raghava Rao (1949). He has presented the picture of Mahāviṣṇu as Śeṣāśāyī involving all these stars and has described the 'eye' structure which is stated in the *R̥gveda* as *tadviṣṇoḥparamam padam. sadā paśyanti sūryāḥ*. Since this is the *paramam padam*, the supreme place, the *pitr̥ devas* are believed to have attained this place. Hence, *pitr̥ yajña* is commenced with the order of *mahāviṣṇu-mahāviṣṇorājñayā pravartamānasya.* This seat of Mahāviṣṇu is also described as *vaikuṇṭha* or an unperturbed status. Is it possible that perturbation commences the process of creation and the unperturbed condition is sought after for total settlement? Is it possible to find a place of unperturbed status or total tranquility in the region of Maghā star or Leo constellation in the celestial expanse?

Pūrvāphālguni

The presiding deity of the star Pūrvāphālgunī is Bhaga and he is propitiated by the following *ṛk*s.

> So may felicity be ours at present, and
> when the day approaches, and at noon-tide;
> And may we still, O Bounteous One, at sunset
> be happy in the deities' loving kindness.
> May Bhaga verily be bliss-bestower, and
> through him, Gods may happiness attend
> us.
> As such, O Bhaga, all with might invoke
> thee, as such be tough our Champion
> here, O Bhaga.
>
> (*ṚV*, VII.42.4-5)

These are attributed to Vasiṣṭharṣi and set to *triṣṭubh* metre.

It has already been mentioned that Aryamā is another name for the Sun. Aryamā, Bhaga and Savitṛ, all synonymous with the Sun, are the presiding deities of the stars Pubbā, Uttarā and Hastā respectively. This assumption on the part of the sages can be understood from the view of depiction of Mahāviṣṇu lying on Ādiśeṣa in the sky connecting these very star groups with others, as has already been mentioned (Raghava Rao, 1949). Aryamā, Bhaga, Savitṛ are different names of the sun who is also identified as Mahāviṣṇu.

Agricultural seeding activities take an advantageous position in this star. In *Maṇḍala* X, hymn 85, *ṛk* 13, there is the statement "*aghāsu hanyante* . . ." which is interpreted by Sāyaṇa as "*maghāsu*", meaning that cattle are beaten/driven to Somagṛha and wedding of the bride takes place in the Arjunī, i.e., Pūrvā and Uttarāphālgunī stars. Why the wedding must take place in these two stars is unclear; but the celestial wedding of Suryā with Soma-Moon and the daughter of the Sun probably took place in the arc of these stars and this may well indicate some astronomical phenomenon.

Uttarāphālgunī

The presiding deity of the star Uttarāphālgunī is Aryamā who is propitiated by the following *ṛks*:

> Thou at thy birth art Varuna, O Agni:
> when thou art kindled thou becomest
> Mitra.
> In thee, O Sun of Strength, all Gods
> are centred, Indra art thou to man who
> brings oblation.
> Aryaman art thou as regardeth maidens:
> mysterious is thy name, O self-sustainer
> As a kind of friend with streams of milk they
> blam thee what time thou markest
> wife and lord one-minded
>
> (*ṚV*, V.3.1-2)

These are attributed to Atreya Vasusṛtaṛṣi and set to *triṣṭubh* metre.

Probably, the latter half of *ṛk*. 3 of this hymn would support Viṣṇu's aspect of Aryamā. That is given as follows:

> That which was fixed as Viṣṇu's loftiest
> station-therewith the secret of the cows
> thou guardest.

It is clear from the above that Pitṛ, Bhaga and Aryamā deities presiding over Maghā, Pubbā and Uttarā stars are the different aspects of Mahāviṣṇu pictured by the stars.

The 12 names of the sun are given as Mitra, Ravi, Sūrya, Bhānu, Khaga, Pūṣā, Hiraṇyagarbha, Marīci, Āditya, Savitṛ, Arka and Bhāskara (Josyer, 1976, p. 140). These12 Suns (each in the 12 *rāśis* of the zodiac) along with all Rudras, the eight Vasus, Indra and Prajāpati make the 33 deities of the *Ṛgveda* addressed usually as *Trayastriṁśaddevatā*.

It is observed that the occurrence of rainbow or halos in the arc of the stars will increase rains. This observation, however, needs to be examined.

Hastā

The star Hastā is presided over by Savitṛ who is propitiated by the following *ṛks*.

> Bless us with shine, bless us with perfect
> daylight, bless us with cold, with
> fervent heat and luster.
> Bestow on us, O Sūrya, varied riches, to
> bless us in our home and when we travel.
> Gods, to our living creatures of both kinds
> vouchsafe protection, both to bipeds
> and quadrupeds,
> That they may drink and eat invigorating
> food. So grant us health and strength
> and perfect innocence.
>
> (*ṚV*, X.37.10-11)

These are attributed to Sūryaputro Abhitapaṛṣi; first is set to *triṣṭubh* metre and the second to *jagatī* metre.

This hymn is attributed to Sūrya and the *ṛks* have been drawn to propitiate the deity in the form of Savitā. This star is also said to favour agricultural seeding. The earlier three stars and this form the concept of *mahāviṣṇu-paramam-padam* beyond the '*Saptarṣi Maṇḍala*'. The name is given to the group of five stars making an impression of a hand.

The *Nakṣatrāṇī Sūkta* in the *Atharvaveda* occurs as the 7th in *kāṇḍa* 19 and is attributed to Gārgya. It is set to *triṣṭubh* metre. The next 8th *sukta* is also called *Nakṣatrāṇī*. In the 7th *sūkta*, it is benedictory and the *ṛṣi* requests for blessings from the stars. The next, i.e., the 8th *sūkta*, is employed along with the 7th *sūkta* in the *Nakṣatrahoma* performed with the express desire to obtain good omens at new jobs undertaken and for warding off bad consequences. Perhaps this *Nakṣatrahoma*, as it is called, is different from the *Nakṣatreṣṭhi*. While the *Nakṣatrahoma* is mentioned in the *Atharvaveda*, it is not certain when the *Nakṣatreṣṭhi* was conceived. The *Nakṣatrahoma* is mentioned by Sāyaṇa while the *Nakṣatreṣṭhi* presented by Bhatta (1991) is not found in any early literature.

Citrā

The presiding deity of Citrā star is Tvaṣṭṛ and the following *ṛks* addressed to Viśvedevas are attributed to Tvaṣṭṛ.

> May Tvastar find our hymn acceptable,
> and may Aramati, seeking wealth, be ours.
> May who lavish gifts bestow those
> treasures; may Rodasi and Varuṇāni listen.
> May he, with the Varutris, be our refuge.
> May beautiful Tvastrar give us store
> of riches.
>
> (*Ṛ*V, VII.34.21-22)

These are attributed to Vasiṣṭharṣi; the first is set to *dvipadā* and the second to *triṣṭubh* metre.

One may view *ṛk* 23 of this hymn which is rather down to earth as having some geological purport:

> So may rich mountains and the liberal waters,
> so may all herbs that grow on ground,
> and heaven,
> And Earth accordant with the Forest-Sovrans,
> and both the world-halves round about
> protect us.

This last *ṛk* has great environmental significance and most of these *ṛk*s give the same meaning indicating the interaction of the Vedic *ṛṣi*s with nature and their appreciation of the natural environment. This is more meaningful in the present-day world where unethical and uncontrolled exploitaion of the natural resources is on all over the world especially with the utmost disregard to the natural protection of life on the earth.

Star Citrā has been equated with Spica and Alpa Virgo and was in the midst of a controversy of Ayanāṁśa — precession of equinoxes — Caitrādi or Aśvinādi, in recent times. This is more probably due to the *Sūrya Siddhānta* statement " . . . should calculate the Ayanāmsa, or when the sun is six signs distant from the Nirayaṇa Meṣādi or Tulādi or at any desired time . . . " Thus, the importance of the star in calculation of the rate of precession of equinoxes is well-established in Indian astronomy.

Swāti

The presiding deity of the star Swāti is Vāyu and it is worshipped by employing the following *ṛk*s:

> Vāyu, the bright is offered thee, best of
> the meath at holy rites.
> Come thou to drink the Soma juice, God,
> longed for, on thy team-drawn car.
> O Vāyu, thou and Indra are meet
> drinkers of these Soma-draughts,

For unto you the drops proceed as water
gather to the vale.

(*Ṛ*V, IV.47.1-2)

These are attributed to Vāmadevarṣi and set to *anuṣṭubh* metre.

The arc of the Swāti star coincides with the solar movement from the last week of October to the first week of November. This was noted by the Vedic sages as a period of severe wind action. Hence, the deity of the star is Vāyu. While the first *ṛk* given above is attributed to God Vāyu, the second is attributed to Indra-Vāyu. Association of Indra with Vāyu is significant here since the severe action of the wind is probably a result of the reaction of the geomagnetic field with the solar magnetic influence charged by the Swāti star.

According to Nirayaṇa system, the sun will be at 8^0 Tulā on the 24th October 1992 which coincides with the position of 2^0 in Vṛścika according to Sāyaṇa system of calculation. This means that the sun would be about to enter Anurādhā star and Nirayaṇa Swāti transit of sun will end about the 6th of November, which is equated with the 15th of Vṛścika when the Sāyaṇa Sun would have transited Anurādhā star. At the present juncture, whether the severe gales due to depressions in the seas surrounding the Indian Peninsula during the first half of November should be equated with Swāti or Anurādhā is a matter of debate. However, the lord of Anurādhā is Mitra who has nothing to do with severe winds. Thus, the Nirayaṇa almanacs do not bear testimony with the natural facts while the Sāyaṇa almanacs correctly bring out the changes noted in nature. If the latter is to be considered, the presiding deities of the stars would not be the same.

Viśākhā

The presiding deity of the star Viśākhā is Indrāgni and the following two *ṛks* are employed to honour this star (Griffiths, 1986):

First Indra-Agni, hatch this Maid come
footless unto those feet.
Stretching her head and speaking loudly
with her tongue, she hath gone down-
ward thirty steps.
E'en now, O Indra-Agni, men hold in their
arms and stretch their bows.
Desert us not in this great fray, in battles
for the sake of kine.

(*ṛV*, VI.59.6-7)

These are attributed to the sage Bārhaspatya-Bhārdvāja; the first *ṛk*. is set to *bṛhatī* metre and the second to *anuṣṭubh* metre.

Commenting on these *ṛk*s. Griffiths (1986) observed that the 'Maid' referred to is Usas or Dawn. Footless is suggestive of moving unsupported in the sky — of course, this is true to all other stars and *graha*s also. Sāyaṇācārya interpreted 'stretching her head' as 'having abandoned the head, being herself headless'. The nomenclature itself is suggestive of *Viśiṣṭā Śākhā-Viśākhā* meaning that which has 'specially branched' hence 'headless'.

Indra-Agni have been described as brothers born of a father with their mother everywhere. This may mean that the geo-electric (magnetic) field and the geothermal field have a common origin and they are omnipresnt (owing to their mother who is everywhere). It is uncertain whether both Indra and Agni had their origin in the arc of this star, Viśākhā. Its two *śākhā*s or branches suggest that it may have given rise to Indra and Agni separately. The significance of this star is shrouded in mythology and its true picture is not understood clearly.

Anurādhā

The presiding deity of the star Anurādhā is Mitra who is celebrated by the following *ṛk*s:

> Joying in sacred food and free from sickness
> with knees bent lowly on the Earth's broad
> surface.
> Following closely the Āditya's statute, may
> we remain in Mitra's gracious favour.
> Auspicious and adorable, this Mitra was
> born with fair dominion, King. Disposer.
> May we enjoy the grace of him the Holy.
> Yea, rest in his propitious loving-kindness.
> (*Ṛ V*, III.59.3-4)

They are attributed to Viśvāmitrar̥ṣi and set to *triṣṭubh* metre.

Mitra, the presiding deity, is here noted to follow the statute of the sun — in the sense that he is probably a facet of the sun. According to Macdonell (1976),

> In the Atharvaveda, Mitra at sunrise is contrasted with Varuna in the evening, and in the Brāhmaṇas. Mitra is connected with day, Varuṇa with night.

This observation suggests that the morning or day aspect of the sun was called Mitra, meaning, a friend. Thus Mitra is noted to be the benevolent aspect of the sun in the day-time. How the star Anurādhā is connected with Mitra is uncertain but it is possible that the benevolent aspect of the sun would be more obvious during the transit of the sun through the arc of this star.

It is observed by Macdonell (1976) that this is the only hymn in which Mitra is praised alone; in many of the hymns, both Mitra and Varuṇa are together praised.

The glorification of Mitra in this hymn — Mitra supports Earth and heaven, Mitra is renowned, he is superior to heaven by his greatness, he is superior to Earth by his glories, etc. — indicate that Mitra as an attribute is that aspect of the sun by which life originates on the earth and there is, thus, always to be found a friendship between life and this aspect of the sun. It is generally said that there is no friend like the sun who is always by your side, advising you to desist from bad works and encouraging you to do good works.

Jyeṣṭhā

The divine aspect of this star is Indra and he is praised by the following hymns:

> Drink Soma, Mighty One, for which,
> when louded thou breakest through the
> cattle-stall, O Indra;
> Thou who, O Bold one, armed with
> thunder smotest Vrtra with might,
> and every hostile being.
> Drink it thou God who art impetous
> Victor, Lord of our hymns, with beauteous
> jaws, the Hero,
> Render of kin-stalls, car-borne, thunder-
> wielding, so pierce thy way to wonderous
> strength, O Indra.
>
> (*RV*, VI.17.1-2)

They are attributed to Bārhaspatya Bhāradvājarṣi and set to *triṣṭubh* metre.

There are other *ṛ̥ks* in this hymn which appear to be scientific in purpose. For example, 'Make the sun visible' in *ṛ̥k* 3 may be a request to the cloudy sky to open itself. *Ṛk* 9 reads "Yea, even that heaven itself of old bent backward before thy bolt", suggesting that the space may be bent backwards during the 'thunderbolt' occurrence. This may probably indicate the existence of a parabolic space when thunder strikes which, in turn, may offer a different explanation to the geometry of space.

Ṛk 12 is simply the surface description of gravity (a form of the geomagnetic field). It reads:

> Though settest free, the rushing wave of
> waters, the floods great swell encompassed
> and obstructed,
> Along steep slopes their course thou, turnest, Indra
> directed downward, speeding to the ocean.

It is again uncertain why these two *r̥ks* only have been selected for propitiating the deity of Jyeṣṭhā star though there are numerous others in praise of Indra, the chief god of the *Ṛgveda*.

Mūlā

The deity ruling this star is Nirr̥ti and he is praised in the following *r̥ks*:

> His life has been renewed and carried
> forward as two men, car borne, by the
> skilful driver.
> One falls then seeks the goal with quickened
> vigour. Let Nirrti depart to distant
> places.
> Here is the psalm for wealth, and food, in
> plenty; let us do many deeds to bring
> us glory.
> All these our doings shall delight the singer.
> Let Nirrti depart to distant places.
>
> (*ṚV*, X.59.1-2)

They are attributed to Gaupāyana Bandhvādaya sages and set to *triṣṭubh* metre.

Nirr̥ti is the god of death; he was believed by the sages to preside over the arc of the star, Mūlā. Hence, the ending of the *r̥ks* is keen to see Nirr̥ti depart to distant places, leaving behind long life. But the scientific aspect of this concept is brought out in *r̥k* 9:

Health-giving medicines descend sent down
from heaven in twos and threes
or wandering singly on the Earth. May
Heaven and Earth uproot and sweep
inequity and shame away; nor
sin nor sorrow trouble thee.

The 'twos' are said to be Aśvins and the 'threes' are stated to be Ilā, Sarasvatī and Bhāratī goddesses by Sāyaṇācārya. This suggests that the heaven sent medicines curing the illness and imparting long life. In this, the arc of Aśvini, Makhā and Mūlā have a trinity relationship. It is difficult to ascertain how the sages came to the conclusion that Nirṛti ruled this arc. It may be that the influence of this arc could result in drastic effects especially death. This point may be further examined for its validity.

Pūrvāṣāḍhā

The arc of Pūrvāṣāḍhā star is presided by the water deity. The following *ṛk*s are noted in this context:

Whatever sin is found in me, whatever
evil I have wrought.
If I have lied or falsely sworn, Waters
remove it far from me.
The Waters I this day have sought, and
to their moisture have we come:
O Agni, rich in milk, come thou, and
with thy splendour cover me.

(*Ṛ̣V*, I.23.22-23)

These *ṛk*s are attributed to Sidhudvīpa or Ambarīṣa and set to *anuṣṭubh* metre.

The arc of Pūrvāṣāḍhā star in the zodiac is very significant and has a triplicity with Bharaṇī and Pubbā arcs. The full moon in this arc occurs in the month of Āṣāḍha and it is a month of the rainy season. Perhaps it is due to this that the sages have attributed waters as the presiding deity of the arc.

The meaning of the *ṛks* is significant. Sin means sickness which may be due to external injury, internal weakness, etc. The waters, thus, happen to be the healing balm. This is expressed also in another *ṛk*:

> Amrita is the Waters; in the Waters
> there is healing balm;
> (*ṚV*, I.23.19)

Most of the diseases are caused by impure waters and most of the diseases are cured by pure water. The healing property of the waters was well-recognised by the sages who elevated the waters to godhood. The waters are *amṛta*, i.e., ambrosia, rightly. Without water, life cannot exist. Water is, in other words, a life-giving or a life-generating medium of the *pañcabhūtas*.

Ṛks 22 and 23 noted above have been included in the daily prayers of the Hindus. It is only to indicate the importance of pure water for life and express appreciation of the clean environment.

Uttarāṣāḍhā

The presiding deity of the arc of Uttarāṣāḍhā star is given to be Viśvedevas. But the commentary by Sāyaṇācārya makes it clear that the deity is the Sun.

The following ṛks are used for propitiation.

> Let every mortal man elect friendship
> so the guiding God.
> Each one solicit him for wealth and seeks
> renown to prosper him
> These, leading God, are thine, and these

here ready to speak after us.
As such may we attain to wealth and wait
with services on thee.

(*ṚV*, V.50.1-2)

These ṛks are attributed to Svastyātreya sage and are set to *anuṣṭubh* metre.

Uttarāṣāḍhā forms a triplicity with Uttarā and Kṛttikā. Uttarā is ruled by Aryamā and Kṛttikā by Agni, the other forms of the Sun.

It is difficult to ascertain how the sages concluded that the Viśvedevas rule this arc of Uttarāṣāḍhā; by the meaning of the ṛks as interpreted by Sāyaṇa, the deity is the Sun and rightly so, interpreted as since this arc has a triplicity with Kṛttikā and Uttarā which are also ruled by the forms of the Sun.

There are many other ṛks of significance applicable to both the gods, Viśvedevas and the Sun and it is not very clear why only these two ṛks, of minor significance, have been selected in praise of the star arc, Uttarāṣāḍhā.

The advantage of this arc has been studied by later astrologers like Vạrāhamihira to describe the Āṣāḍhiyoga and ascertain the nature and timing of the rains in a year in advance. Varāhamihira has described this *yoga* in his famous text *Bṛhatsaṁhitā* (Bhat, 1987) in the section on the annual interpretation of rains.

Śravaṇā

This star is presided by Viṣṇu who is honoured by the following ṛks:

Let the hymn lift itself as strength to
Vishṇu, the Bull far striding, dwelling on
the mountains.
Him who alone with triple step hath

measured this common dwelling-place
long far extended.
Him whose three places that are filled
with sweetness, imperishable, joy as it
may list them,
Who verily alone upholds the threefold,
the Earth, the heaven, and all living
creatures.

(*Ṛ*V, I.154.3-4)

These *ṛ*ks are attributed to Oucathyo-Dīrghatamā sage and set to *triṣṭubh* metre.

The arc of this star means 'hearing'. Normally, the *Ṛgvedins* had their annual performance of the Vedic studies reinforced on the day when the Moon attained fullness, i.e., *Śrāvaṇa śuddha pūrṇimā* under the name *Upākarma*. This is suggestive of the fact that the *Vedas* were taught through word of mouth in early days and the Vedic injunctions imparted in a year studied 'through the ear' (the *Vedas* are called *Śrutis*). Thus, this star meaning 'hearing' was specially respected.

The deity is rightly noted as the Sun, for the entire *Vedas* — *Ṛg*, *Yajus* and *Sāma* — sing the praise of the Sun — *Gāyatrī*, Look at the first two *ṛ*ks of the same hymn.

I will declare the mighty deeds of
Vishṇu, of him who measured out the
earthly regions.
Who propped the highest place of
congregation, thrice setting down his
footstep, widely striding.
For this his mighty deed is Vishṇu lauded etc.

(*Ṛ*V, I.154.1-2)

This only indicates that the Sun governs all creation.

Dhaniṣṭhā

Dhaniṣṭhā is presided over by Indra who is honoured by the following *ṛks*:

> Thou wast born mighty for victorious
> valour, exulting, strongest, full of pride
> and courage.
> There, even there, the Maruts strengthened
> Indra when his most rapid Mother
> Stirred the Hero
> There with friend's ways even Prsni was
> seated: with much laudation they
> exulted Indra.
> As if encompassed by the mighty-footed,
> from darkness, near at hand, forth came
> the children.
>
> (*ṚV*, X.73.1-2)

These are attributed to sage Gaurīvīta and set to *triṣṭubh* metre.

Dhaniṣṭhā arc has been described Indra-Mātā, i.e., mother of Indra in the Sāyaṇācārya's commentary. But how this arc is connected with Indra may be questioned. Here, Indra's valour and his receiving the support of his close friends, the Maruts, have been described. Also implied is that the waters held by Vṛtra were cleared of their darkness by Indra wielding his powerful weapon, thunderbolt. This may indicate the Dhaniṣṭhā rains, the rains which fall when the Sun transits the arc of this star.

Dhaniṣṭhā has a triplicity with Mṛgaśirā and Citrā stars. The deity of Mṛgaśirā is Soma while Citrā is presided by Viśvedevas. How this triplicity came about in later literature is not very clear.

Śatabhiṣā

Śatabhiṣā is presided over by Varuṇa who is honoured by the following hymns:

With bending sown, oblations, sacrifices,
O Varuṇa, we deprecated thine anger;
Wise Asura, thou King of wide domination,
Loosen the bonds of sins by us committed.
Loosen the bonds, O Varuṇa, that hold
me, loosen the bonds above, between,
and under.
So in thy holy law we made sinless
belong to Aditi, O thou Aditya.

(*ṚV*, I.24.14-15)

These are attributed to Ajigarta Śunaḥśepa sage and set to *triṣṭubh* metre.

Varuṇa is described as one who resides in waters and make a note of the bad and good acts of people. He is requested here to loosen the bonds of sin — diseases or sickness — and keep one hale and healthy. Śatabhiṣā arc in the constellation of Aquarius is noted to heal wounds and provide relief from sickness — as the Aśvins. This arc is noted to contain three stars with the symbol of a camel. Again, how this arc is associated with Varuṇa is not clear. Varuṇa's holy law is described as remaining strong or unweakened in another *ṛk* of the same hymn. Macdonell (1976) comments, "Varuṇa is the chief of the lords of natural order. His activity displays itself preeminently, on the control of the most regular phenomena of nature". This is evidently the law of gravitation.

This star is in a triplicity with Ārdrā and Swāti. Ārdrā is ruled by Rudra and Swāti by Vāyu. The Varuṇa, Rudra and Vāyu trinity is difficult to explain for Vāyu or Maruts have been the children of Pṛśnī or Rudra, as noted earlier. Varuṇa being the lord of waters, the relationship of waters or clouds with wind is why they have been clubbed together.

Pūrvābhādrā

The arc of the star Pūrvābhādrā is ruled by Ajaikapād. The

following *r̥ks* are dedicated to him.

> May Ajaikapād and Ahirbudhnya, and
> Earth and ocean hear our invocation;
> All gods who strengthen law, invoked and
> lauded and holy texts uttered by sages,
> help us.
> So with my thoughts and hymns of praise
> the children of Bhardwāja sing aloud to
> please you.
> The Dames invoked, and the resistless
> Vasus, and all Ye Holy ones have been
> exalted.
>
> (*ṚV*, VI.50.14-15)

These are attributed to Ṛjiśva sage and are set to *triṣṭubh* metre.

Ajaikapād is commented upon as a stormer of one foot and he is noted to be the Sun. The Sun is also a form of Rudra. Ahirbudhnya is Rudra and, as meant here, the Sun strengthens the Universal Law, i.e., of gravitation. Most of the *r̥ks* in this hymn suggest this concept. Ṛjiśva may be a Bhārdvājī.

Pūrvābhādrā is described as a group of two stars suggestive of a sword. This star forms a triplicity with Punarvasu and Viśākhā, ruled by Aditi and Indrāgni respectively. The reason why Ajaikapād is the lord of this star arc is not clear.

Though this hymn is attributed to Viśvedevas, Aditi, Indra and Agni have been praised elsewhere in the same hymn. This corroborates the triplicity of this star and the other two stated above. The planet Mercury is noted to have originated in the arc of this star. The origin of planets in the arcs of certain stars appears to have been a matter for study during the *Siddhānta* period. However, the Sanskrit texts tracing the concept from the starry lore of the Ṛgvedic literature to the *Siddhāntas* are missing.

Uttarābhādrā

The star Uttarābhādrā is ruled by Ahirbudhnya who is celebrated in the following hymns:

> Accordant with the Gods choose for our
> Friend the water's Child; may he be
> good to us.
> With lauds I sing the Dragon born of
> floods; he sits beneath the streams in
> middle air.
>
> (*Ṛ̣V*, VII.34.15-16)

These are attributed to Vasiṣṭha sage and are set to *dvipadā virāṭ* metre.

Ahirbudhnya is another name for Rudra who is also described as Mahākāla, Mahānta, etc. according to *Amarakośa*. This star has a triplicity with Puṣyā and Anurādhā stars which are ruled by Bṛhaspati and Mitra. This is also a group of two stars resembling a stick. It is noted that the Moon originated in the arc of this star.

The full moon month in this star, i.e., Bhādrapada *māsa*, is included in *Varṣā-ṛtu* as suggestive of the rainy season. It is perhaps owing to the association of wind with rain that Rudra has been identified with the arc of this star.

The moon's origin in the arc of this star is not very clear. The moon's major period of time being connected to the Rohiṇī-Hastā-Śravaṇā trinity, it is difficult to explain how the moon could originate in the arc of this star. However, modern theories of the origin of the members of the solar system do not give any idea as to the exact arc of the zodiac within which they formed at the time of their consolidation out of the nebular hot clouds or by the accumulation of the numerous meteorites. This is a very important question to ponder over, for, the later Siddhāntic texts have mentioned the arc of the zodiac in which each of the planets, the moon and the sun have been formed. This aspect may be special to Hindu astronomy.

Revatī

The ruler of this star is given to be Pūṣan who is honoured by the following hymns:

> O Pūshan,with thy golden ships that
> travel across the ocean, in the air's
> mid region,
> Thou goest on an embassy to Sūryā.
> subdued by love, desirous of the glory.
> Near kinsmen of the heaven and Earth
> is Pūshan, liberal, lord of food, of
> wonderous lustre.
> Whom strong and vigorous and swiftly-
> moving, sbdued by love, the deities
> gave to Sūryā.
>
> (*RV*, VI.58.3-4)

These are attributed to Bṛahspati Bhāradvāja sage and set to *triṣṭubh* metre.

This star is in a triplicity with Āśleṣā and Jyeṣṭhā — ruled by serpents and Indra respectively. This is described as a group of three stars in the shape of fishes. Ketu — the sensitive point of the zodiac — is said to have commenced in this arc. This gives rise to the idea that Rāhu and Ketu — not visible celestial bodies but sensitive points of the zodiac always separated by 180^0 — originated (commenced their celestial activity) in the arcs of the stars of Hastā and Revatī. It is rather difficult to check the data. These points are the sensitive nodes causing the eclipses. There is also an indication that these points have existed from the time of the formation of the solar system causing eclipses — first recognised in the Vedic literature, specially by the term Svarbhānu for Rāhu. That there are many Ketus has already been stated.

Thus the imaginary Rāhu and Ketu points of the ecliptic causing the eclipses of the luminaries have been identified as very sensitive points.

The Vedic sages used *Nakṣatra* calendar. Their *yuga* of five years commenced when the Sun and the Moon together associated with Dhaniṣṭhā star and they were named as *Saṁvatsara*, *Parivatsara*, *Idāvatsara*, *Anuvatsara* and *Idvatsara*. The *Vedāṅga Jyotiṣa* of Lagadha (Shamasastry, 1936) observes that it is the oldest text known on Hindu astronomy and it is related to the Ṛgvedic period. It is clearly mentioned in the 28th *śloka* of the booklet that they well instituted a calendar consisting of 366 days, etc. The related verse, rendered in English by Shamasastry (1936, p. 61) is given below:

> Three hundred and sixtysix days, one year, six seasons, two ayanas, twelve months are to be considered as solar; this taken five times is a cycle.

Thus the foundation of the modern calendar was laid down by the Ṛgvedic sages and presented in the form of a text by Śuci, a student of Lagadha, in *Vedāṅga Jyotiṣa*.

The development of Hindu astronomy from the Vedic times to the late Siddhāntic times cannot be traced. It has proved difficult to do so. But by the time of the late *Siddhāntas*, i.e., of the *Brahma Siddhānta* and *Sūrya Siddhānta*, much advancement in Hindu astronomy appears to have taken place. There was probably a discussion of the origin of planets, etc. and this has been taken into consideration by the later *Smṛtikāras* including Āśvalāyana and Baudhāyana. In the *Graha-yajña*, i.e., the worshipping of the planets, origin of planets and the luminaries are mentioned as given below:

The Sun	Kṛttikā star
The Moon	Uttarābhādrā star

Mars	Mṛgaśirā star
Mercury	Purvābhādrā star
Jupiter	Bharaṇī star
Venus	Jyeṣṭhā star
Saturn	Swāti star
Rāhu	Hastā star
Ketu	Revatī star

It is interesting to deliberate on this topic for the benefit of astronomers and earth science students. This aspect is further explained in Part II.

Thus the starlore of the Vedic literature is something like a testimony of the universal knowledge of the Vedic sages who had acquainted themselves with the terrestrial and planetary bodies. The material universe with its multitheistic concept later helped them to make observations on the ultimate reality underlying the universe. These sages from the Brahmāvartta — the place where they had originated and which they occupied on the earth — made varied observations and formulated a system of calendar as well to show the influence and interaction of the celestial bodies with the earth. Their understanding of the earth was almost universal.

The hymns selected by each sage or *Smṛtikāra* to propitiate the deity of a particular star varies. The hymns and *ṛk*s of *Nakṣatreṣṭhi* given by Bhatta (1991) is different from the one employed by Baudhāyana. The former group of hymns and *ṛk*s is by Āśvalāyanaṛṣi. It appears that there is scope for the development of conceptual worship of the stars based on their understanding. Only one set of the *ṛk*s given by Bhatta (1991) has been presented in this chapter. Though they lacked the modern data of astronomers relating to brightness, etc. they appear to have paved the way for the study of the starry heavens. They are the first lessons in starlore, especially along the belt of the zodiac. It may be questioned why they did not consider the stars of the hemispheres in their entirety. It is difficult to answer this question. Probably the sages confined themselves to the stars of the zodiacal belt that would have helped them ascertain the seasons by the regular and perfect motions of luminaries and the planets through them in a year. They called it *ṛta* or *satya*, i.e., the reappearance of the seasons at the right time. This helped them formulate an annual calendar for performing their sacrifices at the regular time. Thus, the starry heaven helped them to mark a suitable frame for their planetary calendar. As this was due to the regular motion of the earth, we can say that the calendar so formulated by them was actually a calendar of the earth.

The Vedic sages not only formulated the oldest-known geo-astronomical calendar but also identified the earth's proper place in the universal perspective.

PART II
APPLICATION

4

Formulation of the Theory of the Earth

A STUDY of the *Veda*s has revealed that the sages were the first students of nature. The sages were also great poets living amidst nature's bounty. They had their home in present-day Punjab, Himachal Pradesh and Jammu and Kashmir. The region of the present-day Ambālā district, which used to be drained by the rivers Sarasvatī in the north and Dṛsadvati in the south, was called 'Brahmāvartta' — the abode of *ṛṣi*s. Here, in the calm and sublime surroundings on the foothills of the Western Himālayas, they keenly observed the various geological agents and recorded their first and most effective interactions with nature in the form of poems set to several well-recognised metres. They sang the 'Geological Poetry' in the *Veda*s.

They recognised the action of the heat due to the Sun, the under-sea fire and terrestrial fire; they keenly observed the days and nights; they made acquaintance with the activities of wind, rain, rivers and oceans. They were also the earliest people to study earthquakes and the first to study time. They made a calendar for their day-to-day activities and they could determine the duration of a year by regularly measuring the luni-solar movements. The beautiful scenery surrounding their picturesque location amazed them and the regular occurrence of the seasons made them wonder. They named it *ṛta* or the truth.

They were not only acquainted with the terrestrial agents but also the various members of the solar system though to a lesser extent. Most of their observations were on the movements of the luminaries among the members of the solar system. They admired the starry heaven and recognised as many as 27-28 stars in the zodiacal belt especially for ascertaining the movements of the luminaries.

Thus they laid the foundations for a sound 'Theory of the Earth'. They invested divinity in all the objects of nature. They were extremely good souls who lived in harmony with the natural surroundings. They praised each and every geological agent and natural phenomena and sought their blessings for plenty of cattle, food and prosperity. They realised the importance of rain in the cause and maintenance of life on the earth and named the various seasons of the year by their characteristic quality. After understanding the various geological agencies and natural phenomena in terms of Indra, Varuṇa, Vāyu, Parjanya, etc. and living comfortably on the banks of the river Sarasvatī and its tributaries for hundreds and thousands of years, they must have suffered the vagaries of nature in the form of floods and storms and realised the inadequacy of their prayers. It is said that there are 33 gods in the *Ṛgveda*, viz., 12 Ādityas, 11 Rudras, 8 Vasus, Indra and Prajāpati. While instituting the *Vedas* itself, the sages must have been in search of some superior god who controlled all these. The concept of Viśvedevas came up later but again, they felt some kind of shortcoming there. In some of their hymns they have questioned as to who is the actual creator of this universe. They called him 'Hiraṇyagarbha' who was born earlier than the *Pañcabhūtas* and from whom this Hiraṇyagarbha originated. 'To whom shall we offer our *havis*' — this is the concern of prayer no. 121, *Maṇḍala* X in the *Ṛgveda*. In prayer no. 164 of *Maṇḍala* I of the *Ṛgveda*, the sages have delved deep into the problem of creation. Prayer no. 129 in *Maṇḍala* X of the *Ṛgveda* likewise contemplates on a creation. All these hymns show the earnest search of the Vedic sages to understand the reality underlying the whole of creation.

The Vedic sages were agitated in their minds as to the nature and concept of the fundamental truth underlying the Universe. This is the final object of the 'Theory of the Earth'. The Vedic 'Theory of the Earth' has paved the way to the truth behind universal creation. Though the answers to these questions and problems had not been forthcoming during the Vedic period itself, they were the object of extreme contemplation during the Vedāntic or Upaniṣadic times. With the end of the Vedic literature appeared the Vedāntic literature. Vedāntic literature was a result of deeper contemplation especially in the tranquillity of the forests. These texts were called *Āraṇyaka*s, the best amongst them being the *Bṛhadāraṇyakopaniṣad*. The questions and deep problems put up during the Vedic times found their answers in the *Āraṇyaka*s and *Upaniṣads*.

In this section some sublime points on the universe will be made and the essence of the salient *Upaniṣad*s will be brought out to reveal the fundamental truth of creation including the origin of the earth. The data collected during the Vedic times proved helpful during the period of the *Vedānta* to arrive at a clear and lasting lesson on the fundamental truth.

The 'Theory of the Earth' that emerges as a result may not help us predict the day-to-day behaviour of the earth which is the essential question of the famous *Siddhānta*s of *Jyotiṣa*. Nevertheless, it has been the foundation theory for all later developments and it has been able to reveal the reality of the universal existence in its own way. This type of concept is not known from any literature except Sanskrit literature. Hence, its importance cannot be overexaggerated; there is no modern 'Theory of the Earth' which can compare with this today when the earth sciences have seen spectacular advancement. That this theory may be used to test the philosophy underlying it is the challenge to the modern scientist.

The Concept of the Divine Earth

The earliest concepts of the earth in the *Ṛgveda* are associated with the hymns of *Dyāva-Pṛthvī*, i.e., the earth and the heaven. They have been called the parents of all creatures who, it is observed, do not grow old. They are also noted to be vast. They are supposed to be strengtheners of law, i.e., *ṛta* — the seasons so regulated. Between them, the sun is noted to travel by a fixed decree. Which of these two is elder is undecided. They are unsupported.

By the time of the *Yajurveda*, the ṛṣis understood that the earth was made of fine organic materials like rocks, soil, mountains, hills, sands, oceans, vegetation, gold, silver, iron, lead, tin, copper and steel.

In the *Atharvaveda*, the time of the moon and the sun as measured in the Ṛgvedic period were re-emphasised. Accordingly, they counted 12 moons in a year and 37 moons in three years. They realised that the earth contained oceans and rivers (the Earth was served day and night by the rivers). They noted that the earth was representative of the universe (*Viśvambharā*). They described her as containing the 8 Vasus (*Vasudhā*) namely, Agni, Pṛthvī, Vāyu, Antarikṣa, Āditya, Dyau, Candramā and Nakṣatras. It means that all these facets of nature go to form the earth. The earth is also noted to have magical movements. The earth is described as enveloped by the sky or space and being ambrosia-like. The earth is wide and supporting forests, hills and mountains. She is described to be white, dark, tawny and of variegated colours. The earth is at places raised and at other places lowered. She gave birth to both people and animals. The divine fire is noted to be in the earth, in herbs, waters and rocks and in all life. The earth is said to have a smell which is reflected in the herbs. The earth is made of rocks and dust and enjoys the various seasons. It is the abode of wealth.

The above-mentioned facts are drawn from some six hymns

of the *Ṛgveda*. Some references from the *Yajurveda* and a hymn from the *Atharvaveda* reveal to us the profound understanding that the Vedic bards had about the earth in such a remote period of human history. They can really be considered as the oldest students of geology. Though these facts are the first and the oldest, they do not appear to be raw but display maturity. Their concept of the earth was of a divine nature (they elevated the Earth to divine-hood) as they saw the earth as the giver of food, shelter and prosperity. They described the goddess Earth as Bhūdevī in the iconographic sense as well.

The Vedic bards with their geo-poetry were at home with the elements of the Earth, her movements (without any support), her benevolent nature in supplying food and shelter, and her incessant serving by way of her rivers and her wealth. These observations were the forerunners of later sciences like *Jyotiṣa*, *Āyurveda*, Mining and Metallurgy, Agriculture, etc.

Though the action of the geological agents like heat, wind, water in the form of rivers, oceans, etc. described in the *Veda*s indicate the first lessons in terms of modern physical geology, it is not on the lines of Western thinking. There appears to be a peculiar mix and a total or overall picture of the earth subjected to various natural geological and geophysical agencies is presented. For example, the influence of heat on the earth (the geothermal aspect) is part of the *Agni Sūktas*; the influence of water on the earth (the hydrosphere related activity) is part of the *Varuṇa Sūktas*, *Nadī Sūktas*, *Parjanya Sūktas*, *Samudra Sūktas*, etc.; the action of wind in the atmosphere is part of the *Vāyu Sūktas*; and the role of water in the hydrological cycle causing rain is the essence of the *Indra Sūktas*. In the absence of systematic discussions and in-depth studies, these *Sūkta*s remained as hymns for purposes of recitation only. Analytical logic was little applied to these fields while it was applied in full force to the resolution of the fundamental cause of the universe in the form of *Darśana Śāstras*.

Most of the *Ṛgveda* and parts of the other *Vedas* deal with the various geological and geophysical activities and are centred around the earth. Thus, all the data collected from these sources can easily help us formulate a 'Theory of the Earth'.

Though mining had been practised in the Western countries from about the beginning of the Christian Era or little earlier, the concepts of the modern science of the earth, geology, were crystallised only towards the first half of the nineteenth century when the book *Principles of Geology* was brought out by Charles Lyell (in 1830). Through the centuries the various concepts of modern earth science have been developing. The branch of science called 'Geology' came into being only a couple of centuries ago. Many theories of the Earth have been brought out by Western scientists in this long period (Murthy, 1987). Though much data existed in the Orient, they did not crystallise into a 'theory' — in the Western sense of the term — mostly due to the fact that they were camouflaged under the term *Jyotiṣa*. But now that the various theories of the earth have been brought out (Murthy, 1992), they may be compared with the theories promulgated in the western countries.

Now that the 'Vedic Theory of the Earth' has been pointed out to be the basis on which most of the oriental theories were substantiated in later periods, it is extremely essential to establish the 'Vedic Theory of the Earth' for its intrinsic value. Having brought out the facts from the *Vedas*, we will now show the influence of various geological and geophysical agencies on the earth as evident in the Vedic texts.

Earth's Electric Fieldas noted in the Indra Sūktas

There are many references to *Vidyut* in the *Ṛgveda* and these are mainly connected with the hymns of Indra. Indra is noted to have the thunderbolt or *Vajrāyudha* as his weapon. The close association of thunder and lightning with the rainy clouds is well-known. With his weapon, Indra is said to cause rains to pour from the clouds and thus fill all the rivers with water. This is the first attribute of Indra in many hymns. The second attribute of Indra has to do with the fixation of the trembling earth firmly (terra firma) and shaking the movable and immovable material world, causing earthquakes. These aspects have received much attention from the Vedic sages and Indra's powers have been described in ample terms.

The causing of rains from clouds is a natural phenomenon in the hydrological cycle. Thunder associated with the rainy clouds is the loud noise following the flash of lightning due to discharge of electricity through the air. The electricity in the clouds may be due to the geomagnetic-electric field of the earth generated by the motion of its liquid core of iron and other components. This natural phenomenon was addressed as Indra and thus, Indra may fundamentally mean the geo-magnetic-electric field especially since Indra is described to be omnipresent.

Coming to the second attribute of Indra, it may be recalled that the earth displays several kinds of motions on its orbit. Its regulation, again, is due to the motion in the core which generates the geo-electric (magnetic) field. The shaking of the earth, meaning causing of the earthquakes, is a complex phenomena.

The concept of *Bhū-Vidyunmaṇḍala*—geo-electric-magnetic field — is the meaning of the deity Indra with his attributes and omnipresence. Since the Vedic statements are rather 'suggestive', their actual meaning has to be inferred by conceptual prognostication.

The Geothermal Field as noted in the Agni Sūktas

Agni is said to shine like the sun with a lustre resembling that of the dawn and the lightning of the rain clouds. Hence, he is noted to be the brother of Indra. Here it may be stated that conversion of geothermal energy into geo-electrical energy is intended. Agni is noted to reside in waters as 'Fire under the Sea'. The sun being described as a form of Agni who was brought to earth from the heavens by Mātariśvan, the triplicity of Agni may be observed here. Agni resides in the rocks — the primary rocks are called 'igneous' ('igni' is derivative of Agni), in vegetation, in life and all objects. This proves his omnipresence. Hence, Agni means the Geothermal Field.

Agni is prominently the carrier of *havis* to all other deities. This means that all other natural geological agencies can be approached through the medium of fire. The importance of temperature in controlling the climate, the effective action of the hydrological cycle, the formation of rocks, and the growth of forests, vegetation and all life on earth has been appreciated by the sages. The interaction of the geothermal field with all other field forces including the atmosphere, hydrosphere, lithosphere and with the fields of luminaries is evident. All these fields exist within the earth and they mutually influence one another and individually interact with the earth. In this way, the hymns concerning the aspects of Indrāgni, Agni-Vāyu, Agni-Marut, etc. are relevant. The great sages, for want of technical terms, infused divinity into the field forces and named them as gods.

The attributes of Agni — his omniscience, his being the forehead of the sky and centre of the earth, his close touch making solid things shake, his traversing of the earth — all go to show the activity of the geothermal field. As the medium of *havis* to all gods, Agni, or this agent of the geothermal field, has direct contact with all other field forces. Though other geological agents like the geo-electric, hydro and atmosphere are also omnipresent, Agni is special in that he alone carries the *havis* to all.

The Hydrosphere as described in the Ap Sūktas

A vivid description of the torrential rains attended by roaring thunder and the forming of numerous streams levelling the undulations of the ground is found in the *Parjanya Sūktas*. The rain waters treated by the Sun are described as ambrosia capable of healing all injuries.

Many of the rivers draining the land of Brahmāvartta have been described in the *Nadī Sūktas*. The Sarasvatī which is the most important river of the Vedic Civilization has been elevated to godhood and its most important utility, that of production of food, has been well-described.

The cleansing and active nature of the sea waters has been described in *Samudra Sūktas*. The incessant action of the rivers draining the ground and marching to music as they flow towards their receptical seas is described. *Nadī* means one which produces sound (*nadati*).

The most benevolent aspect of the waters, especially their role in the upkẹep of the environment, was recognised by the Vedic sages. The rivers were seen as a healer of all diseases and sicknesses. Their flooding nature, roaring movement, thundering sound, confluences, and the effect of erosion of the river banks and mountains were understood and these are some of the first and finest lessons in modern physical geology.

Varuṇa is said to reside in the waters and make them flow; his law as well is followed by all gods. This suggests that the gravity flow of the waters in the form of streams and rivers now called the force of gravitation was known to the Vedic sages. Though some of the concepts overlap, their rudimentary aspects can be gleaned. They observed that all the rivers flow into the oceans which maintain a level due to the action of Varuna. It was a wonder to them that in spite of the flow of waters through the rivers of the world into the seas, the seas did not fill up!

Varuna's power of controlling the waters' flow and ordering the motion of the sun, moon and the stars suggests that it is nothing but the force of gravitation known to modern science.

The Atmosphere as noted in the Vāyu Sūktas

Here, both the *Vāyu* and *Marut Sūktas* are taken into consideration. Vāyu and the Maruts are described to be great and mighty; they make a thundering noise and cause mountains to quake. The destruction of forests by gales has been described. Their ability to generate thunder and storms relates them to Indra (geo-electric field) and they are known to be allies of Indra.

The transportation of rainy clouds, the movement of sand and rocks due to heavy gales, storms, cyclones, hurricanes, tornadoes etc. have been recognised by the Vedic bards and recorded. In association with the waters, the winds act swiftly to clean the ground and weather out the rocky surfaces of the mountains.

Thus, the geological activities of the major geological agents have been identified by the Vedic bards in their geo-poetry of the *Ṛgveda*. There may be some exaggerations and shortcomings in the compositions of hymns. The exaggerations, however, may be seen as characteristic of poetry: bereft of such things, the matter would boil down to hard facts many of which are corroborated even today by students of physical geology. These early observations may not compete with those derived from modern study since they are more than five to six thousand years old. But they, very early, realised the global aspects of the geological agents. That, in itself, is something superb. The *Veda*s are thus not only religious spells, as they have been known from the time of their composition, but also the foundation-stones for material philosophy.

The activities of sub-surface geological agents as dealt with in the *Veda*s bring out the geomorphological changes that attend upon them and the changing scenery of the earth (evident in the Vedic observations on seasons). While giving importance to the earth shells of lithosphere, hydrosphere and atmosphere along with the geothermal field and geo-electro (magnetic) fields, the Vedic sages also made a thorough study of time by manipulating the motions of the luminaries against the starry background of the zodiacal belt.

The Luni-Solar Calendar of the Earth

A most important achievement of the Vedic period is the evolution of a calendar to measure time for purposes of performing sacrifices. The luni-solar movement was clearly observed by the Vedic bards and they instituted a *yuga* of five years. The duration of a year was divided by them into two halves based on the northern and southern movements of the sun. The year when both the sun and the moon were in the Dhaniṣṭhā star commenced their *Uttarāyaṇa* and the Āśleṣā star commenced the *Dakṣiṇāyaṇa*. Each *ayaṇa* was further divided into three two-monthly periods called *ṛtus* and they, in all, made 12 months in a year. The months were named as Madhu, Mādhava, Śukra, Śuci, Nabh, Nabhasya, Īśa, Ūrja, Saha, Sahasya, Tapa and Tapasya. A nomenclature was instituted for the days, the half-days, etc. as has been described earlier. All these things were the consequence of the motions of the earth on its orbit round the sun.

The eclipses of the luminaries had a special appeal for the Vedic bards. Many hymns were sung to get the luminaries out of the ecliptic non-existence (*graha-ṇa*) during the eclipses. This aspect has been brought by Shamashastry (1936, p. 61 and 1938, p. 22, xii).

Each planet and luminary was recognised as something divine; and so also was each group of the stars numbering some 27-28 in the zodiac. They were worshipped by employing the Vedic *mantras* or spells as has been explained earlier.

The evolution of the calendar, with some modifications that are followed to this day, is a testimony of the accurate time measurements of the Vedic sages. Though this calendar has undergone a sea change since its inception, its main features and the foundations laid in it have been intact to this day. Most of the festivities, Vedic performances, auspicious celebrations, etc. are done on the basis of such a calendar even to this day in India. In one sense, it is the life and breath of India as it is the country's most prestigious heritage.

It was possible for the Vedic sages to institute such a calendar owing to their close observation of the earth's motions. The Vedic calendar was, however, refined later in the Siddhāntic period. The date of creation in the *Sūrya Siddhānta* can vie with that indicated by any modern geological calendar. The importance of the earth in instituting such a calendar cannot be over-exaggerated.

Formulation of the Theory of the Earth

In order to conceive the 'Vedic Theory of the Earth', the Vedic bards had to study the terrestrial and celestial changes in all their details. The details of their studies have been given in the previous pages. But even after completing their observations on the various natural agencies and phenomena and investing divinity into them, they found that something was lacking in their full knowledge. They performed sacrifices to many deities but felt that some singular force was behind all such superficial forces. They gradually began analysing the existence of a universal authority. They then contemplated and made an in-depth study which constitutes the subject-matter of the *Vedānta*.

Of the many texts of the Vedāntic schools in Sanskrit, i.e., the *Āraṇyakas*, the *Brāhmaṇas* and Upaniṣadic texts, the *Taittirīya Upaniṣad*—a part of the *Kr̥ṣṇa Yajus*—would prove extremely useful for an earth science student. In this *Upaniṣad*, the evolution of the earth has been described in a beautiful manner. The relevant section is that of *Bhr̥guvallī*, (Bhr̥gu being the son of Varuṇa). This *vidyā* goes under the name of *Vāruṇī Vidyā*. Bhr̥gu asks his father to teach him the *Brahman*. His father advises him to meditate on the *Brahman*. After a deep and steady contemplation, Bhṛgu tells his father that *anna* (food) is *Brahman.* In the *Ṛgveda* the cooked rice put to *havis* is called *Brahman* (*haviranna brahma*). But his father asks him to continue his deep studies and ultimately Bhṛgu realises that *prāṇa, manas, vijñāna* and finally *ānanda* are *Brahman.* Thus, the term *Brahman* denotes many meanings including 'That fundamental field out of which all the creation is evolved and dissolved' which is responsible for visible and invisible manifestation. At one instance, the student even asserts that Vāyu is *Brahman* (*namaste vāyo-tvameva pratyakṣam brahmāsi*).

The section called *Ānandavallī* brings out the various stages of evolution of the universe. While Brahmā is declared as *ānanda* in *Vāruṇī-Vidyā,* this section traces the evolution of the universe up to the level of *anna* (food). Accordingly, those who know *Brahman* say that the *Brahman* is Truth-Knowledge-Endless (*satyam-jñānam-anantam brahma*). This may also mean that boundless knowledge of truth is the *Brahman. Brahman* is noted to reside in the 'heart' of the being. From the *ātman* (reflection of the *Brahman*) evolves *ākāśa* or space; from *ākāśa,* Vāyu (wind); from Vāyu, Agni (fire); from Agni, Āpas (water); and from Āpas, Pṛthvī (earth). From the earth is derived herbs and food.

This aspect of the *Upaniṣad* deserves much commentary. First of all, by the time of this *Upaniṣad,* the Vedic bards had gave up all the deities that they had instituted and worshipped in early times. Then they questioned about the one in control of the entire manifest universe. They observed that Vāyu is the *Brahman* and began tracing the evolution of space, air, fire, water and the earth from the *Brahman.* The Upaniṣadic renaissance of the Vedic school is something spectacular: it was an advancement on the earlier understanding and saw the evolution of a monotheistic philosophy from a multitheistic philosophy. All these have come out of a deep study of the earth and its evolution in the manifest universe. The Upaniṣadic texts are rather crisp and do not unfold the evolution of ideas from the Vedic multitheistic stage to the highly-advanced monotheistic stage. It appears that many texts which could have described this evolution of ideas have been lost, leaving us with little, though extremely significant information.

This 'Theory of Evolution' of the earth has not been challenged by any later authority in the entire Sanskrit literature. Rather, they have advocated it as the basis or foundation of their respective theories (Murthy, 1992). That the earth is the final product of space around us is very hard to imagine; and so is its dissolution into space at the end of the present cycle of evolution. Though this theory does not explain stage-by-stage the evolution of the earth and the universal bodies, its major observations have been traced for further study.

The salient features of this 'Theory of the Earth' are enumerated below:

1. The Earth is a representative of the Universe. This concept at once invalidates the understanding that the Earth is independent and can be examined in isolation as per the Theory of Hutton (Murthy, 1987).
2. The mountains, oceans, rivers, plains, deserts and habitable lands are the elements of the earth.
3. The electro-magnetic field of the earth, addressed as the omnipresent 'Indra', causes thunder and lightning and rains which sustain vegetation and life on the earth; it also causes earthquakes.
4. The atmosphere field of the earth called omnipresent 'Vāyu' is responsible for large-scale movements of rain clouds and dust storms, and it also causes earthquakes.
5. The hydrosphere of the earth called the omnipresent 'Āpas' is responsible for the hydrological cycle, flooding

of rivers which join the oceans and maintaining their level.

6. The field of gravitation addressed as 'Varuṇa' is noted to control all the above forces as well as keep the luminaries and stars in their path of motion.

7. The geothermal field addressed as divine 'Agni' is found in the sun, waters, rocks, vegetation and life on the earth.

8. The various fields of Indra, Vāyu, Varuṇa and Agni interact with one another and cause rainfall resulting in floods, vegetation and life on earth as well as earthquakes.

9. The magical movements of the earth with reference to the motions of the luminaries and stars provide a calendar to measure the time on earth.

10. The earth is the home of life. It evolved out of space through air, fire and water according to the orders of the *Brahman*, the fundamental truth underlying universal manifestation and dissolution.

The modern concepts of the evolution of the universe corroborate the above-mentioned features in general. The modern astronomers also believe that the manifest universe is from space. The concept of space in Hindu philosophy has already been presented. A thorough discussion of the ancient Indian concepts of space by applying Indian logic to them will be rewarding.

The time-distance equations were well-established in the Siddhāntic period. Work on decoding the ancient Indian astronomical code given in the *Ṛgveda* is on. A study has revealed that the Vedic Indians determined the earth-sun and the earth-moon distances. An analysis of the code has revealed that the sun was 108 sun-diameters away from the earth and the moon was 108 moon-diameters away from the earth. The modern values are 107.6 for the sun and 110.6 for the moon. (*The Deccan*

Herald, Bangalore, dated 31.3.1993). The Ṛgvedic code has also suggested that the solar year is of 364.24675 days.

It may be added to this that the diameter of the sun is 108 times that of the earth (Murthy, 1987). The diameter of the earth being of the order of 8000 miles, that of the sun is 8000 x 108 = 8,64,000 miles. This multiplied by 108 will be the distance between the sun and the earth = 93,312,000 miles (the actual distance being 92.9 million miles).

According to the *Sūrya Siddhānta* which is being followed to this day to prepare the annual Indian almanac on the Vedic basis, the time equations are as follows:

The duration of one day of Brahmā = 4320 million years
The duration of one night of Brahmā = 4320 million years
The total for a complete day = 8640 million years.

This is the diameter of the sun multiplied by 10000 called the *Brahma-dina* (full day and night). Half the distance between the earth and the sun = 864,000/2 = 432000 solar years constitutes a tenth of a *mahāyuga*. One *mahāyuga* is 4.32 million years; this number multiplied by 1000 yields 4320 million solar years — a Brahmā day. Equal time duration is called *Brahma-rātri*; hence the full day and night of Brahmā will be 8640 million solar years.

Thus, the time-distance relationship established in the *Siddhāntas* has been decoded recently especially from the *Ṛgveda*.

In this connection, it may be interesting to recall Bode's Law of planetary distances from the sun. By doubling the numbers as we go on and adding four to each we get the following:

0	3	6	12	24	48	96	192	384
4	4	4	4	4	4	4	4	4
4	7	10	16	28	52	100	196	388

Dividing these numbers by 10, we have

0.4 0.7 1.0 1.6 2.8 5.2 10.0 19.6 38.8

These numbers indicate the mean distance of the planets from the sun expressed in astronomical units. The astronomical unit is the distance of the earth from the sun. The actual astronomical units are; 0.39, 0.72, 1.00, 1.52, 2.77, 5.2, 9.54, 19.18, 30.06. The planets indicated here are Mercury, Venus, the Earth, Mars, Ceres, Jupiter, Saturn, Uranus and Neptune respectively, an exception being Pluto. The ratio of distance appears to be in multiples of three for inferior planets and in multiples of three and four for the superior planets (Baker, 1965, p. 557). This may bear some resemblance to the Vedic code.

The number 108 is noted to be significant as in the table of 9, the total of digits amounts to 9 only. In the calculations of the *ayanāṁśa*, i.e., the precession of equinoxes, the *Sūrya Siddhānta* theory states that it is oscillatory within the arc of 27^0 from nil-*ayanāṁṣa* position on the zodiac. Its forward motion to 27^0 and backward motion to 54^0 and, again, forward motion to 27^0 would constitute 108^0 accounting for 7200 solar years per oscillation. 600 such oscillations will be there in a *mahāyuga* accounting for 4.32 million years.

Similarly, the Vedic sages have identified 27 stars each with 4 quarters accounting for 108 quarters. The actual significance of the number 108 is difficult to unravel with all its details. But suffice it to say that it was evolved and known to the Vedic people.

A critical evaluation of the material presented here in suggests that the Vedic bards were thorough students of nature and understood many of the intricate things by sustained study. They appreciated the hydrological cycle in all its vividity and acquainted themselves with the geo-electric (magnetic) field, geothermal field, hydrosphere, atmosphere and space and various phenomena of nature. But they had their own system of describing the natural things in personification and did not use the terms we employ today. They invested divinity in them and searched for the most fundamental truth in their philosophical pursuit. Their multitheistic philosophy, to start with, identified monotheism to be the end of their pursuit. They established the concept of the *Brahman* in the end. They evolved the earth from space and related the earth to the entire universe. Though the *Veda*s 'appear' to be of religious significance alone, an in-depth study of these texts will lay open data relating to various fields, the most important being earth sciences.

A major portion of the Vedic literature comprises the early geological studies carried out by Vedic students in search of truth. This aspect has usually got camouflaged in the religious versions of the Vedic exposition. The statement by Vālmīki in his *Rāmāyaṇa* that without the application of the *Veda*s the science subjects do not shine, is true. But why then did the science of the earth not flower and develop here as it did in the Western circles? The only answer to this question is, the orthodox school of the *Veda*s did not make this aspect available for detailed logical discussions like they did for proving the core of Indian philosophy.

As has already been made clear, the great extent of the *Veda*s (*anantā vai vedāḥ*) that prevailed in the pre-Vyāsa period was rendered into the present 10 *maṇḍala*s of the *Ṛgveda*. The edition of Vyāsa has stood the test of time but many details wanted by the students of the earth are missing in this version. The present-day *Veda*s require a thorough reading of the hymns pertaining to various fields. Then, a detailed and logical discussion on the specific literature needs to be carried out to come to scientific conclusions. Such a discussion may also lead to decoding of a lot of interesting information contained in the *Veda*s.

One may feel that one is not really aware of the true meanings of the Vedic hymns but their meanings are not very distant from the truth of careful analysis. Most of the commentaries on the *Vedas* which are available to us from the Yāskan times deal with religious ideas and there is hardly any commentary on them worthy of examination by modern scientists. Since the Vedic statements are only generally suggestive in nature, it may be necessary for students of various branches of science to take interest in the *Vedas* and interpret them from their own points of view.

5

The 'Vedic Theory of the Earth' in Practice

A REVIEW of the Vedic Theory of the Earth presented in Part I of this book would reveal that the Vedic and post-Vedic treatment of the earth and its surroundings is rather partial to what can be called 'Geocosmology' than to any other field of scientific study. The Vedic sages discovered the early foundations of mathematics in order to study the earth and the universe and the mathematical foundation was laid in order to properly base their astronomical studies. Unlike modern geological studies which are based essentially on studies of earth substances, the Vedic bards dealt with the origin, age, shape, movements, etc. of the earth from an astronomical point of view. Since there is a close affinity between astronomy and geology especially with regard to ages in terms of millions of years, which has been realised only recently in geology, the astronomical deductions of the Vedic and post-Vedic earth literature have a close resemblance. This will be brought out in specific sections dealing with them. Here, let it suffice to state that in the earliest part of the development of human civilisation, the Vedic scientists did advanced studies purely from a mathematical angle but with a good deal of first-hand observation. This would be sufficient to keep the Vedic heritage unrivalled at all times to come.

Why the Vedic sages resorted to astronomy and not geology is a question which cannot be answered. Instead of looking at the earth, they looked at the heavens to understand the earth. This can be noticed even in the early European ideas about earth till the time of Hutton who with his statements like "Present is the key to the past" and "No traces of a beginning and no prospect of an end" directed the students of the earth to look into the earth rather than outside for geological deductions. He said that "no powers are to be employed that are not natural to the globe" in the study of the earth. Then the disciplines of geology, like petrology, palaeontology, stratigraphy, structural geology and others, followed. But these studies and even the geochronological studies could not make much alterations in the deduction of the Vedic students; they rather supplemented them. Even the laws of uniformitarianism which resulted in the concept of the present being the key to the past has been in vogue in the East as in the Hindu philosophy. According to the Indian school of logic, "by means of repeated observations of this kind we have established the principle of the Uniformity of Nature and also of Causality" (Seal, 1991, p. 313). Nature includes geology, botany, zoology and other similar fields which have been compartmentalised in later history. The principle of uniformitarianism in geological sciences is true of botanical and zoological sciences as well as other fields. The Indian logical truth sweeps at once all the disciplines of nature. The principle of uniformitarianism found in nature year after year, season after season, was identified by the Vedic bards as *ṛta* or *satya* (truth). This was the foundation stone of their school of logic.

The discovery of numbers and the origin of early mathematics in the *Vedas* has been discussed by Satya Prakash (1990, p. 601). From the geocosmological ideas presented in the *Vedas* and post-Vedic literature on the earth, it becomes clear that the ancient Indian scientists viewed the earth with a broad vision in respect of the universe. This perhaps is the result of their open attempts to know the nature of the earth. The Western school which developed during the age of scientific cosmogony (Murthy, 1987, p. 127) long after the Vedic school did not present the kind of concepts extended by the ancient Indian geo-astronomers. Having been partial to the earth, the modern students of geology suffer from a kind of isolation. This is true of the Vedic students also even though they have been exposed to a broader vision. An integrated study from both the schools is the need of the hour.

Though much of the material about the earth being presented in this volume is post-Vedic, its real foundations are in the *Vedas*. The Vedic foundations of the post-Vedic literature are strong but no scientific text of the post-Vedic times can boast that it is independent of Vedic thoughts and ideas. All these texts look to the *Vedas* with great veneration so much so that the *Vedas* have been held in very high respect from the beginning to this day Also, unless one delves deep into the Vedic lore, one will not be able to justify the later study. Moreover, it is a matter of great pleasure to trace the developments as they occurred over the ages

It is intended to cover the later developments on the earth sciences briefly in this part of the book especially from the point of view of the early observations. That is, the practice of such a theory of the earth is now going to be discussed in various chapters. The development of the Hindu almanacs being followed to this day is the most important from the point of view of geology and astronomy, so much so it can be easily termed a 'Geo-astronomical Calendar'. The many almanacs in India at present take the data from modern observatories and prepare the Annual Calendar (*Pañcāṅgas*). This is due to the advancement in modern astronomy. While modern astronomy has been integrated with the ancient Indian in these almanacs, this is not true for the other fields. For example, the meteorological, geological, seismological forecasts have not seen such integration in these almanacs though some kind of vague observations have been attempted. As such, these almanacs need to be appraised for the benefit of humanity. In this connection, a method of forecasting the timing of earthquakes will be presented which may require scrutiny and improvement since no such method has been given by either the modern or the ancient scientists of India. This has been possible by my efforts over the past three decades to study this problem.

Though the implications of the 'Theory of the Earth' from the Vedic point of view is very wide including sociological, political, industrial, medical, environmental and other aspects, here I confine myself to the geological field only. This may enable the modern students of the earth to appreciate the Indian views from the Vedic times. The modern Indian almanacs, numbering more than 50 and catering to various parts of India, attempt to bring out events in the above fields as well as agriculture, famine, metal production, marketing, etc. In a wide sense, all these facts are part and parcel of 'A Grand Theory of the Earth'.

The modern trends predicted in these fields have got a restricted duration of time while those given in the Indian almanacs have a longer duration as their basis and are, perhaps, more dependable. Their examination by competent scientists would lead to their practise in an effective manner.

It is difficult to emphasise the implications of the 'Vedic Theory of the Earth'. In order to understand the movements of the earth through its heavenly path, the sages discovered the numerals essential for advancement in mathematics, discovered the computer perfect language — Sanskrit — to communicate the Vedic material, prepared the calendar by measuring the time in terms of millions of years, prepared the almanacs for day-to-day transactions and helped predict many things. Thus the entire Vedic and post-Vedic field of observations can be seen as constituting a grand stage of earth science development in India. This is unique to this nation on the earth.

The immediate need of the hour is to expand the observational base of this theory as the interpretations in the present form cover only the present Indian territory so that the theory is applicable to the whole world and is more useful for humanity. A theory of the earth without all such predictions is rather futile notwithstanding the tremendous amount of funds which are expended on researches in earth science observations being carried out all over the globe.

The utilitarian aspects of such an Integrated Theory of the Earth are tremendous and invaluable in scope. The sound predictions of such a theory can be the basis of developmental planning of a nation or the world at large. It will indicate the right direction the planners of a nation must adopt to ensure a balanced environment. That will be the key for happy human development and sustenance. A theory better than such an 'Integrated Theory of the Earth' cannot be there as this theory abounds in its implications.

The Formation of Luminaries, Planets and Nodes

A discourse on the earth in geology inevitably commences with the origin of the earth and its development in the solar system. Many hypotheses exist to describe the origin of the earth and various members of the solar system. The earliest was that of Immanuel Kant (1755) followed by that of Laplace, called the Nebular Hypothesis; they were followed by the hypothesis of T.C. Chamberlin and F.R. Moulton in 1900. Then came the concepts of C.F. Von Weizsacker in 1945 and of G.P. Kuiper in 1949 (Baker, 1964, p. 557).

Though considerable information can be found in the *Veda*s with regard to the node Rāhu under the title Svarbhānu, Rāhu's origin has hardly been mentioned. Similarly, considerable literature exists about the sun and the moon but there is nothing about their origin. The same is true of the planets and the earth. But the Vedāntic school has described their origin from space through wind, fire and water. But again, details of their formation are wanting.

The Siddhāntic school advanced very much on the Vedic and Vedāntic schools. Though five *Siddhāntas* — astronomical treatises — have been enumerated by Varāhamihira (AD 505) from possibly the time of the *Vedāṅga Jyotiṣa* of Lagadha, the detailed texts of these five *Siddhāntas* are not available to us now. Their summary presented by Varāhamihira in his *Pañca-Siddhāntikā* excludes many details. The *Graha-yajña* school of Hindu *Saṁskāras* appears to have been formulated by *Saṁskāra-karas* like Āśvalāyana and Baudhāyana in Siddhāntic or post-Siddhāntic times. It includes in its deliberations a section of information on the formation (origin) of the celestial bodies. It is difficult, however, to account for its authenticity in the absence of more detailed information. But it may also be borne in mind that such details are not available even in the best hypotheses available in modern times.

According to Shastry (1938, p. 105) the formation of the luminaries, planets and the nodes has been presented possibly based on some Siddhāntic school which is not mentioned. Some details on the formation of these luminaries, planets, etc. are given below:

Luminaries, etc.	*Star*	*Arc of the Zodiac*
The Sun	Kṛttikā	$26^0 40'$ - $40^0 00'$
Moon	Uttarābhādrā	$333^0 20'$ - $346^0 40'$
Mars	Mṛgaśirā	$53^0 20'$ - $66^0 40'$
Mercury	Pūrvābhādrā	$320^0 00'$ - $333^0 20'$
Jupiter	Bharaṇī	$13^0 20'$ - $26^0 40'$
Venus	Jyeṣṭhā	$226^0 40'$ - $240^0 00'$
Saturn	Swāti	$186^0 40'$ - $200^0 00'$
Rāhu	Hastā	$160^0 00'$ - $173^0 20'$
Ketu	Revatī	$346^0 40'$ - $360^0 00'$

A plot of these details is presented in *Plate* I. It can be seen that the stars of these luminaries, etc. have been read out from a geocentric point of view. Their general disposition is in the form of a reverse 'S' Shape. This disposition would suggest that the earth, with reference to the sun from a heliocentric point of view, will mark that it formed in the arc of the star Anurādhā.

These facts go to suggest that the planets and the earth formed out of possible reversed 'S'-shaped solar clouds at different orbital distances. The formation of these planetary bodies may have been at any of the stages suggested by recent hypotheses which need confirmation.

The extension of the reversed 'S' form to the ecliptic circle will give us the disposition of the nodes. These, according to ancient Indian texts, are very sensitive points and the eclipses of the luminaries are determined for the earth based on these points.

It is difficult to explain how the sages came to identify the formation of luminaries, etc. in the specific star arcs. But the theory may be examined for its veracity.

In the school of *Jyotiṣa* it is considered that there are two groups of vibrations generated by the luminaries and planets. The first group of vibrations is generated by the Sun, Mars and Jupiter while the second group is generated by Mercury, Venus and Saturn. It is also stated that Ketu, the sensitive point, is similar to Mars and Rāhu is similar to Saturn. These concepts receive support from the disposition of the nodes, planets and the luminaries. While the Sun, Mars, Jupiter and Ketu are disposed on one section of the reversed 'S' arc, Mercury, Venus, Saturn and Rāhu are disposed on the other side of the 'S' arc. Of course, the position of Mercury is not entirely towards the second portion of the arc but it is somewhere in the middle. This fact would suggest that the original solar cloud (Nebula) could have formed the planets from the different portions of the arc. Perhaps, the earth-moon system was formed of a third chunk which got separated from the solar cloud so as to be in the region dividing the inner and outer planets.

Age of the Earth

'The age of the earth' is a topic that has attracted the attention of scientists for long. Kelvin suggested that the earth is about 40 million years old to account for the dissipation of original heat and in consideration of its present status. Then Jolly estimated that the age of the earth is not less than 100 million years considering the purity of the original oceans which are becoming increasingly saline due to the salt transported and added to the oceans by the rivers of the earth. Then the stratigraphic record giving the details of the fossils estimated the age of the earth to be not less than some 600 million years (Kummel, 1961). Based on radiometric methods, the age of the earth has been estimated to be about 4,500 million years.

Prior to these scientific deliberations, religious texts like the *Bible* had a different concept. According to Kummel (1961, p. 610),

> Archbishop of Armagh (Ireland), calculated in 1654, from studies of the Scriptures, that the Creation has taken place on the twentysixth of October, in the year 4004 BC, at about 9 o' clock in the morning. This date, inserted as a marginal reference by some unknown authority into the later editions of the King James version of the Bible, became implanted in religious thinking, and for long afterward it was an act of heresy among English-speaking Protestants to deny its validity.

Kummel continues,

> Other estimates came close to Ussher's and the genealogies of the Bible do, in fact, require approximately such dating.

The age of the earth according to the Mohammedan Scripture is not known.

These accounts have successfully avoided the age of the earth given in the Vedic and related texts. The only observation made by modern scientists on the Vedic age of the earth is the views of Arthur Holmes (1965, p. 1288) who has been quoted earlier.

Arthur Holmes has been recognised as the architect of modern geochronology. His observations on the age of the earth from Vedic texts is something which the Vedic and post-Vedic students of the earth must be proud of. Further, it may be remarked that the accuracy that the Vedic chronology has maintained is not seen in the modern scientific deliberations. Even the most accurate geochronological dating of the earth in the present state of our knowledge would go by a margin of + or – 100 million years or so.

The Vedic school had instituted a five-year cycle of measuring time by the time of *Ṛg Vedāṅga Jyotiṣa* as per Lagadha's version (Shamashastry, 1936). The cyclic measurement of time, however, progressed further and the *Siddhānta* school improved it very much. The most important of the *Siddhānta*s — the *Sūrya Siddhānta* — adopted a highly improved version of the measurement of time in terms of cycles.

It appears that many astronomical texts (*Siddhānta*s) were in existence from the time of the *Vedāṅga Jyotiṣa* of Lagadha. Of all, five *Siddhānta*s were available to Varāhamihira (AD 505) and he has summarised these in his text *Pañcasiddhāntikā* (Tibhaut & Dvivedi, 1968). The *Siddhānta*s happen to be the Pauliṣa, the Romaka, the Vasiṣṭha, the Śaura and the Pitāmaha. According to Varāhamihira, the *Śaura* or the *Sūrya Siddhānta* is the most accurate. The Pauliṣa and Romaka are also accurate but the Vasiṣṭha and the Pitāmaha are not accurate. However, this version of the *Sūrya Siddhānta* appears to have undergone a lot of correction, emendation and modification in later times as the version found at present is very different from the one edited by Varāhamihira.

Since Varāhamihira certifies that the *Sūrya Siddhānta* which he edited is the most accurate of all the then existing *Siddhāntas*, we may take it for our discussion. In contrast to the cycle of five years propounded by Lagadha in his *Vedānga Jyotiṣa*, Varāhamihira's edition of the *Sūrya Siddhānta* has a cycle of 4.32 million years as a cycle of *mahāyuga*. This jump in the years of cycles is shrouded in mystery for Siddhāntic texts which were present during the period between Lagadha and Varāhamihira are not available to us. This large number of solar years constituting the *mahāyuga* is given to be the common factor derived from the revolutions of planets in that period. They are as follows:

Saturn	146564
Jupiter	364220
Mars	2296824
Venus	7022388
Mercury	17937000

(Shukla, 1957; Tibhaut & Dvivedi. 1968).

It can be seen from *Plate* I that from a geocentric point of view, the planets Mercury, Venus, the Sun, Mars, Jupiter and Saturn succeed in order. This is mentioned in verse 39, chapter XIII of *Pañcasiddhāntikā*:

> Above the moon there are Mercury, Venus, the Sun, Mars, Jupiter and Saturn (in succession), and then the stars.

According to verse 42 of the same chapter:

> The products arranged in the ascending order upwards

from the moon are the lords of the months (in succession); in their descending order downwards from Saturn, they are the lords of the hours; if we take each fifth member of the ascending series we have the Lords of the Days. The Lords of the years are clear (as explained in the first chapter).

The weekdays then can be instituted as given below:

	1	Moon	1	
Order of distance	2	Mercury	3	Order of the weekdays (the successive 5th)
	3	Venus	5	
	4	The Sun	7	
	5	Mars	2	
	6	Jupiter	4	
	7	Saturn	6	

While the cycle of the *Vedāṅga Jyotiṣa* commenced from Dhanisthā star when the luminaries happened to be there, Varāhamihira's *Sūrya Siddhānta* has Meṣa or Aśvini 1^0 to commence the year. When the old system changed to the new system is not very clear, but it must be taken for granted that much development had taken place in the period between Lagadha and Varāhamihira.

This cycle of 4.32 million years called one *mahāyuga* has been instituted in Varāhamihira's edition of the *Sūrya Siddhānta*. It has been retained even by the modern redaction of the *Sūrya Siddhānta*. But there are slight differences in the number of revolutions of the planets excepting Jupiter. The differences in the number of revolutions of planets are: Mars – 8, Mercury + 60, Venus – 12. and Saturn + 4. Similarly some more corrections have been effected by the modern *Sūrya Siddhānta*.

In the modern *Sūrya Siddhānta* (Shukla, 1957), it is given that 1000 *mahāyugas* will make a day of Brahmā and the same number of *mahāyugas*, his night. 360 x 2000 = 720,000 *mahāyugas* will make a year of Brahmā and 100 such years will be his life. The present creation has seen the first 50 years of Brahmā and in the second 50 years, it is first year, first month, first day, day time and 3rd *muhūrta* and the first *kāla* of *prāṇāyāma* (Bhatta, 1991).

According to the modern *Sūrya Siddhānta*, the rate of precession of equinoxes is 54'' per year and it is noted to be oscillatory, with one oscillation of 108^0 being completed in 7200 years. 600 such oscillations of the precession of equinoxes is required to make one *mahāyuga*. 71 *mahāyugas* will make one *Manvantara* and 14 *Manvantaras* with junction periods equal to 6 *mahāyugas* will make one day of Brahmā.

The *Mahāsaṁkalpa* or the order of 'Great Creation' states that "there are seven *Kalpas*, 14 *Manvantaras* and 4 *Yugas*":

Kalpas	***Manvantaras***	***Yugas***
Pārthiva	Svambhūva	28th Mahāyuga-
Kūrma	Svārociṣa	Kr̥tayuga is
Pralaya	Uttama	current
Ananta	Tāmasa	Tretāyuga
Śvetavarāha;	Raivata	Dvāparayuga
Brahmā	Cākśuṣa	Kaliyuga = 3102 BC
Sāvitrī	*Vaivasvata;*	17/18th Feb. —
	Suryasāvarṇī	current Yuga

Dharmasāvarṇi

Dakṣasāvarṇī

Rudrasāvarṇī

Brahmasāvarṇi

Indrasāvarṇi

Vedasāvarṇi

This, for instance, would give 1955,885,094 years from the starting of Śvetavarāha *kalpa* to that of the Śrīmukha year beginning from 24.3.1993.

The concept of the large numbers in the *Sūrya Siddhānta* for the 'Kalpa Theory' has been examined by Karnik (1991). According to him, the *Sūrya Siddhānta* makes use of the real time as well as non-real time reckonings. He has based his study on the kind of simulation done in high-tech uses of computer technology. He argues that no number however large can give an integer multiple of the number of years required for the completion of the orbit. Hence the L.C.M. theory of the number of revolutions of the planets making one *mahāyuga* cannot be substantiated. Karnik (1991, pp. 131-41) observes,

> But the accuracy of one kalā in a year is not adequate for the planetary computations for which a higher accuracy, two hundred times higher, is needed. To give an accuracy of one/two hundredth of a kalā in a year a period two hundred of 21,600 or 4,320,000 years is necessary. The first number of 21,600 years is the real one and the other number of 4,320,000 years taken for Mahāyuga is the frame time or the non-real time. That there is no misunderstanding about this, the Sūryasiddhānta gives a 1:10.

Karnik continues,

> Maya was father of Mandodari the wife of Rāvana of the Rāmāyaṇa fame. It is stated in the Sūrya Siddhānta that it was revealed to Maya by Sūryapurusha when there was still some years to be elapsed for the closure of Krtayuga. Maya is stated to have run away to the present region of Maya civilisation i.e. Central Americas. This knowledge from an asura or demon was to be practiced surreptitiously otherwise one would have incurred the wrath of the royalty. Hence this knowledge was kept secret till Varāhamihira gave it in his Panchasiddhāntika about the beginning of the 6th century AD.

If 21,600 years make up a *mahāyuga*, then the duration of different *yugas* will be as below:

Kaliyuga	2160 years
Dvāparayuga	4320 years
Tretāyuga	6480 years
Kṛtayuga	8640 years

Now the *Kaliyuga* is running 1993 years past 3102 BC, accounting for some 5095 years. As per the above, *Kaliyuga* would have ended by 942 BC (3102 – 2160 = 942). From 942 BC, *Kṛtayuga* would be on in which 287 years (942 = 1992) have been completed.

In that case, to substantiate the statement from the *Sūrya Siddhānta* that the total text was revealed at a time when some years of the *Kṛtayuga* were remaining, we may have to account as follows:

The current *Kṛtayuga*	=	2874 years
Kaliyuga	=	2160 years

Dvāparayuga	=	4320 years
Tretāyuga	=	6480 years
		15834 years

This would bring us to the interval of the third and the fourth ice age and the evolution of man to a highly advanced stage would have taken a few more millennia. This theory may need further examination to be established as a scientifically authentic concept.

Karnik (1991) has not mentioned the reason why the ancients tried to give an accuracy of one to two hundredth of a *kalā* in a year and not three hundredth or more. What is special about 'two hundredth' is not clear excepting that 4.32 million is 200 times of 21600. In the absence of definite evidence, it is rather difficult to subscribe to the concepts of Karnik.

According to Amarasiṁha (Rice, 1970, p. 408) 71 *mahāyugas* will make one *Manvantara*. It would amount to: 4,320,000 x71= 30Є,420,000 years. This would mean that the Sun himself being addressed as Manu (measurer of time), his sojourn around the centre of the galaxy may be equated with one *Manvantara*. Fourteen such *Manvantaras* along with the junctional periods of 15 *Kṛtayugas* (equal to 6 *Mahāyugas*) will make up the 1000 *Mahāyugas* of a *Kalpa*, or a *Brahmā dina*.

It would be an interesting exercise to compare and contrast the periods of orogeny on the earth considering the movements of the sun round the centre of the Milky Way galaxy to find any sensitive points on the solar orbital ring. I have attempted to do this in my book, *Glimpses of Hindu Astrology and Some Aspects of Indology* (1993, p. 308).

A look into the 'Kalpa Theory' will allow us to calculate a yet longer period for the Creatio

Kalpas	*Years*
Pārthiva	4320 million years
Kūrma	4320 million years
Pralaya	4320 million years
Ananta	4320 million years

The total comes to 17200 million years to the beginning of the present Śvetavarāha *kalpa* and1955,885,094 years from the beginning of this *kalpa* to 24.3.1993. This would amount = 19235.885.094 years. Perhaps this is the time of the "Big Bang" of modern cosmology (Hawking, 1994, p. 196).

This is within the present cycle of *kalpas*. It is not known how many *kalpas* have been completed accounting for the completion of Brahmā's *parārdha.*

Whether these numbers of years are substantiated by the creative cycle and whether they can be supported by modern radiometry may have to be examined.

One of the most important outcomes of the Ṛgvedic studies is, as mentioned, the evolution of the Hindu calendar. The precise observations traceable to remote antiquity make up one of the most interesting and lasting calendars in the world. We see an important and dynamic practice of the 'Vedic Theory of the Earth' in the forging of this calendar that is common to the earth/creation. This calendar is unique to any civilisation on the earth. The time reckoned in terms of five components called *Pañcāṅgas* of the time, namely, *tithi, vāra, nakṣatra, yoga* and *karaṇa,* each with their specific effects, is calculated ahead of every year and circulated for all daily purposes. Some 50 almanacs are in vogue in India at present (Anon, 1973, p. 263). They are serving the people in social, religious, meteorological, agricultural and other fields.

Tithi is the difference in the longitudes of the moon and the sun (30 in number, 15 each in the bright and dark halves). *Vāra* has been described already. *Nakṣatra* is the star of the day, the star in which the moon transits. The *yoga* is obtained by adding the longitudes of the sun and the moon and dividing it by 200. They are also 27 like the stars. They are named as Viskambha, Prīti, Āyuṣmān, Saubhāgya, Śobhana, Atiganda, Sukarma, Dhṛti, Śūla, Ganda, Vṛddhi, Dhruva, Vyāghāta, Harsana, Vajra, Siddhi, Vyatipāta, Variyān, Parigha, Śiva, Siddha, Sādhya, Śubha, Śukla, Brahmā, Indra and Vaidhṛti. Half the *tithi* is *karana.* The *karaṇas* are 11 in number, namely, Bava, Bālava, Kaulava, Taitule, Garaje, Vanija, Bhadra, Śakuni, Catuṣpāt, Nāgavān and Kimsthughna.

The nature of the time is indicated by their proper names. The disposition of the planets is calculated on the lines of the *Sūrya-Siddhānta*, *Vākya*, Aryabhata and Dṛgganita styles. The *Pañcāṅgas* have existed for such a long time that different systems of calculations, difference in ending of *tithis*, etc. have crept in. But it may be useful to study the depth of the variations and set right the *Pañcāṅgas*.

Thirty *tithis* make up one *masa* or month and the name of the month is the name of the star in which the full moon appears. Two of such months will make one *ṛtu* (season) and three of such *ṛtus* will make one *ayana*, i.e., the movement of the sun to the north or south of the earth. The 12 months are Caitra, Vaisakha, Jyestha, Āsādha, Śrāvana, Bhādrapada, Asvayuja, Kārttika, Mārgaśirṣa, Puṣya, Māgha and Phālguna. Two months successively from Caitra will constitute *ṛtus* *Vasanta*, *Grīṣma*, *Varṣā*, *Śarad*, *Hemanta* and *Sisır*. The *ayanas* are *daksina* and *uttara*.

The nomenclature of the solar months, *ardhamāsas*, days of the *pakṣas*, etc. was changed by the time of the later *Siddhāntas*.

Thus, the Hindu calendar sounds scientific and appears to be totally based on the movement of the heavenly bodies. This entire system has been based on the movement of the earth with respect to the movement of the celestial bodies.

The Vedic sages also recognised five types of years, viz., the Solar, the Lunar, the Sāvana (360 days), Nakṣatra and Bārhaspatya, the last based on the movements of the planet Jupiter. The last one is in vogue probably from the time of Varāhamihira. This forms a cycle of 60 years commencing from Prabhava and ending with Akṣaya.

It appears that prior to the introduction of the Gregorian calendar by the British, the *Pancangas* were in abundant use. But now, the Gregorian calendar has been totally adopted relegating the Hindu almanacs to the background — they are now used for religious and festive occasions only.

This sixty-year cycle instituted by Varāhamihira (Bhat, 1986, p. 1106) appears to have its basis as two rounds of Saturn closing with five rounds of Jupiter of the zodiac. Since they are the two major planets, their influence on the earth must have been felt to be decisive. The spirit originated in the Prabhava year is noted to undergo changes through the years of the 60-year cycle and come to an end by the end of the 60th year, i.e., Kṣaya.

It is nearly fifteen centuries ago that this system was instituted by Varāhamihira. It appears that the later generations have been satisfied with this calendar and its observations and they did not seem to have desired any change.

It is evident from world history that each and every civilisation developed its own concepts about the earth and other celestial objects. As the civilisations advanced, there was the need for a calendar, the need to understand the nature and motion of celestial objects and the origin and nature of universe at large, etc. While the Mid-East, European and Mediterranean people's concepts have been relatively well-documented and are being taught in modern schools, it is not the same case with the Indian and Chinese concepts. For a balanced and unbiased outlook, it is necessary to look into all the views and come to definite conclusions.

Shape of the Earth

According to Ronan (1964, p. 232),

> To them (Babylonians) the earth was a round generally flat area and although what we could call a 'flat Earth', it was considered to be higher in the centre than at the edges, and to be floating on water.

This would suggest that the earth was like a disc to the Babylonian people. He further says,

> However, in spite of their careful observations of the planets and of the Sun and the Moon, Babylonians appear to have come to no conclusions about what made them move, nor did they ever go so far as formulating a theory of planetary motions. Why we do not know. . .

Though Egyptians also have a long history, Ronan (1991) observes,

> Yet in the field of science, and more particularly in the science of Astronomy, they contributed nothing. . . . To the Egyptians the heavens were shaped like a dome and the Earth was flat and oblong in shape. So far their conception of things appears to differ little from that of the Babylonians.

Like the Babylonians, the Greeks also believed in a disc-like Earth. According to Ronan.

> The early Greeks were influenced by some of the Egyptian ideas. . . In brief the Earth, flat disc though it might be,

was fixed in the middle of the whole sphere of creation.

Anaximander also subscribed to the above views but with a little change. Ronan states that Pythagoras accepted the Homeric idea of a spherical universe but rejected the belief that the earth was a flat disc. Pythagoras, instead, claimed that the earth itself was a sphere. It may be noted that Pythagoras lived about fifth-sixth century BC for Ronan observes that "it also seems evident that he (Pythagoras) cannot have been born before 570 BC" and he died around 497 BC.

Plato who lived between the first quarter of the fifth century BC and the middle of the fourth century BC accepted the Pythagorean idea of a spherical earth stationary in the centre of a spherical universe. Aristotle also taught that the universe was spherical with the earth stationary at its centre. He agreed that the Earth was made of elements like fire, air, water — an idea attributed to Plato. According to Ronan, "He (Aristotle) considered first the apparent movement of stars and planets across the sky"; this, Aristotle pointed out, must be due either to the motion of the stars themselves, or to the motion of the whole heaven or to both at once unless, as he was quick to percieve, neither moved and the whole apparent motion was due to the movement of the earth. But the last possibility Aristotle cast aside because he concluded that the earth must be stationary in the centre of the Universe. Aristotle was the first to suggest that the Earth is round for during an eclipse of the moon the shadow of the Earth is carved. His five elements appear to be direct derivatives of the *Taittirīya Upaniṣad.*

Eratosthenes in the third century BC determined the circumference of the earth, which is very close to the modern value. Claudius Ptolemaius or Ptolemy, who flourished in Alexandria between AD 127 and 151, wrote the *Almagest*—'The Mathematical Calculations'. According to Ronan (1964, p. 232), "Beginning with broad outlines, Ptolemy places himself fairly and squarely on the side of Aristotle and accepts a spherical

Earth immoveable in the centre of a spherical Universe". The picture of the solar system and 'Ptolemy's plan of the Universe, with the Earth immoveable at the centre' given by Ronan is the same as the one propounded by some *Siddhāntas* — mainly the *Sūrya Siddhānta* — presented by Varāhamihira in his *Pañcasiddhāntikā* (Verse no. 39, Chapter XII — On the Constitution of the Universe; Thibaut & Dvivedi, 1968, p. 110). Ptolemy's plan of the universe was a subsequent version, of course, and an improvement upon the epicyclic plan proposed by Appollonius. By about the same time Hipparchus (middle of the second century BC) established the concept of 'precession of the equinox'.

The next most important contribution was that of Copernicus in AD 1543. He established the Heliocentric theory of the solar system in his famous book, *De Revolutionibus*. Then Kepler established the laws of motion of planets in his book, *The New Astronomy* in AD 1609. Galileo supported the views of Copernicus and he was subsequently condemned to prison for the publication of *Dialogue on the Great World Systems* in AD 1686 which showed the cause for the motion of the earth and other celestial bodies. This was clearly understood and expressed by Einstein in his general theory of relativity later in 1920 and 1950. The mathematical reasoning of the general theory of relativity has been observed by Eddington (Ronan, 1964) who says,

> All the laws of nature which we formulate have their origin in the workings of men's minds and that only the fact that the Universe is made up of atoms which are themselves composed of smaller basic particles is the real essence of the material world. Because of this he sought to express in numbers what were to him the essential things in the physical Universe.

Ronan concludes his book *Astronomers* with the following statement:

> In one very real sense it can be said that both Eddington and Einstein had much in common with Pythagoras and Plato, who also believed that in numbers lay the clue to the Universe.

All these principles of natural philosphy have been gathered from observations around the earth and through a clear understanding of the origin, existence and dissolution of the earth it has been possible to probe into the realities of the universe. The origin of the theory of numbers is due to Vedic sages (Satyaprakash Saraswati, 1990, p. 675) and it is a result of grasping the universal truths which also implies exercise of the human mind. This cannot be the final truth of the universe since it is man-made. We may now turn to the concepts of the earth in the Indian school.

The *Pañcamahābhūta* theory of the evolution of the universe has already been dealt with earlier. Taking this into consideration, Varāhamihira in his *Pañcasiddhāntikā* (Thibaut & Dvivedi, 1968, p. 105 and Subbarayappa & Sarma, 1985, p. 338) described the earth as given below:

> The spherical Earth, which is constituted of the five elements, stands poised in the region of space as if it is an iron ball held in position in a cage of magnet.

The same opinion is also expressed by Lalla (Subbarayappa and Sarma, 1985, p. 338):

> This sphere of Earth, made of ākāśa, air, fire, watcr and clay and thus having all the properties of the five elements, surrounded by the orbits (of the Moon, etc.), and extending up to the sphere of stars, remains in (the centre of) space.
>
> Just as a ball of iron, when suspended amidst pieces of magnets, remains suspended in space, in the same

> manner this globe of Earth remains in space unsupported, while itself remaining the abode of all.

In all these texts the earth has been described as a globe and the term *Bhūgola* is first round in the *Pañcasiddhāntikā* text edited by Varāhamihira (6th century AD). It is very much probable that the word featured in the *Sūrya Siddhānta* text which was in existence prior to Varāhamihira. That would be the period from the *Vedāṅga Jyotiṣa* of Lagadha to the time of Varāhamihira. With its base of vast information from the Vedic, Vedāntic and *Brāhmaṇa* literatures, the concept of the global earth has been buried and it is difficult to cull out the exact reference at present. Since the Ṛgvedic age ended with the battle of the ten kings (David Frawley quoted by Rajaram, 1993, pp. 113-37) in *c.* 3730 BC, the concept of the global earth must be as old as this period in the Hindu astronomical texts.

The change in the concept of the disc-like earth to spherical earth took place in Europe about fifth/sixth century BC during the period of Pythagoras. Even then, they did not know how the spherical earth could exist in space unsupported until Newton explained it by his "Theory of Gravitation" in AD 1686. But in the absence of prolonged observations there as those carried out by the Ṛgvedic sages and assimilated and employed by the *Siddhānta* school, it is difficult to subscribe to the recent European school of thought that the astronomical knowledge was flowing from Greece to India than the reverse. Even the concept of the force of attraction of the sun on the planets and the earth is described in the *Ṛgveda* as has already been mentioned. But its quantification as was done by Newton was not done in the eastern school at least from the time of Alexander's invasion in the third century BC. Even if there had been any other texts — certainly there must have been as the advancement in mathematics indicates — these have not been found until now. It may be that they have got destroyed over time.

The concept that the earth is in the shape of a globe and is just suspended in space like a magnet was something novel even at the time of the late nineteenth century. The concept has been supported only in this century by advances made in astronomy, geology and allied sciences, like space, geophysics and others. Could it be treated as something trivial when such a concept prevailed in the Vedic school ages ago?

Dimensions of the Earth

The earliest calculation of the circumference of the earth was attempted before Aristotle but it is Hipparchus who has been credited for a calculation close to modern values in 240 BC (Ronan, 1964, p. 232). Newton is noted to have demonstrated that the earth is not a perfect sphere but an oblate spheroid. In modern times great improvements have been made over these values.

According to the *Pañcasiddhāntikā* of Varāhamihira (Thibaut & Dvivedi, 1968), Chapter XIII, verse 15 states:

> One degree answers to nine yojanas minus one ninth of a yojana (on the earth) : this fact is manifest to those who dwell on the same meridian, from the deflection (of the heavenly bodies) from the zenith
>
> Thus there is effected by ninety degrees (a difference of) eight hundred yojanas. What is sunrise for one observer is noon (for another observer) in a place distant to that extent.
>
> The circumference of the earth being equal to 3200 yojanas, 9-1/9 yojanas correspond to one degree and 800 yojanas to 90 degrees.

The views of later authorities like the modern *Sūrya Siddhānta*, Brahmagupta, Deva Keralam, Bhāskara II, Nilakantha and others have been presented by Subbarayappa & Sarma (1985, p. 338). According to the modern *Sūrya Siddhanta*, and Bhāskara II. the circumference of the earth is 4967 *yojanas* and the surface area of the earth is 785,034 square *yojanas*. The Deva Keralam and Bhāskara I gave 3299 *yojanas* as the circumference of the earth. According to Nilakantha the diameter of the earth is 1050 *yojanas*.

The date of the text which Varāhamihira has edited in his *Pañcasiddhāntikā* is uncertain but Subbarayappa and Sarma (1985) give the date of the five *siddhāntas* as third century BC (on the authority of Sen, INSA, 1966).

It can be seen from the above texts that the data on the circumference of the earth is not mentioned by Lagadha in his *Vedāṅga Jyotiṣa* dated to 1140 BC (Subbarayappa & Sarma, 1985 on the authority of Sen, 1966) but is given by Varāhamihira in his *Pañcasiddhāntikā*. These dates fixed for the astronomical texts are arbitrary and they need to be revised in the light of researches being carried out by American Indologists (Rajaram, 1993) who have fixed the end period of *Ṛgveda* at 3730 BC. The composition by Lagadha being just the age of the *Ṛgveda*, it is untenable to trace the date of the five later *Siddhāntas* of *Pañcasiddhāntikā* to third century BC. They must have spread over a period of 38 + 5 centuries by the time of Varāhamihira. In view of these uncertainties, it is conjectured that the Siddhāntic calculation of the circumference of the earth in terms of *yojanas* far precedes the calculations attemped by Hipparchus.

Modern calculations give a little less than 40,000 km as the circumference of the earth. This would give 111-1/9 km per radian, comparable to 8 and 8/9 *yojanas*. On the same lines the diameter of the earth would be

$$\frac{1050 \times 9 \times 1000}{80 \times 9} = 13155 \text{ km or about 8220 miles.}$$

Nilakantha arrived at this data by about AD 144 (Subbarayappa & Sarma, 1985).

Constitution of the Earth

The Vedic and the Upaniṣadic concept of the earth has already been presented. In the light of what has already been mentioned, the earth evolved out of space, wind, fire and water. The successive stages of evolution would include the characteristics and properties of the previous stages and so, the earth has all the characteristics of the previous stages of evolution which include qualities of sound, touch, form, juices and smell respectively. Also, as has already been mentioned, all these evolutionary phases are also present within the earth. All these fields of space, wind, fire and water are omnipresent in the earth simultaneously.

The modern conceptions of the earth also believe in the existence of the geothermal, hydrothermal, atmospheric fields within the solid earth. While the geomagnetic field is not mentioned in the literature that existed prior to *Pañcasiddhāntikā* of Varāhamihira, the concept of a geomagnetic field is not original to Varāhamihira; it must have been mentioned in some *Siddhānta* which he had edited — most probably, the old *Sūrya Siddhānta*.

Going back to the Vedic concept, the earth is described to have originated out of the cosmic gold egg. Based on this concept, it would be reasonable to presume that the earth has a gold-womb. The modern school describes the earth as made of crust, mantle and core shells and the core compensating for the lesser density of the crust by being denser to the tune of 11 to 13 or so but it is only a conjecture. The core is known to be made up of nickel and iron called 'NIFE'. The crust of the earth is the shell which is above the 'Moho' level which may vary from 35 to 60 km at the surface. The mantle is known to extend up to 2900 km from the surface where the boundary of the core commences towards the centre. These have been recognised by the propagation of earthquake waves within the earth, and it is noted that as 'S' waves do not transverse the core, the core must be at least partly liquid in condition. (Gutenburg, 1951, p. 439).

Bullen (Richter, 1958, p. 768) suggested that below 5000 km the core material may be solid and it could transmit the transverse waves. But the core is found not to transmit transverse waves because of its plastic condition. It has been suggested that the 'S' waves arriving at the boundary of the core do not enter it but transform into longitudinal waves by refracting and transit the core. A fund of information is being collected by studies on propagation of earthquake waves within the earth and a good deal of speculation exists regarding the actual nature of the core and various discontinuities in the mantle.

Could it be that the inner core is made of gold? What will be the overall specific gravity of the earth if the inner core is of gold? Do the transverse earthquake waves transit the mass of gold? Experiments may be done in these lines to find out whether the earth is 'Hiraṇyagarbihiṇī' or gold-wombed.

The geological agencies like geothermal, geomagnetic, hydrothermal and wind present within the earth make us question their activity within the earth. Their activity on the crustal surface has been well understood by the Vedic and modern physical-geological students. But their activity within the earth, if any, needs to be studied. It may be recalled that the earthquakes occur in the Indra, Agni, Vāyu and Varuṇa *maṇḍalas*. Their restricted motion within the earth and their tendency to escape outside the earth may be the cause of some earthquakes. This will be dealt with in detail later. However, the concept that these geological agencies are also active within the earth was very well-known to the Ṛgvedic sages.

Movements of the Earth

The movements of the sun attracting the celestial dust (Including celestial bodies) through the firmament was described by the sage 'Hiraṇyastūpa (*ṚV*, I.35.2). And that the sun never sets or rises is describes in the *Aitareya Brāhmaṇa* (Subbarayappa & Sarma, 1985) as given below:

> He (the Sun) never sets or rises. When (men) think that he is setting, he is only turning round, after reaching the end of the day, and makes night here and day below. Then when (men) think he is rising in the morning, he is only turning round after reaching the end of the night, and makes day here and night below. Thus, he (the sun) never sets at all.

This idea is also supported by the *Chāndogyopaniṣad*. But the concept of the geocentric theory was so strong that scientists later did not venture to think that the earth was also moving. Though Varāhamihira and Lalla stated that the Earth is suspended in space like a magnet without support, they do not appear to have subscribed to the concept of the motion of the earth. However, Varāhamihira mentioned that (verses 6 and 7):

> Others maintain that the earth revolves as if it were placed in a revolving engine, and not the sphere; if that were the case, falcons and other (winged creatures) could not return from the ether to their nests.
>
> And, to mention another argument, if the earth revolved in one day, flags and similar things would, owing to the quickness of the revolution, stream constantly towards the west. If the earth, on the other hand, moves slowly, how does it revolve (once within 24 hours)?.

These ideas indicate that even though some *Siddhāntas* prior to Varāhamihira rightly thought that the earth revolved, Varāhamihira appears to have thought that it did not. But he has not mentioned who actually believed in the revolution of the earth prior to his time (Thibaut & Dvivedi, 1968).

But Āryabhaṭa (Murthy, 1978, p. 105) who presented his text of *Āryabhaṭiyam* to the Academy of Kusumapura in AD 499 was clear in his exposition that the earth revolved on its axis causing day and night (verse 10, *Golapāda* Chapter). His description of a person moving in the boat witnessing the motion of the mounts, etc. on the sides in opposite direction is something superb. This would herald the 'Spaceship Earth' concept. However, it appears that Bhāskara II who wrote *Siddhāntaśiromaṇi* in AD 1077 did not appreciate the view of Āryabhaṭa. But like Varāhamihira, Bhāskara II enters into an argument with the Jains and Buddhists condemning their viewpoints. The most important contribution of Bhāskara II is his theory of attraction exercised by the earth. Bhāskara observes that (Singh, 1905, p. 112) :

> The earth has got force of attraction. By this force the earth attracts heavier bodies towards it. During this action, it appears that the body is falling on to the earth. However, space is extended on all four sides. As such, how does the fall of the earth takes place?
>
> (Verse 6, *Buvanakośa* chapter in *Golādhyāya*)

The concept that the earth revolved which is attributable to an unknown author of some *Siddhānta* prior to Varāhamihira preceded a similar concept by Copernicus (AD 1543) and Galileo (1609) at least by a millennia; the concept of the force of attraction of the earth given by Bhāskara II in AD 1077 preceded a similar concept of Newton (AD 1686) at least by six centuries. It is a pity that the Indian scientists did not proceed further and quantify the same in terms of mathematical procedures!

The concept of the rotation of the earth was adopted by the author of *Brahmasphoṭasiddhānta-Brahmagupta* in AD 598. The commentary on this work by Pr̥thūdakaswāmī in AD 864 (Subbarayappa & Sarma, 1985) states,

> The sphere of the star is fixed. It is only the Earth that

> is regularly rotating once a day, causing the rising and setting of the stars and the planets.

Pṛthūdakaswāmī observes,

> The Earth's rotation had been accepted by Āryabhata also, vide his words 'The Earth rotates through (an angle of) one second per one *prāna* (of time)' (Āryabhaṭīyam, i.6). On account of (possible) adverse criticism by people, Bhaskara I and others explained the verse to give it a different meaning. (Subbarayappa & Sarma, 1985).

In AD 1491 Appaya Dikṣita again went back to an old idea based on the Vedic statement *Pṛthivī Pratiṣṭhā*. According to Subbarayappa & Sarma (1985),

> On the authority of the Vedic statement — 'The Earth is Stable', the views of Āryabhata and others to the effect that the Earth is rotating had to be discarded as being against scripture and logic.

All these observations go to show that the eastern geoastronomers also had a long discussion on the rotation of the earth. In spite of the idea being established as early as the (probable) old *Sūrya Siddhānta* and gaining credence in later times owing to celebrated geo-astronomers, some authorities hesitated to accept the view as it went against what was stated in the scriptures. This stituation is comparable to a similar one in Europe.

Even Lalla (Subbarayappa & Sarma, 1985) who clarified many erroneous points of view held earlier by traditions or authorities like the existence of the mountain Meru, falling down of the Earth, two suns and two moons theory of the Jains, a view explaining the eclipses' cause, etc. questions the movement of the earth. He asserted that neither could the earth be moving from west to east nor from east to west. This was the situation even by *c.* AD 788 at the time of Lalla's *Śiṣyādhivṛddhidā* text.

The stationary position of the sun was proclaimed as early as the text of *Aitareya Brāhmaṇa*, and this should have opened the eyes of later authorities as a corrollary to the effect that the earth must be rotating to account for the motion of *Bhūcakra*. But it was not to be and the crude idea that the earth was not moving continued to rule the day. As a result, in spite of the advancement in observations and developments in mathematical astronomy concerning the motions of the planets and the luminaries in later ages, the stationary earth concept remained unaffected and the motion of the earth was not recognised.

They believed that the celestial sphere at the earth's equator is constantly carried towards the west by the Pravāha wind. The seven winds that surround the earth were recognised as Avaha, Pravaha, Udvaha, Samvaha, Parivaha, Suvaha and Pravāha. (Lalla quoted by Subbarayappa & Sarma, 1985). In spite of the fact that the sun moves along with all the members of the solar system (celestial dust) entering the various celestial mansions by force of attraction *Ākr̥ṣṇena*, the later authorities believed in the motion of these planets by certain wind forces.

According to the *Pañcasiddhāntikā* (Thibaut & Dvivedi, 1968), Chapter XIII, verse 39 :

> Above the moon there are Mercury, Venus, the Sun, Mars, Jupiter and Saturn (in succession), and then the stars. All planets move towards the east with the same velocity, each in its own orbit.

Verse 41 says:

> The moon which is placed (farthest) below the sphere of the stars revolves quickly in her small orbit; Saturn which is placed highest above revolves in his large orbit with the same velocity.

In the modern *Sūrya Siddhānta* (Kapileswara Chowdhury,

1946, p. 298) eight kinds of movements of planets have been described. They are Vakra, Ativakra, Vikala, Manda, Mandatara, Sama, Śīghratara, and Śīghra. Special movements, Atiśīghra, Manda, Sama, Vikala and Vakra are also known. But no such movement appears to refer to the earth.

The same order of disposition of planets has been given by the modern *Sūrya Siddhānta* also. From that period onwards, it appears that no research has been made in the movements of the earth as has been witnessed in Europe.

Based on the data that was available till his time, Kepler formulated the laws of planetary motion. Of Kepler's three laws, two are concerned with the motion of planets. He describes the two laws in his *Commentaries on the Motion of Mars* which appeared in AD 1609 and the third in his *The Harmony of the World* which appeared in 1618. The conclusions drawn by Kepler, Galileo and Copernicus paved the way for the formation of the laws of gravitation by Issac Newton in AD 1687 (Baker, 1965, p. 557).

These developments indicate that though the Indian geo-astronomers had a lead in the post-Vedic Siddhāntic period, they lagged behind the European scholars in the post-modern *Sūrya Siddhānta* period. The Vedic concept of the attraction of celestial bodies, though brought out by Bhāskara II about the twelfth century AD, did not pave way for the formulation of the theory of gravitational attraction in India. That was left to Kepler, Galileo, Copernicus and Newton in Europe.

Similar is the story of the concept of precession of equinoxes. According to Suryadevayajvan (Subbarayappa & Sarma, 1985) in the year 3600 — at the beginning of this *kaliyuga*— the northern solstice was exactly at the beginning of Cancer and the southern solstice at the beginning of Capricorn. He suggested methods to calculate the amount of precession of equinoxes from that zero point. Before Āryabhata (AD 476), the *Pañcasiddhāntikā* of

Varāhamihira which has presented the essence of five *Siddhānta*s gives methods for arriving at *nirāṁśa* position of planets in several verses including 69,72,73,75,76 and 78 of chapter XVIII dealing with the courses of planets (Thibaut & Dvivedi, 1968). These facts suggest that the precession of equinoxes was recognised much before the *Pañcasiddhāntikā* date (AD 505).

The modern *Sūrya Siddhānta* (Kapileswara Choudhary, 1946) has given the average rate of precession of equinoxes as 54″ per year on the basis of which has been established the school of *mahāyuga*s and *kalpa*s. It is stated that the precession of equinoxes is oscillatory and one oscillation of 108° (27° westwards from the nil-*ayanāṁśa* position to 27° eastwards totalling 108°) takes place in 7200 years. The duration of one *mahāyuga* is brought by 600 such oscillations.

There is considerable argument between the traditional astronomical school and the modern astronomical school on the nature of the precession of equinoxes. The traditional school believes that it is oscillational while the modern school which gives the rate as 50″ per year believes that it is rotational.

Manjula in his *Laghumānasa* in AD 932 is noted to have mentioned that the *Krānti-pāta* has a revolution of 1,99,669 during a *kalpa* amounting to 59.86″ *ayanāṁśa* per year. (Subbarayappa & Sarma, 1985). According to *Samrāṭ Siddhānta* of Jagannātha Samrāṭ (AD 1720) the rate of precession of equinoxes is 51″ per year (Subbarayappa & Sarma, *ibid*). The rate of precession of equinoxes has been given by different authorities. Parāśara (about 3200 BC) is noted to have given 46.5″ per year ; Bhāskara II (AD 1150) has given the value of 59.9″ per year. (Murthy, 1976, pp. 29-42).

Though a considerable database was established by the Indian geo-astronomers from the Vedic times, all the data were relating to the motion of planets, luminaries and stars, etc. and there was not much on the actual movements of the earth. This is perhaps not without any reason; it may be due to the fact that they believed that the earth is stationary in the centre of the universe. This geo-centred universal theory was responsible to a large extent for their lack of observation on the movements of the earth.

The Earthquakes

The problem of earthquakes is as old as the *Ṛgveda*. There are umpteen *sūktas* in the *Ṛgveda* praising Indra, Agni, Varuṇa and Vāyu while describing them as shakers of the earth. There is the story that the Earth being shaken severely by the winged mountains approached Brahmā who ordered Indra to cut off the wings of the flying mounts. Indra did so and the Earth is noted to have been rendered relatively stable. Indra also said to the Earth that wind, fire, himself and Varuṇa will shake the earth in the four parts of the day and night put together respectively in order to reveal the good and bad effects of action to the world.

According to Varāhamihira (Bhat, 1986) some sages believed that the earthquakes occur due to the motion of huge animals in the oceans. Garga is stated to have observed that the earthquakes are caused due to the unrest of the elephants supporting the earth in eight directions. Vasiṣṭha is said to have held that the earthquakes are caused by the atmospheric wind colliding with another and falling to the earth with a booming sound. Vṛddha Garga is stated to have observed that the earthquakes are caused due to some unseen power. According to Parāśara the earthquakes are caused by the eclipses of the luminaries, unnatural phenomena occurring in the planets and special movements of the heavenly bodies. According to Raman (1993, p. 87),

> As early as the beginning of *kaliyuga* (3102 BC) Parāśara had observed: *arka candra grahaṇa gṛha vikṛtacārajāṁśca kampana hāyulu* meaning that when the course of a planet is disturbed from the normal path owing to the attractive force of other planets there is

> shaking of the planet which is perceived as earthquake. Though sage Garga says that earthquakes are due to volcanic erruptions, Parāśara's view seems to be more reasonable as it can be proved astrologically. In fact, planetary movements as an exciting cause of earthquakes is only doubted by those who have never made any fair and complete inquiry into it. Aristotle placed on record the fact that it sometimes happens that there is an earthquake about the time of eclipse of the moon.

I have examined the issue of earthquakes from various angles in one of my works (Murthy, 1993, p. 308). It is a fact that there is no method at present by which the earthquakes can be forecast. In spite of spectacular developments in the modern discipline of seismology, it has been very difficult to deal with this aspect. All that is being done at present is the post-mortem study of earthquakes. The discipline of seismology took the shape of a scientific attitude from the deep study of the 1897 Assam earthquake by R.D. Oldham (1899). Since then scientists are of the opinion that the earthquakes occur due to differential movements along fault planes. Now based on the theory of plate tectonics, the earthquakes are stated to occur along the plate margins where a considerable amount of strain is accumulated which gets released suddenly due to unknown causes. Recently Green (1994, pp. 50-57) has proposed a model of Olivin-Spinel phase transformation to account for the deep focus earthquakes. But the problem of predicting the quakes remains unsolved.

THE PROBLEM OF PREDICTING EARTHQUAKES

In spite of using very sophisticated instruments like lasers, etc. to trace the slightest movements in the ground when micro-seisms occur, it is not possible to take any concrete action between the onset of the microseisms and the immediately-following megaseisms because of the time gap. If an earthquake is predicted at least by a few hours ahead, it may be possible to shift people from the earthquake-affected regions to safer places. But no instrument has been found so far that can indicate earthquakes a few days, nay, a few hours beforehand.

The earthquakes are classified on the basis of depth of focus or origin into three categories. There are shallow quakes with depths not exceeding 60 km and there are intermediate ones ranging in depth from 70 km to 300 km. The deep focus earthquakes, however, have depths of 300 km and above (Richter, 1969). The causes of these earthquakes may also vary. The shallow depth earthquakes may be due to falling of portions of the earth from top due to landslides and may also be due to the pressure exerted by water reservoir areas. The intermediate focus earthquakes may be due to reservoir effects and shallow level faults. The deep focus earthquakes may not be due to both the above causes but owing to a sudden shift in the centre of the earth mass. The prediction of the shallow and intermediate level earthquakes is rather difficult. But the deep focus earthquakes may be predicted by a method explained here.

VEDIC METHOD FOR PREDICTING DEEP SHOCK EARTHQUAKES

The method given by Varāhamihira in the chapter on *Bhūkampalakṣaṇādhyāya* of his *Bṛhatsaṁhitā* has already been brought out. The accompanying diagram depicts the theory (*fig.* 11). The deep focus earthquake which occurred during the first half of the twentieth century (Richter, 1969, p. 768) has been plotted using this diagram. The nine earthquakes which are plotted indicate that they might have been due to various causes which include geo-magneto-electrical disturbances, geothermal disturbances, hydrospherical disturbances and atmospheric disturbances, as read out from the starry circle indicating the various *maṇḍalas* like Indra, Agni, Varuṇa and Vāyu. But the thumb rule presented by Varāhamihira does not help in determining the time of the earthquake and the place of its occurrence.

The fact underlying the theory is to find out a path of the total angular momenta of the solar system during the first half of the twentieth century. The total angular momenta of the solar system being constant when unaffected by external influences, its path in space must be smooth. But as the orbits of all the planets in the solar system are not perfectly circular but slightly elliptical, the planets accumulate a certain amount of strain over a long period of time, the sudden release of which shifts the mass centre causing earthquakes.

The unit angular momentum of the earth is described as mvR = mass x velocity x radius. This would give us (Gutenberg, 1951, p. 439):

mass of the earth = 5.975×10^{27} g

angular velocity of the earth = $7.292115851 \times 10^{-5}$ radians/sec

radius of the earth = 145.5×10^{6} km

Full angular momenta of the planets is given below (Boris Levin, p. 91):

Mercury	0.03
Venus	0.69
Earth	1.00
Mars	0.13
Jupiter	723.00
Saturn	294.00
Uranus	64.00
Neptune	95.00
Pluto	1.00

Accordingly, the angular momenta of the sun has been noted to be about 20. From the table it can be seen that the sun, which enjoys the lion share of the mass of the solar system, does not share even 2 per cent of the aggregate angular momentum of the entire solar system. The remaining 98.99 per cent of the total angular momentum of the solar system is concentrated with the planets. Thus, it can be seen that superior planets exercise their greater angular momenta on the system to balance it.

Hence the disposition of the superior planets (excepting Pluto which has but only one unit) at the time of the deep shock earthquakes for the first half of the twentieth century was plotted and the centre of the angular momenta of the solar system was brought out in *figs*. 1-9 by employing a computer (substantiated by geometric method, Murthy, 1990 pp. 535-38). Then it was plotted against the time axis in the graph (*fig*. 10). The abrupt change in the direction of the path of the total angular momenta of the solar system became evident indicating the earthquakes. Had the orbits of the planets around the sun been perfectly circular, the path of the total angular momenta would have been a smooth curve, with no scope for earthquakes (*fig*. 12). The same points are plotted in *fig*. 11 to find out the exact cause of the earthquakes in terms of the Vedic geological forces.

If the assumption is correct, then it can be stated that whenever there is abrupt change in the path of the total angular momenta (the dynamic centre) of the solar system, we must expect an earthquake of deep focus. This can be accomplished by the advanced calculation of the planetary positions. This can be done based on the Nautical Almanac or any other system prevailing at present. It is necessary to trace the path of the total angular momenta of the solar system continuously. This can be done by employing computers.

There are two aspects of earthquakes. One is timing and the other is location. By the method proposed above, it is possible to determine the timing of earthquakes. But the location cannot be predicted. For locating the focus of the earthquake, one has to subject the strain map of the earth to the timing determined by the above method. It would give us the probable focus of the deep shock earthquake far in advance. Further, it can also be read in the context of *Plate* 11 to discover the cause of the earthquake in terms of the Vedic geological agencies.

This method can be refined making use of the various other parameters. The angular momenta of the inner planets and that of the moon may also be corrected. One more point of consideration from the Vedic angle is the occurrence of earthquakes during eclipses of the luminaries. Changes can be effected to ascertain how the eclipses are responsible for the occurrence of the deep shock earthquakes. The full pull exercised by the luminaries, being on one side during the solar eclipse, and the pull of the sun and moon on either side during the lunar eclipse can also be determined.

THE ADVANCED EPHEMERIS

In order to predict the timing of a deep focus earthquake, it is necessary to have the advanced ephemeris calculated as accurately as possible. It may be for a day, a month or a year. Having calculated the advanced position of all the planets, the sun and the moon, it is necessary to draw the path of the centre of the angular momenta of the solar system, preferably continuously, so that its behaviour through space can easily be determined. This may be done by the help of a computer with a software program prepared for the purpose.

A thorough inspection of the motion or the tracing of the path of the dynamic centre will indicate the timing of the impending earthquake on the time axis. It may be indicated in advance in terms of hours, days, or months depending upon the exercise undertaken. This is the greatest advantage of this method of earthquake prediction. Such an effort is not possible by using any method known to the science of seismology today. The path that is traced by the dynamic centre of the solar system through space and time is a clear indication of the disturbance that the solar system is undergoing through its motion. The graph showing the path of the dynamic centre of the solar system through space and time will speak volumes of celestial dynamics (*Fig.*10).

When once the timing is known, the gravity map of the earth should be examined for places where the lithospheric plates, especially their margins, are under great strain. Such places indicate to us the focus of the impending deep shock earthquakes. Thus it is possible to arrive at both the time and place of a deep focus earthquake by determining the kinks in the path of the dynamic centre of the solar system and the areas of extreme strain on the margin of the lithospheric plates subject to that timing. Based on these exercises, information about an impending earthquake may be made available in advance so that precautionary measures can be taken for shifting human population from the area or making alternative protection to tide over the calamity.

Some scientists believe that the deterministic approach evident here in forecasting deep shock earthquakes goes against the principle of uncertainity. According to Hawking (1994, p. 198), "One certainly cannot predict future events exactly if one cannot even measure the present state of the universe precisely!" This situation may be true of particle physics. But many things connected with the earth are being predicted to man's satisfaction by various methods propounded after a long period of observations and practised even to this day. Under this category, however, one may not find any prevailing method to predict earthquakes. The method proposed by me here may not take one to the level of particle physics; but it may be attempted for whatever it is worth to trace the deep shock earthquakes especially based on planetary dynamics. For further refinement and sophistication, one may turn to the application of Heisenberg's principle of uncertainty but this will only make one realise that it is futile to speak of future predictions. I believe that when there is hardly any attempt in predictive seismology by application of Newtonian mechanics, it is far-fetched to apply the ideas of the principle of uncertainty.

6

Résumé

Now that we have come to the end of this work, we may take the liberty to slightly digress to mention some very important points which would provide the finishing touches. Though people are born, bred and they die on this earth, they devote hardly any time to knowing something of value about the earth. They little realise that it is their home and their only home in the vast universe. Hence, like geography and history, geology also must feature in our educational curricula, preferably at the middle level of education, to make students realise this important aspect.

Regarding a 'Theory of the Earth' there is no doubt that it is much needed in all walks of life. This aspect is, in actual life, very little appreciated. Whether it is agriculture, meteorology, navigation — air or sea, city or town planning, planning for development, space study, archaeology, anthropology or any other field of study, it must rest on the foundation of a 'Theory of the Earth'. The roots of this theory are in the *Veda*s, the oldest texts of mankind; that is why, this 'Vedic Theory of the Earth' is pre-eminent and most desirable to be understood by all. The application of such a theory is almost universal and it is left to the educated world to make one and all realise this aspect. For prediction of rains, cultivating certain crops, earthquake prediction, prediction of volcanic activity, sociological upheavals and political changes, etc. this theory is the basis or the foundation. One must realise that such a powerful, influential and decisive role is being played by this theory on environmental aspects that all other factors just disappear like snow in the heat of the sun.

Hence, it is my earnest desire to see a wide base of this theory developed as applicable to the entire earth so that 'world almanacs' can be prepared for the four quarters of the earth (at 90^0 interval) and many activities forecasted for the benefit of humanity. If this is done, many calamities can be averted and mankind may be saved from the natural catastrophes.

oṁ tat sat

Figures

Fig. 1

January 4th 1903

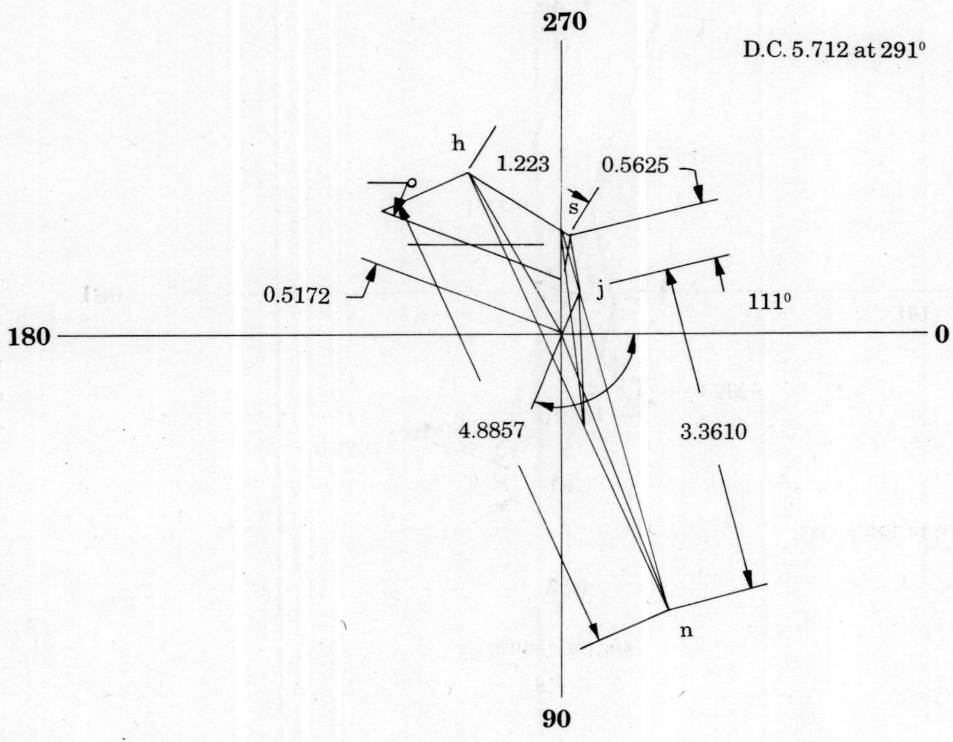

Fig. 2

June 7th 1904

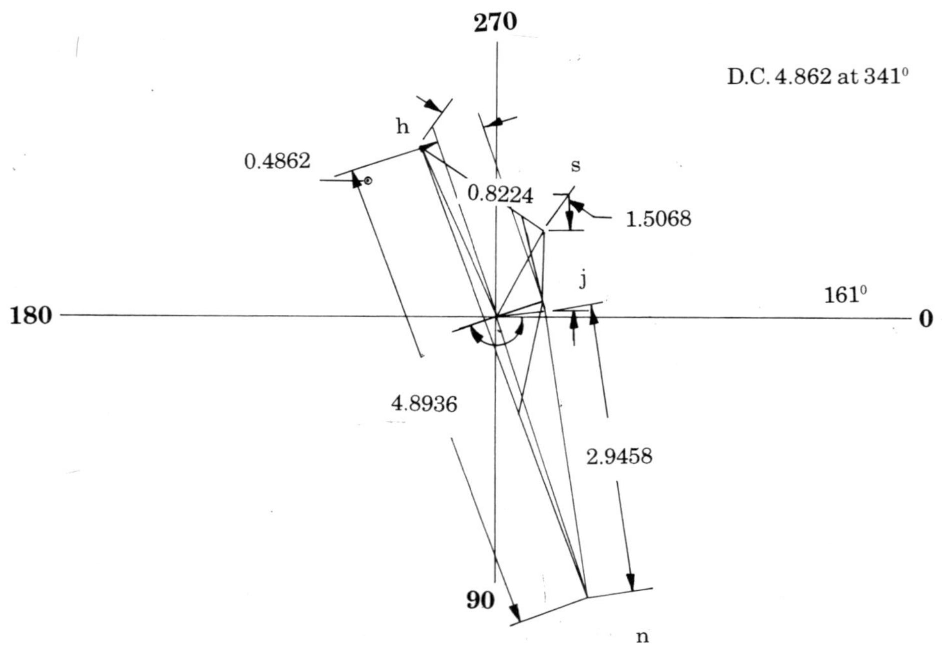

Fig. 3

January 21st 1906

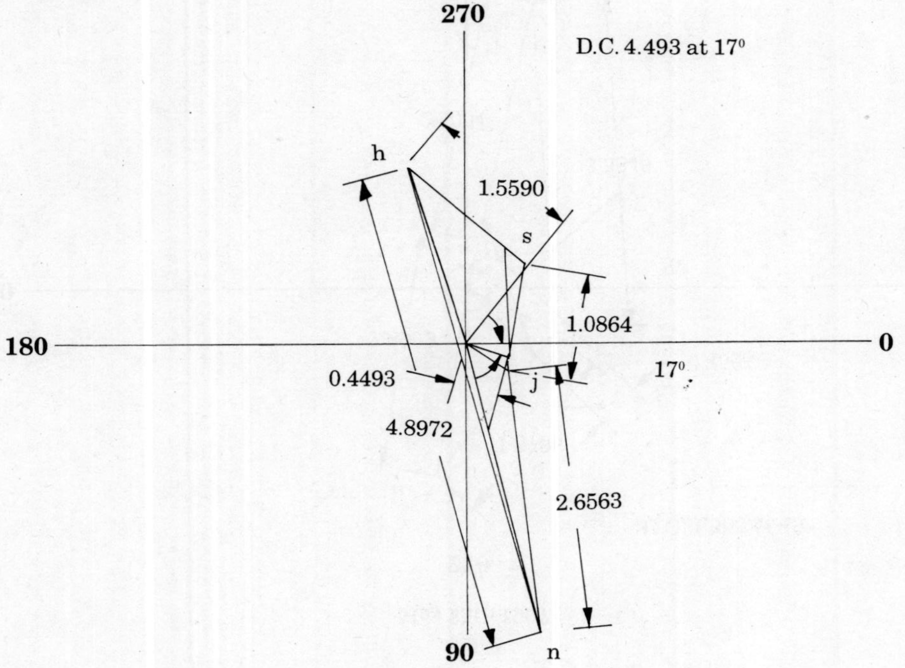

Fig. 4

May 25th 1907

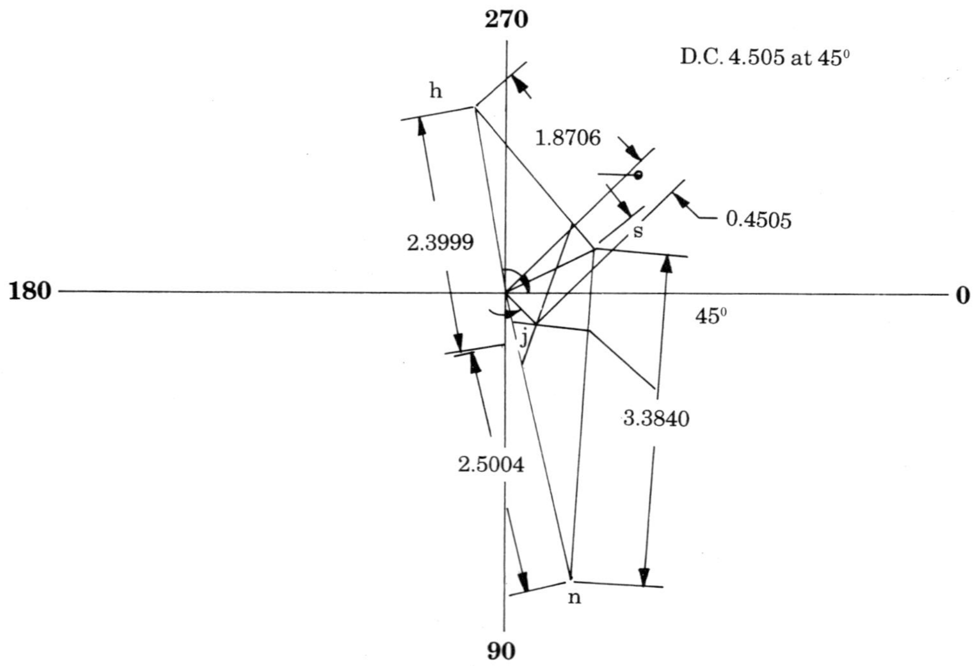

Fig. 5

February 22nd 1909

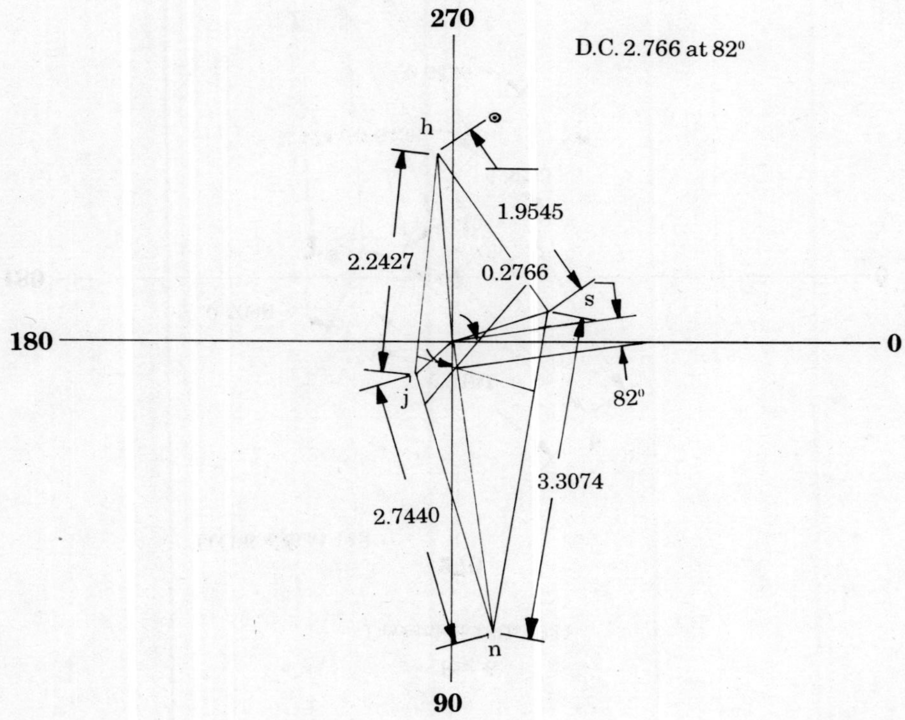

Fig. 6

December 18th 1921

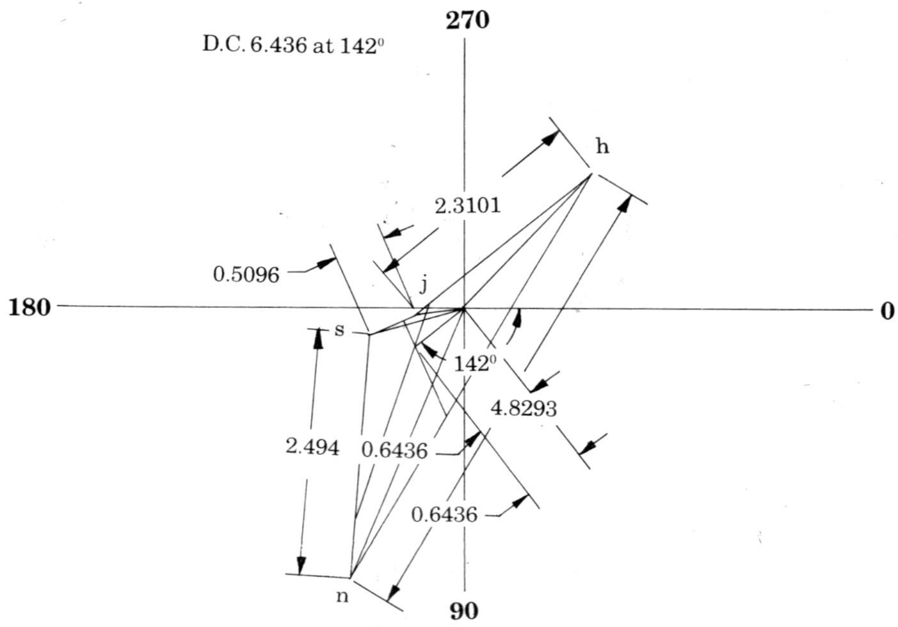

Fig. 7

May 26th 1932

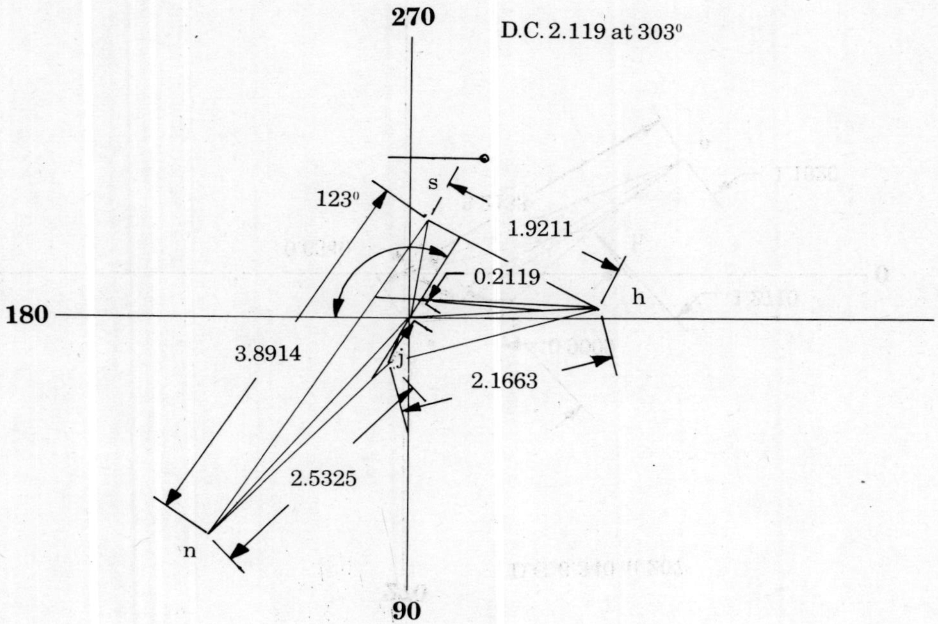

Fig. 8

April 16th 1937

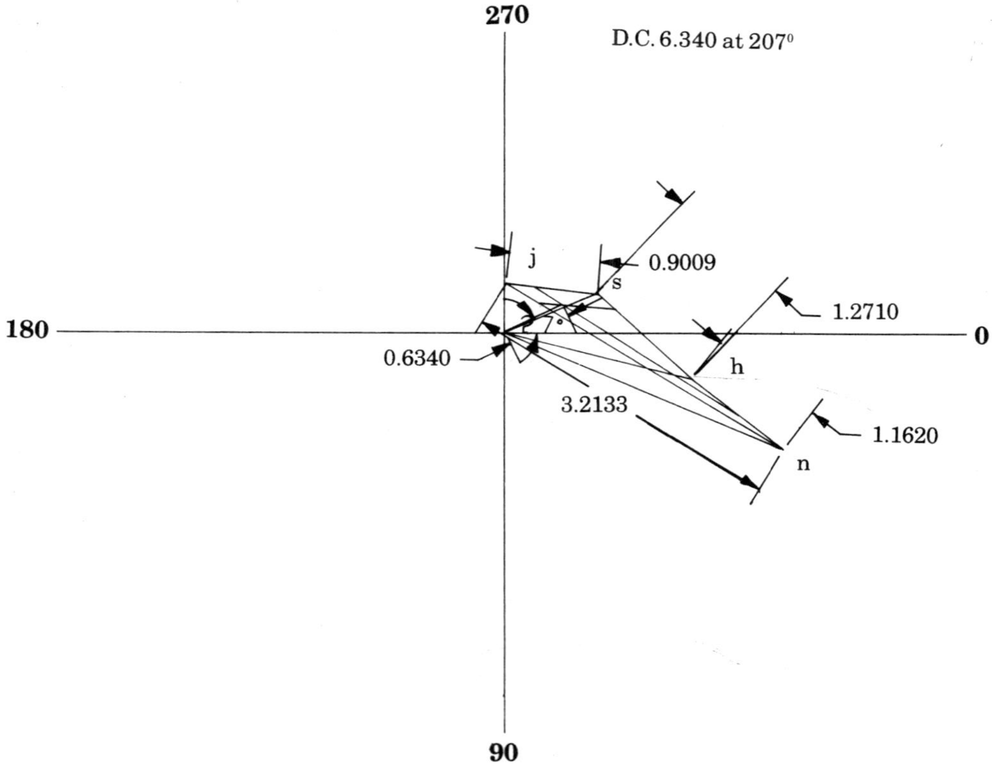

Fig. 9

February 28th 1950

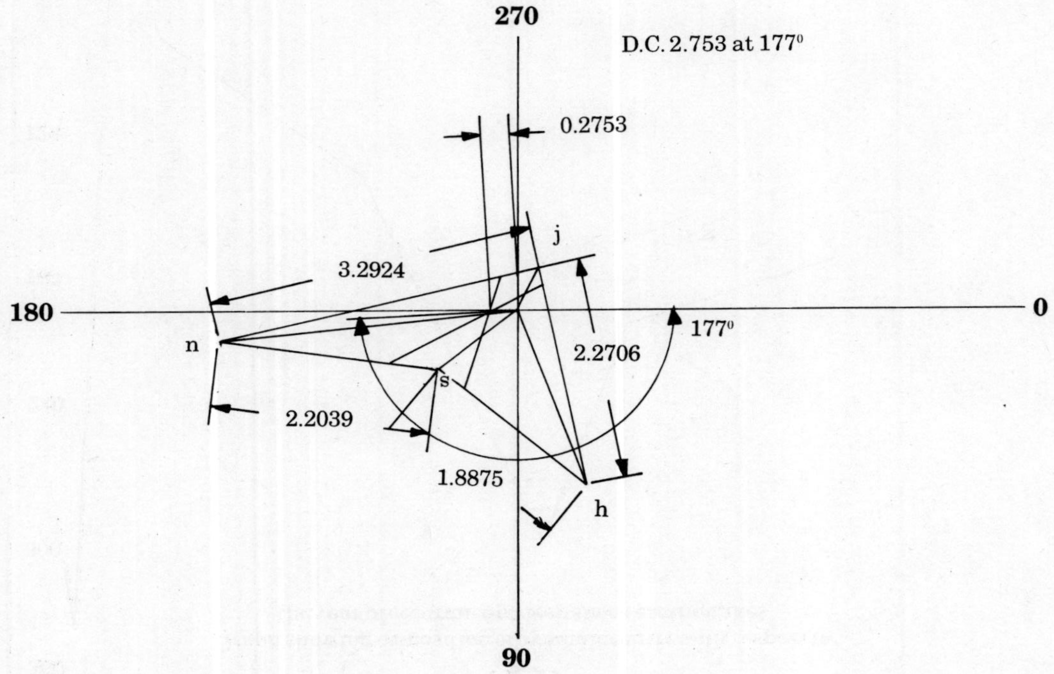

Fig. 10

Graph showing disposition of dynamic centre with respect to the year of occurance of deep shock earthquakes

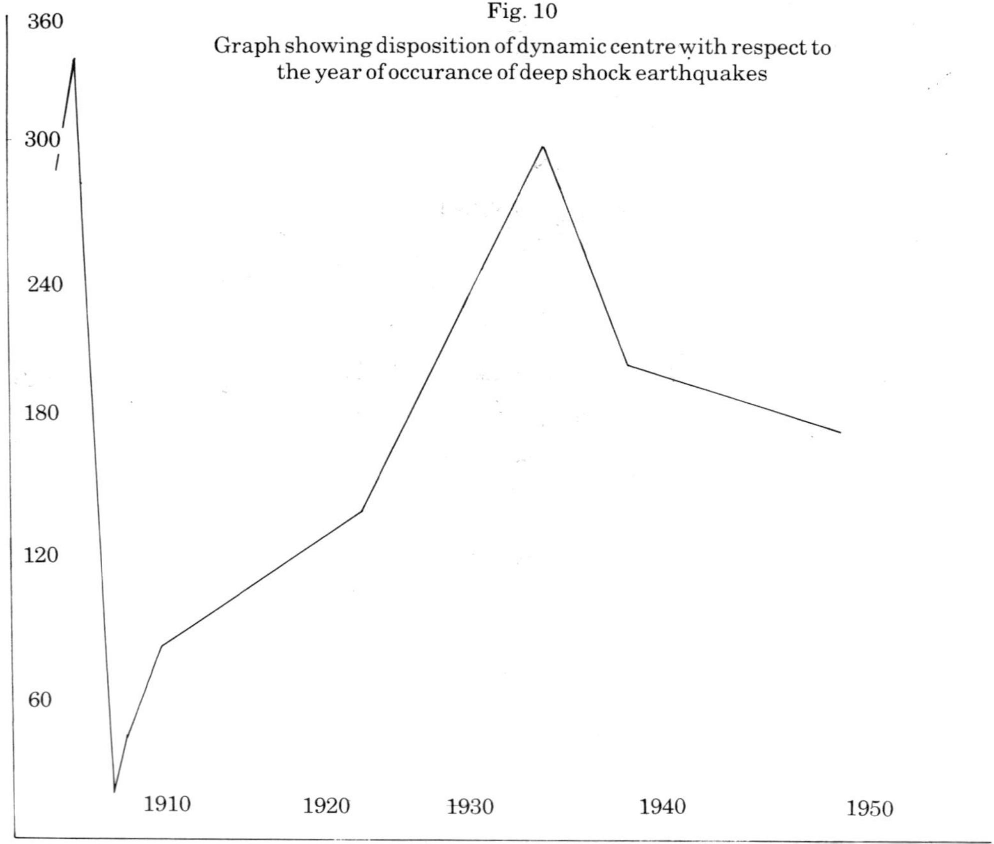

Fig. 11

Diagram indicating the origin of earthquakes due to different geological agencies

(Of deep shock earthquakes for the period 1900-1950 AD)

(Richter, 1969, page 715)

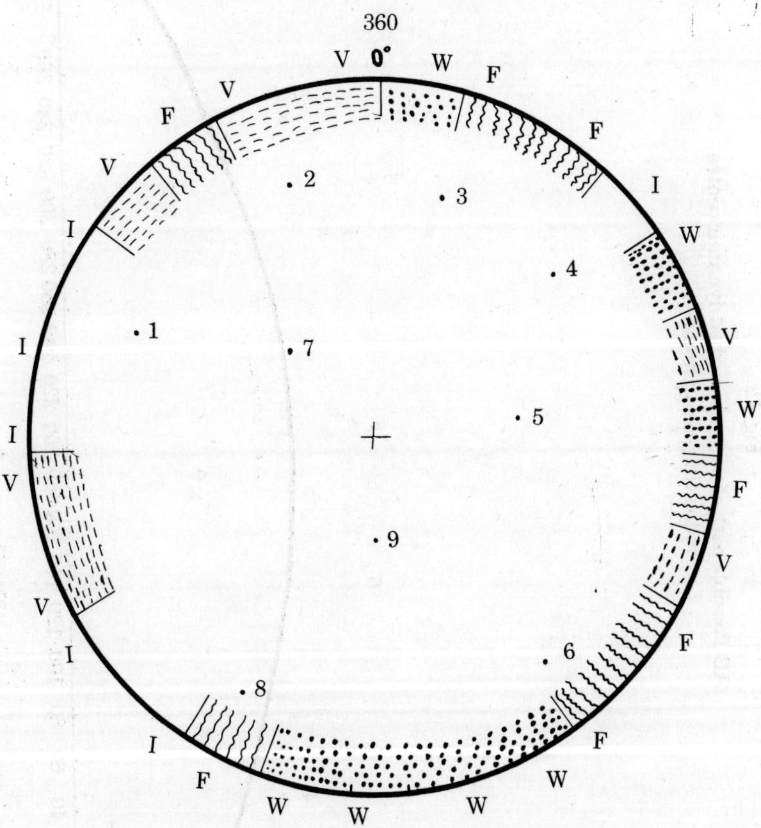

I Indra Geoelectrical/Magnetic disturbances points 1, 4

F Agni Geothermal disturbances points 3,6,8

V Varuna Hydrospherical disturbances points 2, 7

W Vāyu Atmospheric disturbances or gases inside the earth points 5, 9

Fig. 12

AB Possible path of the undisturbed dynamic centre indicating no earthquakes

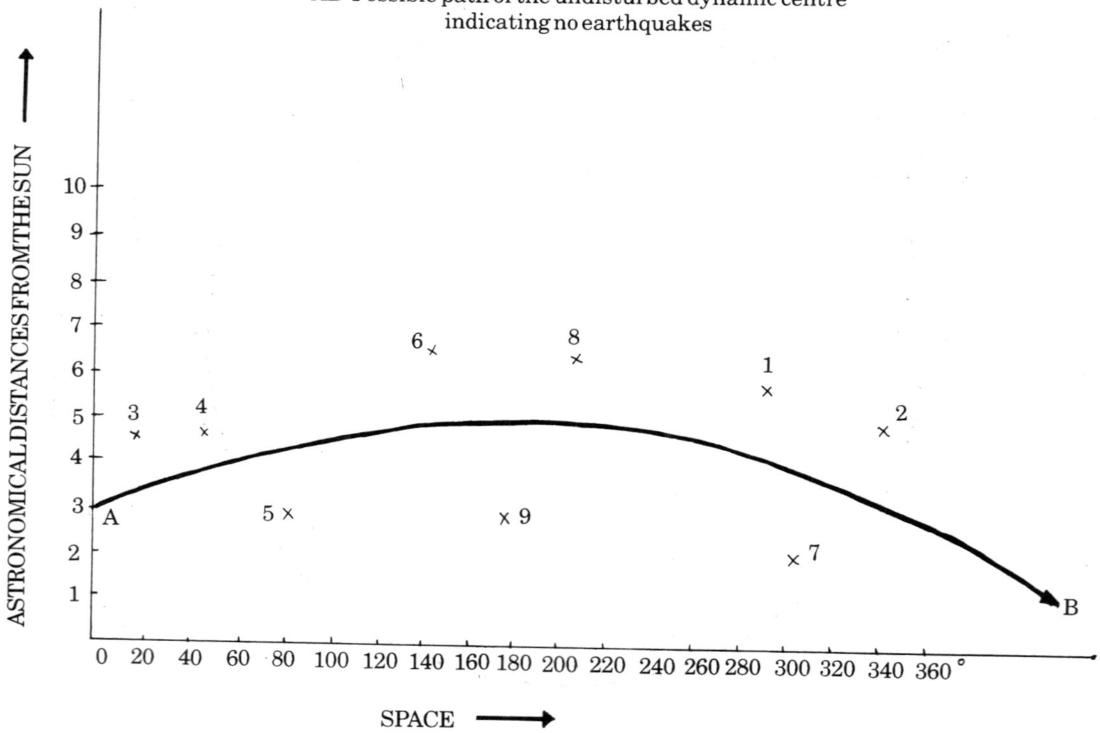

Glossary

Adhidevatā	:	additional god.
Aditi	:	the oldest period in the Āryan age; wife of Kaśyaparṣi.
Ādityācāra	:	movements of the sun.
Ādityas	:	they are 12 in number and represent the sun in the 12 constellations of the zodiac.
Adri	:	hill or cloud.
Agni	:	the Vedic god of fire — here, interpreted as geothermal field.
Agninakṣatra doṣa	:	the atmospheric and, in turn, human and animal health pollution due to the movement of the sun through the arc of the star Kṛttikā during the months of Meṣa/Vṛṣabha, i.e., May.
Āgrahāyaṇi	:	Mṛgaśirā star/full moon in Mṛgaśirā was the first day of the year.
Ākāśa	:	sky/space/mind.
Ānanda	:	joy/heavenly bliss.
Ananta	:	endless/eternal.
Antarikṣa	:	sky.
Anuṣṭubh	:	a metre of the Vedic poetry.
Āpas	:	waters.

Āraṇyakas	contemplative texts on Vedic injunctions closely related to the *Upaṇisads*.
Aśvaratna	best of the horses.
Āśvins	twin gods of the same star.
Atharva	the last (in chronology) of the *Vedas* and the fourth *Veda* which includes Hindu science of spells, black magic, archery and medicine.
Āyudha	weapon.
Āyurveda	Hindu science of health and longevity.
Bādarāyaṇa	Vyāsa.
Bhaga	the Sun.
Bharadvāja	*Kulapati* of the sixth book of the *Ṛgveda*.
Bhū-Maṇḍala	circle of the earth.
Bhūtagrāma	the universe.
Brahmā	the Creator.
Brahman	knowledge of the Supreme by knowing which nothing remains to be known.
Brāhmaṇas	detailed Vedic literature dealing with sacrifices.
Brahmāśtra	weapon on the spell of the *Gāyatrī*.
Brahmāvartta	area first populated by the Āryans — now the region of the Ambālā district in the foothills of the Himālayan range, i.e., the Śiwālik hills.
Bṛhatī	a metre of the Vedic poetry.
Darśanas	revelations.
Dikpāla	lord of direction.
Dvipadī	a metre of Vedic poetry.
Gajaratna	best of the elephants.

Gautama	:	founder of the *Nyāya* school of Indian philosophy.
Gāyatrī	:	a metre of Vedic poetry; the Vedic spell supreme.
Grahamaṇḍala	:	circle of the planets, etc.
Graha-yajña	:	sacrifice to the planets.
Ghṛtsamada	:	*Kulapati* of the second book of the *Ṛgveda.*
Havis	:	sacrificial material offered to the gods through the divine fire.
Indra	:	the king of Vedic Gods, ruler of rains, thunder — here interpreted as electromagnetic field.
Jagatī	:	a metre of Vedic poetry.
Jaimini	:	founder of *Pūrva Mīmāṁsā* school of Indian philosophy.
Kakup	:	a metre of Vedic poetry.
Kaṇāda	:	founder of the *Vaiśeṣika* school of Indian philosophy.
Kapila	:	founder of the *Sāṁkhya* school of Indian philosophy.
Kaśyapa	:	a great sage and one of the seven *Brahmarṣis.*
Kavandha	:	cask or clouds.
Kāvyas	:	Sanskrit poetics.
Khila	:	means, not in use or outdated.
Kośa	:	pail/clouds/treasury/dictionary.
Madhvācārya	:	re-establisher of the *Dvaita* school of Indian philosophy.
Mahāśaura	:	hymns of the great sun.

Manas	:	mind.
Maṇiratna	:	gems.
Manu	:	the sage who first gave mankind the human code of conduct.
Manvantaras	:	the time interval between successive Manus which equals 71 *mahāyugas* or 306.72 million solar years.
Maruts	:	group of winds.
Māsakṛt	:	the Moon.
Māyā	:	magic.
Nadī	:	river.
Nadyaḥ	:	rivers.
Nakṣatrahoma	:	sacrifice to the stars.
Nakṣatra maṇḍala	:	circle of the stars.
Nakṣatreṣṭhi	:	sacrifice to the stars.
Nārāyaṇāśtra	:	weapon on the spell of Nārāyaṇa (Mahāviṣṇu).
Oṣadhīśa	:	the moon-lord of herbs.
Pañcagrahas	:	five planets — Mars, Mercury, Jupiter, Venus and Saturn.
Pañcamahābhūtas	:	five fundamental elements of nature, viz., space, wind, fire, water and earth.
Paṅkti	:	a metre of Vedic poetry.
Parjanya	:	rain.
Patañjali	:	founder of the *Yoga* school of Indian philosophy.
Pavamāna	:	hymns attributed to the wind.
Pitṛyajña	:	sacrifice to the manes.
Prajāpati	:	Creator.

Pratyādhidevatā	:	second additional god.
Pr̥thvī	:	the Earth.
Purāṇas	:	Hindu esoteric historiography.
Pūṣan	:	the Sun.
Rāmānuja	:	re-establisher of the *Viśiṣṭādvaita* school of Indian philosophy.
Ṛgveda	:	the oldest texts of Āryan thought employed for purposes of nature worship in the form of hymns.
Ṛk	:	unit of a hymn.
Ṛta	:	truth; seasons.
Rudras	:	11 in number — 10 kinds of human breaths viz., *Prāṇa*, *Apāna*, *Udāna*, *Samāna*, *Nāga*, *Kūrma*, *Krakara*, *Devadatta* and *Dhanañjaya*, with the eleventh being the soul.
Śaci	:	wife of Indra.
Śākhās	:	divisions or branches.
Sāmaveda	:	the *Veda* which is employed for music or singing.
Śaṁbara	:	a demon killed by Indra.
Samudra	:	sea.
Sandhyā	:	morning and evening.
Śaṅkara	:	Re-establisher of the *Advaita* school of Indian philosophy.
Sarasvatī	:	Goddess of learning; an extinct river on the banks of which Indian sages composed the *Vedas*.
Śāstra	:	Hindu science.
Satya	:	truth; living; manifest.

Śaura : spells of the sun.

Sāvitrī : the Sun.

Sāyaṇa : Also, Madhva — a thirteenth century Śaṅkarācārya of the Śṛṅgerī *pīṭha* in Karnataka who wrote a grand commentary on the *Vedas*, the latest of its type, after the establishment of the famous Vijayanagara Empire.

Śeṣāśāyī : sleeper on the serpent Ādiśeṣa — Mahāviṣṇu.

Siddhānta : Geo-astronomical texts in Sanskrit.

Śilpas : Vedic sculpture.

Soma : the Moon or an enlivening herbal juice.

Somapā : Indra or one who drinks *soma*-juice.

Strīratna : best among women.

Sūkta : hymn.

Svarbhānu : the ascending node, Rāhu — a point on the ecliptic crossed by the orbit of the moon.

Udher : Udder or clouds.

Upaniṣads : An in-depth study of the Vedic injunctions that form a principal triad of Indian philosophy.

Uṣas : dawn.

Uṣṇīk : a metre of Vedic poetry.

Utsa : spring season or clouds.

Vala : a demon sacrificed by gods.

Vāmadeva : *Kulapati* of the fourth book of the *Ṛgveda*.

Varṣā-ṛtu : rainy season — the months of Śrāvaṇa and Bhādrapada.

Varuṇa	:	the Vedic god of waters or hydrosphere.
Vasiṣṭha	:	*Kulapati* of the seventh book of the *Ṛgveda*.
Vāstu	:	Vedic science of architecture and civil engineering.
Vasus	:	the gods of fire, earth, atmosphere, sky, the sun, the moon and the stars residing in the earth.
Vāyu	:	the Vedic god of atmosphere.
Veda(s)	:	the sacred and the religious texts of knowledge of the Āryans — the oldest such in the library of mankind. They were three earlier, viz., *Ṛg*, *Yajur* and *Sāma* and the *Atharva* was later added.
Vedāṅgas	:	Adjuncts of the *Veda*s are six, viz., *Śikṣā*, *Vyākaraṇa*, *Chandas*, *Nirukta*, *Jyotiṣa* and *Kalpa*.
Vedānta	:	the end or the essence of the *Veda*s. They constitute the subject-matter of Indian philosophy. They are six in number, viz., *Sāṁkhya*, *Yoga*, *Nyāya*, *Vaiśeṣikas*, *Pūrva* and *Uttara Mīmāṁsā*.
Vedī	:	sacrificial platform.
Vidyut	:	electricity.
Vijñāna	:	science.
Viṣṇu	:	One of the trinities of Hindu pantheon of gods responsible for the maintenance of the universe.
Viśvāmitra	:	*Kulapati* of the third book of the *Ṛgveda*.

Viśvedevas	:	all gods.
Vṛtra	:	a demon killed by Indra.
Yajña	:	sacrifice.
Yajurveda	:	Vedic texts employed for purposes of performing sacrifices.
Yama	:	the god of death or a regime of management.
Yāska	:	an ancient commentator on the *Vedas*.

Bibliography

Achyuta Krishnananda Tirtha (1913), *Vanamālā commentary on the Taittirīyopaniṣadbhāṣya*, Srirangam.

Anon (1973), (in Kannada), The Calendar Reform Committee, Government of India, New Delhi.

Aurobindo (1993), *The Secret of the Veda*, Pondicherry.

Baker, R.H. (1965), *Astronomy*, Van Nostrand.

Bhargava, M.L. (1964), *The Geography of Vedic India*, Lucknow.

Bhat Ramakrishna, M. (1986), *Varāhamihira's Bṛhat Saṁhitā*, Motilal Banarsidass, 2 vols.

Bhatta, Dhali Laxminarasimha (1991), *Ṛgveda Prayoga Dipika*, (in Kannada), Veda Prakashna Samstha, Bangalore.

Bose, A.C. (1970), *The Call of the Vedas*, Bharatiya Vidya Bhavan, Bombay.

Dayānanda Sarasvatī Maharṣi (1976), *Ṛg Vedādībhāṣyabhūmikā*, Ajmer.

Choudhary, Kapileshwara (1946), *Sūryasiddhānta*, Kashi Sanskrit Series, No. 144, Banaras.

The Deccan Herald, a daily, (31.3.1993), Vedic Star Codes, Bangalore.

Feynman, R.P., Leighton, R.B. and Sands, M. (1986), *Lectures on Physics*, Narosa, New Delhi.

Frawley, David (1992), *The Astrology of the Seers*, Motilal Banarsidass.

Ganguli, H.K. (1989), "The Rationals and Irrationals in Ancient Mīmāṁsā", in Jha (ed.) *New Horizons of Research in Indology*, Centre of Advanced Study in Sanskrit, Pune.

Giekie, A. (1903), A *Text Book of Geology*, vol. 1, London.

Green, H.W. (1994), "Solving the Paradox of the Deep Earthquakes", in *Scientific American*, September 1994.

Griffiths, R.T.H. (1986), *The Hymns of the Ṛg Veda*, Motilal Banarsidass.

Gutenberg, B. (1951), (ed.), *Internal Constitution of the Earth*, Dover.

Hawking, S.W. (1994), *A Brief History of Time*, Bantam, New York.

Hegde, K.T.M. (1991), *An Introduction to Ancient Indian Metallurgy*, Geol. Soc. India, Bangalore.

Holmes, A. (1964), *Principles of Physical Geology*, English Language Book Society.

Iyer, Paramashiva T. (1911), *The Riks*, Bangalore.

Jha, Acyutānanda (1959), *Bṛhatsaṁhitā — Vidyabhavan Samskrita Granthamālā*, No. 41, Varanasi.

Josyer, G.R. (1950), *Āśvalāyana Pūrva Prayoga*, Mysore.

——— (1996), *Sanskrit Civilisation*, Coronation Press, Mysore.

——— (1976), *Shānti Ratnākara*, (in Kannada), Mysore.

Karnik, P.R. (1991), Yuga, Mahayuga and Kalpa, *Jour. Mythic Society*, Bangalore, vol. 82.

Krishnan, M.S. (1956), *Geology of India and Burma*,

Higginbothams, Madras.

Kummel, B. (1961), *History of the Earth*, Eurasia Publishing House, New Delhi.

Levin, Boris (year not given), *The Origin of the Earth and Planets*, ed. by J. Gibbons and Translated from the Russian by A. Shkarovsky, Foreign Language Publishing House, Moscow.

Lyell, Charles (1833), *The Principles of Geology*.

Macdonnell, A.A. (1976), *A Vedic Reader for Students*, Oxford Press.

Max Müller, F. (1961), *India — What can it Teach us?*, Munshiram Manoharlal, Delhi.

——— (1976), *My Autobiography*, New Delhi.

Murthy, Narasimha, N.K. (1978), *Āryabhaṭīyam* (in Kannada), Bangalore University.

Murthy, S.R.N. (1976), "Earth Science Studies in Sanskrit — An Outline", *Indian Minerals*, vol. 30, No. 3, Geological Survey of India, Calcutta.

——— (1978), "Varahamihira's Contribution to the Vedic Theory of the Earth", in Proceedings of the Third World Sanskrit Conference, Paris.

——— (1980), "The Vedic River Saraswati, A Myth or Fact — A Geological Approach", *Ind. Jour. His. Sci.*, vol. 15, no. 2.

——— (1982), "The Age of the Earth according to the Hindu Calendar", *Jour. Geol. Soc. Ind.*, vol. 21.

——— (1987), An *Integrated Theory of the Earth*, Kalpataru Research Academy, Bangalore.

———(1990), "Correlation of Deep Shock Earthquakes with the Dynamic Centre of the Solar System", in *Jour. Geo. Soc. Ind.*, vol. 36.

Murthy, S.R.N., et al. (1991), "Tin in Ancient India", *Journal, Geological Society of India*, vol. 38, no. 1.

Murthy, S.R.N. (1992), *Ancient Indian Theories of the Earth*, Centre of Advanced Study in Sanskrit, Poona University, Pune.

——— (1992), "The Geoscientific Aspects of Vedic Spiritualism" in *Journal of Oriental Research*, vol. 63, Kuppuswamy Sastry Research Institute, Madras.

——— (1993), *Glimpses of Hindu Astrology and Some Aspects of Indology*, Sadguru Publications, Delhi.

——— (1993), "The Geological Foundations of the Vedic Civilisation", in Summaries of Papers, AIOC, 36th Session, Poona.

——— (1994), Ge*ological Foundations of Indology*, Kalpataru Research Academy, Bangalore.

Nilakantha Shastry, A. (1940), *A History of South India*, Oxford Press.

Oka, K.G. (1913), *The Nāmaliṅgānuśāsana of Amarasiṁha with the commentary of Kshiraswamin*, Poona.

Oldham, R.D. (1899), Memoir in *Geo. Sur. Ind.* 29, Calcutta.

Pandurangi, K.T. (1988), "The Concept of Space and Time in Indian Philosophy" in *Scientific Heritage of India*, Mythic Society, Bangalore.

Pascoe, E.H. (1973), *A Manual of Geology of India and Burma*, Third Edition, Government of India, New Delhi, vol. 3.

Pingree, D. (1981), "Jyotishshastra: Astrol and Mathematical

Literature", vol. 4 of *A History of Indian Literature*, Otto Harrassowitz, Weisbaden.

Prasad, K.N. (1975), "Review of Miocene Anthropoidea from India", in *Journ. Pal. Soc. India*, vol. 20.

——— (1989), "Some Observations on Hominid Evolution" in *Perspectives in Human Evolution*, Delhi.

Raghava Rao, G.V. (1949), *Scripture of the Heavens*, Vizag (A.P.).

Rajaram, N.S. (1993), "Vedic and Harappan Culture: New Findings", in *Jour. Mythic Soc.*, vol. 84, Bangalore.

Raman, B.V. (1993), *Astrology in Predicting Weather and Earthquakes*, Bangalore.

Ray, P. and Gupta, H.N. (1965), *Caraka Samhita*, Indian National Science Academy, New Delhi.

Rice, L. (1970), *Amarakosha of Amarasimha*, (in Kannada), Mysore.

Richter, C.F. (1958), *Elementary Seismology*, Eurasia Publishing House, New Delhi.

Ronan, C.A. (1964), *The Astronomers*, London.

Sarada, H.B. (1975), *Hindu Superiority*, Hindu Academy, New Delhi.

Satavalekar, S.D. (1944), *Atharvaveda Saṁhitā*, Swādhyāya Maṇḍala, Pāradī, Gujarat.

——— (1990), *Krishna Yajurvediya Taittarīya Saṁhita*, Pāradi.

——— (1990), *Taittirīya Saṁhitā*, Swādhyāya Maṇḍala, Pāradī, Gujarat.

Satyaprakash, Saraswati Swami (1990), *Founders of Sciences in Ancient India*, 2 vols., Delhi.

Seal, Brajendranath (1991), *The Positive Sciences of the Ancient Hindus*, Motilal Banarsidass.

Shamasastry, R. (1936), *Vedāṅgajotiṣa*, Mysore.

——— (1938), *Drapsa: The Vedic Cycle of Eclipses*, Mysore.

Shankara Narayan, P.V. (1989), *Geomagnetism and Life Processes*, Madras Science Foundation, Madras.

Shastry, Laxminarasimha (1938), *Navagraha homamu-Navagrahashanti Vidhānamu* (Telugu Script), Bandaru, Musalipatnam.

Shastry, Nanjunda (1924), Nakshatra Cūdāmani of Padmanābha, (in Kannada), Bellary.

Singh, Pandit Udaya Narayan (1905), *The Siddhānta Śiromaṇi — Golādhyāya*, Bombay.

Sontakka, N.S. et al. (1951-92), *Ṛgveda Saṁhitā* (5 volumes), Vaidic Somshodhan Mandala, Pune.

Sontakka, N.S. & Kashmir, C.G. (1983), *Ṛgveda-Saṁhitā with the commentary of Sāyaṇācārya*, 5 vols., Poona.

Srikantasastry, S. (1962), *Harappa and Mohanjo Daro in Bharatiya Samskriti Darshana* ed. by A.N. Krishna Rao, (in Kannada), Bangalore.

Subbarayappa, B.V. and Sarma, K.V. (1985), *Indian Astronomy — A Source Book*, Nehru Centre, Bombay.

Thibaut, G. and Sudhakara Dwivedi (1968), *Pañcasiddhāntikā of Varāhamihira*, Varanasi.

Tilak, B.G. (1936), *The Arctic Home in the Vedas*, Messers Tilak Brothers, Pune.

——— (1972), The *Orion*, Messers Tilak Brothers, Pune.

Index